Security and strategy in the new Europe

D0186616

The end of the Cold War has brought new concerns over the nature of European security to the fore and uncovered major differences in the approaches of individual states to the changed circumstances.

This book examines the debate over the future of European security conducted during the period from the revolutions of 1989 to the failed Soviet coup of August 1991. In so doing it aims to clarify the options for a new security order and contribute to the growing debate over European security. It demonstrates that the apparently new policies of Western governments are not as radical as might have been thought. Most are developments of existing policies and based on existing institutions. These have been moulded in reaction to the new circumstances, but they have not been replaced.

The book is divided into three parts, covering the nature and structure of security and the implications of Europe's resurgent nationalism; military strategy, with particular reference to the NATO perspective and to the European Community; and the distinctive security concerns of individual states. It looks at both Eastern and Western Europe and the Soviet Union, and it analyses the role of the United States in European security.

Security and strategy in the new Europe

Edited by Colin McInnes

London and New York

First published 1992
by Routledge
11 New Fetter Lane, London EC4P 4EE

Simultaneously published in the USA and Canada
by Routledge
a division of Routledge, Chapman and Hall, Inc.
29 West 35th Street, New York, NY 10001

© 1992 Colin McInnes

Typeset in Times by Michael Mepham, Frome, Somerset
Printed and bound in Great Britain by Biddles Ltd, Guildford
and King's Lynn.

British Library Cataloguing in Publication Data
A catalogue record for this book is available from the British Library.

Library of Congress Cataloging in Publication Data
Security and strategy in the new Europe / edited by Colin McInnes.
    p.   cm.
Includes bibliographical references and index.
1. Europe—National security.   2. North Atlantic
Treaty Organization.   I. McInnes, Colin.
UA646.S398   1992
355'.03304—dc20   92–9285
                                                             CIP

ISBN 0–415–07120–8
    0–415–08303–6 (pbk)

Contents

Part III   National concerns and perspectives

Contributors

Dr Colin McInnes is Defence Lecturer in the Department of International Politics, University College of Wales, Aberystwyth. He was formerly a lecturer in the Department of War Studies, The Royal Military Academy Sandhurst. His published works include *Trident: The Only Option?*, *NATO's Changing Strategic Agenda* and *Warfare in the Twentieth Century* (co-editor).

Dr John Baylis is a Reader in the Department of International Politics and is Dean of the Faculty of Economic and Social Studies, University College of Wales, Aberystwyth. His publications include *Contemporary Strategy* (co-author, 2 vols), *Anglo-American Defence Relations 1939–84*, *British Defence Policy in a Changing World* (editor), *Nuclear War, Nuclear Peace* (co-author), *Soviet Strategy* (co-editor), *Alternative Approaches to British Defence Policy* (editor), *Britain, NATO and Nuclear Weapons* (co-author), *British Defence Policy*, and *Makers of Nuclear Strategy* (co-editor).

Professor Ken Booth holds a personal chair in the Department of International Politics, University College of Wales, Aberystwyth. He was the first Scholar-in-Residence at the US Naval War College and was a Senior Research Fellow at the Centre for Foreign Policy Studies, Dalhousie University, Canada. His books include *Navies and Foreign Policy*, *Strategy and Ethnocentrism*, *American Thinking about Peace and War*(co-editor), *Law, Force and Diplomacy at Sea*, *Contemporary Strategy: Theories and Policies* (co-author), *Britain, NATO and Nuclear Weapons* (co-author), and *New Thinking about Strategy and International Security* (editor).

Frederic Bozo was educated at the Ecole normale superieure in Paris, at the Sorbonne and at Harvard University. He is currently a Research Fellow at the French Institute of International Relations (IFRI), specialising in European security affairs. He also teaches at the Institut d'Etudes Politiques de Paris. His publications include *La France et l'OTAN: de la Guerre Froide au Nouvel Ordre Européen.*

Michael Brenner is Professor of International Affairs at the University of Pittsburgh. He is currently preparing a study of multilateralism within the Atlantic Alliance under a NATO Fellowship. His recent publications on European security include articles in *Foreign Policy*, *International Affairs*, *Politique Etrangère* and *Relazion Internazionale*.

Dr Stuart Croft is Deputy Director of the Graduate School of International Studies, University of Birmingham, and was formerly Research Fellow at the International Institute for Strategic Studies. His publications include *British Security Policy: The Thatcher Years and the End of the Cold War* (editor).

Dr Peter Foot is Principal Lecturer at the Royal Naval College, Greenwich. Formerly working in international business and subsequently as a Research Fellow at the Centre for Defence Studies, University of Aberdeen, he has published widely in the fields of contemporary history, strategy, defence economics and international economics.

Stephen Iwan Griffiths is a Research Fellow at the Institute for International Studies, University of Leeds. He formerly taught at the University of Aberdeen, and was a Research Fellow at the Stockholm International Peace Research Institute.

Dr Adrian G. V. Hyde-Price is a lecturer in the Department of Politics, University of Southampton. He previously lectured at the University of Manchester, and was a Research Fellow at the Royal Institute of International Affairs. His publications include *European Security Beyond the Cold War*.

Caroline Kennedy is a lecturer in the School of International Studies, University of Leeds. She previously lectured at the University of East Anglia, and at the University College of Wales, Aberystwyth. Her publications include *British Army Strategy in Northern Ireland* and *The Soviet Union and the US Military Presence in Europe* (both forthcoming).

Dr Norbert Ropers is Executive Director of the Institute for Development of Peace, University of Duisburg. His previous posts include Senior Researcher at the Peace Research Institute of Frankfurt, and Research Consultant for the German Society for Peace and Conflict Research. His publications include *Tourismus zwischen Ost und West – Ein Beitrag zum*

Frieden?, *Grünbuch zu den Folgewirkungen der KSZE* (co-editor), and *Globale Trends 1991* (co-editor).

Dr Len Scott is a lecturer in the Department of International Politics, University College of Wales, Aberystwyth. From 1984–87 he was Political Adviser to the Shadow Foreign Secretary, the Rt. Hon. Denis Healey MP. He has co-authored two Fabian pamphlets, 'Working for common security' and 'Disarmament in a changing world', and has written *Conscription and the Attlee Government*.

Dr Nicholas Wheeler is a lecturer in the Department of Politics, University of Hull. His previous posts include Research Fellow in the Department of War Studies, King's College London, and Research Associate at the International Institute for Strategic Studies. He is the co-author of *The British Origins of Nuclear Strategy, 1945–55*.

Professor Phil Williams is Professor of International Security in the Graduate School of Public and International Affairs, University of Pittsburgh. He was formerly in the Departments of Politics at Aberdeen and Southampton, and Head of the International Security Programme at the Royal Institute of International Affairs. He is the author of *Crisis Management, The Senate and US Troops in Europe*, and co-author of *Contemporary Strategy* and *Superpower Détente: A Reappraisal*. He is also a co-editor of *Soviet and American Policies in Central America and the Middle East* and *Superpower Competition and Crisis Prevention in the Third World*.

Acknowledgements

This book originated with a conference jointly sponsored by the Ministry of Defence and the Department of International Politics, University College of Wales, Aberystwyth, at Gregynog in September 1990. The chapters by Adrian Hyde-Price, Stuart Croft and Caroline Kennedy all received an initial airing at that conference. The structure of and thinking behind the book, however, was developed in the period September-December 1990, and I would like to thank Stuart Croft and Ken Booth for their helpful and imaginative advice at that time. I would also like to thank Alan Macmillan for preparing the index. I owe Sally more than I can ever hope to express, not least for putting up with my 'summer of discontent'. Finally I would like to dedicate this book to Stevie, Luke and Joanna: the new Europe will be their Europe.

Abbreviations

ATTU	Atlantic to the Urals
BAOR	British Army of the Rhine
BERD	Bank for European Reconstruction and Development
CFE	Conventional Forces in Europe (Treaty)
CFSP	Common foreign and security policy
CMEA	Council of Mutual Economic Assistance
CND	Campaign for Nuclear Disarmament
CPC	Conflict Prevention Centre
CSBM	Confidence and Security Building Measure
CSCE	Conference on Security and Cooperation in Europe
CSO	Committee of Senior Officials
C3I	Command, control, communications and intelligence
DPC	Defence Planning Committee
EC	European Community
EDC	European Defence Community
EFTA	European Free Trade Area
END	European Nuclear Disarmament
EPC	European Political Cooperation
FAR	Force d'Action Rapide
FOFA	Follow-on Forces Attack
FOTL	Follow-on to Lance
FRG	Federal Republic of Germany
FRWA	Federal Republic without an Army
GATT	General Agreement on Tariffs and Trade
GDR	German Democratic Republic (East Germany)
GLCM	Ground Launched Cruise Missile
GNP	Gross National Product
G7	Group of Seven
ICBM	Inter-continental ballistic missile
IEPG	Independent European Programme Group

IGC	Inter-governmental conference
IISS	International Institute for Strategic Studies
IMEMO	Institute of World Economy and International Relations, Moscow
IMF	International Monetary Fund
INF	Intermediate Range Nuclear Forces
INGO	International non-governmental organisation
JCS	Joint Chiefs of Staff
LDCs	Less developed countries
LTDP	Long Term Defence Programme
MAD	Mutual assured destruction
MIRV	Multiple Independently-Targeted Re-entry Vehicle
NBC	Nuclear, biological, chemical (weapons)
NAC	North Atlantic Council
NATO	North Atlantic Treaty Organisation
NIC	Non-industrialised country
NNA	Neutral and non-aligned states
NPG	Nuclear Planning Group
NVA	National Volksarmee
OAU	Organisation of African Unity
OECD	Organisation for Economic Cooperation and Development
RRF/C	Rapid Reaction Force/Corps
SACEUR	Supreme Commander in Europe
SALT	Strategic Arms Limitation Talks
SDI	Strategic Defence Initiative
SHAPE	Supreme Headquarters, Allied Powers Europe
SLBM	Submarine Launched Ballistic Missile
SNF	Sub-strategic Nuclear Forces
SNP	Slovak National Party
SSBN	Strategic missile carrying submarine
START	Strategic Arms Reduction Treaty
TASM	Tactical air to surface missile
UN	United Nations
WEU	Western European Union
WEDC	West European Defence Community

Introduction

This book was conceived in the wake of the 1989 'revolutions' in Eastern Europe, and completed in the aftermath of the failed August 1991 coup in the Soviet Union. There can be little doubt that the period 1989–91 marks a watershed in the history of Europe. Although some new trends were apparent from the mid-1980s on (particularly in the Soviet Union,[1] but also in Poland, in the European Community with its movement towards political and economic union, in the changed nature of superpower relations, and in the new emphasis on nuclear disarmament), the period 1989–91 decisively changed the political context in which these trends were being developed.

What this book examines is the development of thinking in the period 1989–91 about the nature and the future of European security. Its focus is on change: how old ideas and institutions are being adapted, developed or abandoned to meet the new circumstances of European security. Ken Booth has suggested that we are in an interregnum, when established structures are collapsing, and when there is 'tension between old and new ways of thought and action' (Booth, 1991: 1). Booth quotes Gramsci:

> The old is dying and the new cannot be born; in this interregnum there arises a great diversity of morbid symptoms.
>
> (Gramsci in Booth, 1991: 1)

What this book suggests is something subtly different: that current thinking and policies about the future of European security are much less radical and much more firmly rooted in the past. Although there is a clear acceptance that radical change has occurred, the policies and institutions prescribed for meeting these are by and large developments of what currently exists rather than forays into radical new territory. Thus the institutions under discussion have substantial histories prior to 1989, but are emerging with new roles for the 1990s: a 'political' NATO; a more politically significant Western European Union; an EC with a security function; and a stronger Conference on Security and Cooperation in Europe. Similarly, although there is widespread agreement in theory on a new, broader security agenda rather than the narrow, state-centric military conception of the Cold War, in practice movement towards this has been slow, and military security still holds centre-stage (though its position is under threat from economic security issues, and the European Bank for Reconstruction and Development may prove the first of a series of new institutions). Thus change has been incremental and based on what existed prior to 1989. This is not to say that the end result might not prove to be radically different; nor is it to suggest that institutions will be capable of successfully adapting their roles and functions – indeed, some may soon disappear almost without trace; rather it is that the process of change in thinking about European security and in institution building has been much less radical and dramatic than the changes in the political context. New institutions have been slow to emerge, and 'new thinking' is being accepted only gradually.

This book is organised into three parts. The first (Chapters 1 to 4) deals with security in the new European system. This is the most forward looking part of the book, and it is here that the most radical ideas are developed. Its two major concerns are the changed nature of security in Europe, and the changed nature of the European system. As regards the first concern, there is general agreement over a widened security agenda and the development of a more holistic approach in the long run, compared to the narrow, military focus of the Cold War. On the second, the growth of interdependence in security, the decline of state-centrism, and the linkage of European security to wider, global issues (particularly North–South issues) receive considerable emphasis.

The second part deals with military (and particularly nuclear) strategy. Its main concern is how this, the centre-piece of Cold War security, is being adapted to meet the challenges of a new Europe. The focus is on NATO as the sole surviving military alliance (Soviet strategic concerns are discussed in Chapter 9). The argument presented is, again, that change has so far proved to be incremental rather than radical. In Chapter 5, John Baylis argues that NATO has reacted to change in the past by continuity in strategic planning, and that despite the disappearance of the Soviet threat pressures for continuity remain strong. This argument is reinforced in the following Chapter by Stuart Croft, who argues that NATO's review of nuclear strategy is more superficial than substantive. In the final chapter of this part of the book, the ideas of alternative defence which were developed in the 1980s are applied to the new Europe. In the longer term these ideas might become the new orthodoxy, and it is indeed apparent that many of their concerns are reflected in the new Europe. Nevertheless it is equally clear that in the nearer term these ideas remain 'alternatives'.

This argument is borne out by the final part, which examines the security policies and perspectives of five key states in the new European system.[2] Two concerns are common to all five: the strategic requirements of the new Europe; and the institutional framework. Although the balance is not always the same, the security policies examined here suggest that the two key questions occupying policy makers are military strategies for post-Cold War Europe (and particularly the role of nuclear weapons), and the institutional/organisational framework in which security is to be pursued. Of particular interest is the relative failure of French and Soviet 'grand schemes', and the emphasis placed in Britain and the United States on the development of existing institutions.

That Europe has entered a new phase in its history cannot be denied; but equally it is apparent that much of the thinking about the policies and institutions for security in Europe are rooted in the past. Booth is correct that we are in an interregnum; but this is not (as yet) an interregnum marked by two conflicting camps jostling for primacy, but rather the development of existing security institutions to meet new challenges. The end result of this evolution may be radically new; but at present there is much still in common with the past.

Aberystwyth
September 1991

NOTES

1 The term '(former) Soviet Union' is used throughout the book to refer both to the pre-August 1991 USSR, and to the post-coup remnants. Although the term is perhaps no longer technically correct, its continued common usage and the lack of a satisfactory new term at the time of writing has led to its retention here.
2 As Booth and Wheeler note in Chapter 1, the definition of Europe is a contested issue. I have chosen a broad definition 'from Vladivostok to Vancouver', and therefore include US security policy as a key concern for the new Europe. With the exception of the Soviet Union, no East European state is examined in detail. Rather East European concerns are dealt with in Chapter 3.

REFERENCE

Booth, K. (1991) 'Introduction: the interregnum: world politics in transition', in K. Booth (ed.), *New Thinking about Strategy and International Security* London: Harper Collins.

Part I

Security and the new European system

1 Contending philosophies about security in Europe

Ken Booth and Nicholas Wheeler

For the first forty years after the ending of the Second World War 'European security' was a lively but well-focused political issue. There was a consensus, East and West, on priorities and parameters. When people opened a book or attended a seminar on 'Security in Europe' they knew what to expect. The questions had become very familiar. What is the state of the NATO/Warsaw Pact conventional balance? How dependable is the US nuclear guarantee? Is the Soviet military threat growing? Would the introduction of a particular missile be stabilising? How flexible is flexible response? These trusty questions were defined by weapons, and were concerned with strategic problem-solving within a two-bloc framework. Since the mid-1980s the issue 'Security in Europe' has been revolutionised. It is no longer well focused. It has become increasingly apparent that 'security' cannot sensibly be conceived narrowly, and that dealing with 'Security in Europe' in the 1990s and beyond depends upon more than strategic problem-solving. The response of Western governments to the news of the anti-Gorbachev coup in August 1991 perfectly illustrated the new era. Some Cold War muscles twitched, and guns began to be counted, but the prevailing reaction was one of uncertainty about what to do next to enhance 'security'. What precisely was the nature of the 'threat' posed by the possible changes in the Soviet Union? And was the most appropriate response a military gesture, the use of economic instruments, a diplomatic initiative or human rights protests? The failure of the Moscow coup, which then precipitated the fragmenting of the Soviet state, led to even more possibilities. It became clearer to almost everyone except unreconstructed old thinkers, that the European security agenda no longer consisted of the old questions or the old answers.

Before successful security policies can be conceived for the next decade and beyond, more discussion and self-awareness is required about the philosophical assumptions underpinning our concepts and political beliefs. The aim of this introductory chapter, therefore, is to clarify the fundamental assumptions which pervade the subject of this book. For forty years, the Iron

Curtain, to a greater or lesser extent, put us all behind the wire, psychologically speaking. It enforced, for the most part, old ways of thinking about the game of nations. Now the Iron Curtain has been dismantled across central Europe we need to begin to dismantle all its manifestations in our minds. By so doing we should become more self-aware about the roots of our arguments on security, and also about the new priorities and parameters. This chapter is therefore not primarily concerned with what is happening, or what might happen, in European security; it is more concerned with the way the subject has and might be thought about.

WHAT IS 'SECURITY'? WHAT IS 'EUROPE'?

Today even the most basic elements of the subject are not as clear as they were formerly. The very concepts of 'security' and 'Europe' are now disputed. Most observers of international politics since 1945 have had a shared understanding of the concept of 'security', though there remains no generally accepted definition (Buzan, 1983, 1990). During most of this period security and defence were virtually synonymous (Booth 1990). As traditionally conceived, security implied some or all of the following: that a state is free from the threat of war; that it is able to pursue its 'national interests' and preserve its 'core values'; and that it feels safe against potential aggressors (that is, war is believed to be unlikely, but should one occur, the state in question does not expect defeat). These traditional ideas about security were based upon three assumptions: the belief that security is centred upon states, that security policy seeks to preserve the status quo, and that military threats and the need for effective military defence are the primary concerns. Consequently, security policy has been primarily concerned with the military power of individual states and general order in the states system.

Despite the strength of traditional ideas, there was through the 1980s a growing unease with the established concept of security, which privileged the state and military power (Booth 1990, 1991a,b; Buzan 1983, 1990). There was a regular call for a 'broadening' or 'updating' of the notion. What emerged was a growing recognition of the desirability of a more holistic and dynamic concept. This implies: first, a concept of security which focuses not just on the state, but which includes individuals and the world community as a whole; second a concept which is not status quo oriented, but which is future oriented and seeks progressive change; and third, a concept which is not synonymous with military problems but which encompasses a broad agenda of threats (economic, environmental and human rights for example) which prevent people and groups living full and free lives. Security, as will be brought out later, has therefore become an 'essentially contested concept' in contemporary world politics.

On the face of it, the definition of 'Europe' would not seem to pose similar problems, but it does. There is today much more to identifying 'Europe' than looking on a map: politics is more important than geography. How people choose to define Europe will have a significant impact on how they think both about security in Europe and Europe's relations with the outside world. The chosen definition will provide the basis of the answer to the crucial question: who is 'us' and who is 'them' politically speaking?

Ole Waever has usefully identified four 'Europes' in security terms (Buzan et al, 1990: 45–9):

1 The European Community (basically Western Europe, with the potentiality for some broadening).
2 Europe from Poland to Portugal (non-superpower Europe).
3 Europe from the Atlantic to the Urals ('Gaullist Europe' or Gorbachev's 'Common European Home').
4 Europe from Vancouver to Vladivostok (CSCE Europe).

According to Waever, each of these four Europes represent 'competing organising principles' and have sharply different implications for European security. To expand this important point: each of the four Europes has different histories (especially in relation to the Cold War), geographies, defence potentials, relationships with the Soviet Union and the United States, political and cultural identities, scope for common decision-making, likelihood of evolution in a 'security' direction, and possible role in future world politics. It remains to be seen which, if any, of these 'Europes' will emerge triumphant: 'Europe's' identity will therefore remain a dynamic issue, as Germany is unified, the 'European Community' broadens and deepens, 'Eastern' Europe struggles to find its location, the Soviet Union breaks up, and the landscape of the post-Cold War world evolves into new patterns.

Part of the present confusion is that 'Europe' is neither simply a geographical expression nor a patchwork of given political states. Each of the Europes identified is made up of complex identity patterns. No 'Europe' can be defined simply in terms of states. Each consists of different nations, ethnic communities, regions, religious and political associations, social movements and individuals (the latter being recognised by states in some human rights legislation). To a greater or lesser extent, in each of the main European geopolitical spaces, there are agents other than states. Identity patterns, as well as politics, have become more complex. Clearly, therefore, 'who and what is Europe?' is another contested issue. The answers people will give, again, will decisively shape their future choices about security policy.

THE 'PRIMARY CONCERNS' OF CLASSICAL APPROACHES

How we come to think about 'security in Europe' will depend not only on how we choose to define these two key terms, but also on our basic philosophical assumptions about the nature of world politics. Different philosophical assumptions offer not only competing explanations but also competing organising principles when it comes to political practice. Students of international relations are usually taught to think in terms of three philosophical traditions, each of which is associated with a classical philosopher (Bull 1977: 24–52; Wight 1966: 89–131).

The Hobbesian tradition

This is the idea that the international system is akin to the Hobbesian 'state of nature', dominated by self-interest and with no legal or moral rules. 'Anarchy' – the absence of overriding authority or government – is the key concept. From this perspective the drive for security is the main preoccupation. Peace and cooperation (like alliances) can only be a temporary arrangement between states, and there can be no international 'society'. Self-interest and expediency determine behaviour; it is a 'self-help' world of – to paraphrase Hobbes – 'everystate against everystate'. To the extent that order can exist in such interstate relations, it will be based upon a balance of power. Academically, the Hobbesian philosophy is represented by the 'realist' tradition of 'power politics' (Bull 1977: 24–5, 46–51; Hobbes 1962; Morgenthau 1960).

The Grotian tradition

This is the idea that although the states-system is anarchical (without overriding authority) it need neither be violent nor chaotic. Anarchy, tempered by society, will allow a degree of order between states. 'Society' is defined as a consciousness among states of common interests and values, and a commitment to common rules and institutions. Sovereignty, international law and diplomacy are some of the shared ideas of the society of states. Academically, this philosophy is represented by the 'rationalist' tradition of 'internationalism' (Bull 1977; Roberts et al, 1991; Wight 1977).

The Kantian tradition

This is the idea that states are a device which, for a prolonged time, have organised humanity, but that the fundamental reality of world politics is the potentiality of a universal community of people. The (individual) units of this universal community are believed to be already joined by the possession of common faculties (such as reason) and common potentialities (for pleasure or justice). 'Community' – the idea of breaking down barriers between people by extending moral obligation and kinship – is a key feature of this approach. Unlike both the earlier traditions, which take states as the fundamental units of analysis, the Kantian tradition seeks, in different ways, to transcend the states-system and its cultural manifestations such as war. The Kantian tradition, it should be noted, has been somewhat less statist than is apparent in Kant's own writing (Hurrell, 1990). Academically, the Kantian approach is represented by the 'revolutionist' tradition of 'universalism' or 'cosmopolitanism' (for example, Falk, 1988).

The three traditions of thought about world politics just identified generate different descriptions of the security problem facing states and people, and offer competing principles when it comes to dealing with them. Andrew Linklater has usefully described the 'primary concerns' of the three traditions as power, order and emancipation (1990: 8).

Power

In what is seen to be a 'self-help' world, each state must attend to its own security, and not assume the support of others. Security is therefore believed to lie in the accumulation of power. Power refers to those material and non-material assets which enable actors to shape the behaviour of others in desired ways. Power is therefore seen as the central preoccupation of state activity; in the much-quoted words of Hans J. Morgenthau, 'International politics, like all politics, is a struggle for power' (Morgenthau, 1960: 28). The interests of states are defined in terms of power, and military power has traditionally been its ultimate expression. As Chairman Mao famously put it: 'power proceeds from the barrel of a gun'. Hobbesian theorists believe that a level of order is possible between states, but only as a result of prudential calculations, with power checking power.

Order

Grotians recognise the importance of power, but believe that order – and therefore security – can be achieved not simply through the manipulation of power but through the growth of a society of states. Order therefore consists of a situation in which the goals of the actors are predictably maintained through shared norms and values. These goals are identified as follows: preservation of the states-system and international 'society'; the maintenance of the sovereignty of individual states; peace; and the 'common goals' of all social life, namely 'life, truth and property' – the limitation of violence, the keeping of promises, and the stabilisation of possession (Bull 1977: 16–20). Tension can and often does exist, in theory and practice, between order among states ('international order') and among people ('world order'). This is a manifestation of the age old and pervasive tensions between justice, power and order which will reappear through the subsequent discussion.

Emancipation

From the Kantian perspective power and order are not seen as appropriate bases for planning security because they are inherently unstable; this is because power and order can only be achieved, as traditionally conceived, at somebody else's expense (Booth 1990: 1–7). The accumulation of power tends to provoke fear while the tightening of order can promote injustice. Consequently, stable security can only be achieved by people and groups if they do not deprive others of it; this can be achieved if security is conceived as a process of emancipation (Booth 1991b). Emancipation means the freeing of humans from those constraints which stop them carrying out what they would freely choose to do; such a goal implies the lifting of unacceptable legal, social, economic, moral, political and physical constraints. People should be treated as ends and not means, whereas states should be treated as means and not ends. Freedom, however, needs to be tempered by the acknowledgement of the equal rights of others.

MODERN EXPONENTS AND POSTWAR PRACTICE

Having established the basic philosophical traditions and their primary concerns, it is now necessary to identify relevant intellectual guidance, and how the traditions have been manifest in security policies in Europe since 1945. When we move from theory to practice, the lines between the different traditions – simplified earlier for clarity – will tend to blur. But before that point is explored, it is useful to discuss briefly the modern exponents of the three traditions.[1]

The Realists

The chief modern exponents of the power politics approach have been the realists, who have dominated the academic study of international politics since the Second World War. The realist tradition contains several schools, though many assumptions are held in common. The chief split is that between the founding figures of realism in the 1940s, notably Reinhold Niebuhr, who saw a flawed human nature at the root of international problems, and the 'neo-realists' of the 1980s, notably Kenneth Waltz, who explained international phenomena in terms of the structure of the system (Smith, 1986; Waltz, 1979). Within realism, a dominating sub-field since the mid-1950s has been strategic studies. The nuclear and other strategists, such as Thomas Schelling and Herman Kahn, have been labelled 'neo-Clausewitzians' by Anatol Rapaport, because of their attempt to conceive war in the nuclear age in a characteristically Clausewitzian fashion, that is, as rational, national and instrumental (Rapaport, 1968, 'Introduction').

The rationalists

In recent international politics literature, the so-called rationalists have attracted the title 'English school', though some of the chief exponents have not been English (Wilson, 1989). The approach has sometimes been more usefully characterised as the 'international society' school, and key writers have been Hedley Bull, Charles Manning and Martin Wight. Strong links are shared with realism; in particular there is a commitment to order. Major themes include the belief that international relations take place within a framework of normative rules which are, essential for order, the rejection of 'Utopian' schemes for the radical restructuring of the international system, and the rejection of behavioural or scientific methodology (Wilson, 1989: 55–6). In the security field the rationalist approach can be seen in those writings which have explored ideas such as 'common security' and 'security regimes' (George, 1988; Jervis, 1982; Palme, 1982).

The revolutionists

Mainstream literature in international relations has marginalised 'radical' traditions in general, but in the 1970s and 1980s increasing numbers of students of the subject saw flaws in traditional realism and explored 'alternative' approaches. In the last decade the 'revolutionist' tradition has been most influentially represented by the world order school and 'critical theory'. World order thinking, seen in the writings of Richard Falk, makes individuals living in a global community the primary referent of its normative theory (Falk, 1988). The approach emphasises the plurality of actors in world affairs, discusses human needs and not just national interests, and examines all significant interactions and not merely those of interest from a power political perspective. World order thinking is explicitly value-oriented, as is critical theory. The latter rejects mainstream theory's claim to objectivity, seeing all theory as ideological and self-interested. Prevailing ideas and institutions are not seen as immutable; instead politics is seen to be open-ended and based in ethics. This approach grew out of the Frankfurt

School in the inter-war years and it achieved visibility in international relations literature through the writing of Robert Cox and Andrew Linklater (Cox, 1981; Hoffman, 1987; Linklater, 1990). The security dimension of emancipatory projects have been explored only to a limited extent, in ideas such as 'citizen's security' and 'non-offensive defence',[2] though the notion of 'security community', developed by Karl Deutsch and his associates in the 1950s, remains an important guiding principle (Deutsch, 1957).

When we move from theory to practice we can expect the different traditions to be more mixed, since politics is a pragmatic business. Few governments, organisations, pressure groups or individuals will consistently represent a pure position on all issues. Nevertheless, the framework that has been established earlier should help clarify postwar policy debates and outcomes and also help the reader locate the intellectual homelands of the subsequent chapters in this book.

The practice of power

The power politics tradition found its fullest expression in the postwar European security field in the bipolar confrontation between the two blocs, each organised around a permanently integrated alliance (NATO versus the Warsaw Pact). During the Cold War, security could only be achieved, in the thinking of many on both sides, if military power was balanced by countervailing military power. As a result, Europe became the site of the two most powerful armed camps in history, and even towards the end of the Cold War half of the military spending in the world was focused on Europe. One result of this balancing of military power, realists argue, was that for nearly half a century Europe was able to enjoy an unprecedented period of peace. There was, undoubtedly, a high degree of military stability during the Cold War – neither side could secure an advantage by striking first – but the cost of a military breakdown between the alliances would have been a catastrophe beyond imagination. It was power politics with the ultimate stakes.

Security in the Cold War became synonymous with deterrence theory. As a result, questions of 'balance', 'stability', 'guarantees' and 'credibility' tended to dominate security thinking. The alleged 'lessons' of the 1930s were thought to be particularly pertinent: draw clear lines, do not give an inch, avoid appeasement, acquire the ability to inflict 'unacceptable damage' in all cirumstances, and follow through the implications of the idea that safety comes from the fear and respect of potential aggressors.

The power politics outlook was particularly evident in postwar Soviet strategic culture, with its themes – until Gorbachev – of military over-insurance, attack is the best form of defence, and respect comes from fear (Jacobsen, 1990). The epitome of this approach was Stalin's 'two-camp' image of the world, and his famous question 'How many divisions has the Pope?'. Together these attitudes reflected the realist view of a world of power political struggle (the idea that 'if you are not with us you are against us') and the assumption that the only serious players in international politics are those with material (and especially military) power. The corollary of such a viewpoint is the belief that without power a state is likely to be, at worst, the victim of aggression, and, at best, the victim of 'Finlandisation'. In contrast, Soviet 'new thinkers' in the early and mid-1980s looked at the record and concluded that Stalinist pessimism and Brezhnevite over-insurance had proved counterproductive. Soviet strategic policies for forty years were seen as having exacerbated the problem they had been designed to counter through the dynamics of the security dilemma.

The practice of order

Rationalism can be regarded as a branch of realism, and so its practice will reflect a mixture of the two traditions. Consequently, the proponents of the practice of order in postwar Europe accepted the importance of power, including deterrence, but they also believed that power should be tempered by the search for common norms, rules and values. Expressed baldly, the massing of power was seen as the business of defence ministries, whereas the creation of order was the profession of foreign ministries. Security, from this latter perspective, has been conceived as a mixture of both threats and reassurance. NATO's Harmel Report of 1967, which embraced both deterrence and détente, was a significant illustration of this approach.

One of the most notable exponents of the theory and practice of order in postwar international politics was the academic-decisionmaker Henry Kissinger. As US Secretary of State, his conception of détente in the 1970s was designed to enmesh what he believed to be the rising power of the Soviet Union in a web of mutual relationships and issue linkages. Behind his thinking was what he had earlier called a 'legitimate international order', the idea that all the major powers reach agreement on the aims and methods of foreign policy, and that their satisfaction with the status quo would thereby ensure that no power need express its dissatisfaction against the prevailing order by a revolutionary foreign policy (Kissinger, 1957). Diplomatically, most aspects of the Conference on Security and Cooperation in Europe, which was completed in Helsinki in 1975, reflected international society thinking. Ten years after the failure of Kissinger's attempt to create a legitimate international order, a similar Soviet conception emerged with Gorbachev's idea of a 'Common European Home'.

Kissinger's strategy, with its strong echoes of the nineteenth-century Concert of Europe, assumed that order was necessary not only between states and blocs, but also within them. This outlook was evident in the 'Sonnenfeldt doctrine', which in the mid-1970s looked to the Soviet Union to carry out what was seen as its historic superpower responsibility of imposing order on Eastern Europe (Talbott, 1984: 191–3). This in turn meant accepting the so-called Brezhnev doctrine of 1968 – the doctrine of limited sovereignty within the 'socialist commonwealth' which rationalised Soviet hegemony over Eastern Europe. One school of thought has given explanatory primacy not to the search by the superpowers for order *between* the blocs, but rather to their mutual desire for order *within* them. According to this argument the primary problem of European security from the perspective of the super-powers during the Cold War was not keeping at bay the imminent military threat of the adversary – the stuff of NATO and Warsaw Pact propaganda – but rather the maintenance of hegemony within their own spheres of in-fluence. For the countries in the two halves of divided Europe the primary problem was that of achieving a greater degree of independence from the oppressive and threatening order imposed by the superpowers (Kaldor, 1990a).

The dangerous and costly cycle of Cold War punctuated by temporary détentes stimulated, by the early 1980s, a variety of ideas about 'common security'. Earlier, at the turn of the 1950s/1960s, superpower arms control had represented the first exploration of the idea that adversaries can have common security interests. By the mid-1980s this notion had evolved into a comprehensive strategy for winding down the spiral of armaments building, tension and mistrust (Buzan, 1987; Palme, 1982; Smoke and Kortunov, 1991). This involved maintaining deterrence but with much more reassur-ance; as a result, it was hoped that there would be stability at lower levels of cost and danger, and that the security dilemma between the blocs would be ameliorated. The realism within the rationalist perspective, however, meant that it was not conceivable that the security dilemma between states could be ultimately transcended. Nevertheless, in the 1980s deterrence tempered by common security came to be seen by increasing numbers of people, East and West, as preferable to traditional deterrence resting upon common insecurity. At the same time there was a growing body of mainly European opinion for whom common security was not enough, since its statist assumptions and privileging of order were seen to be at the cost of justice, and hence could not be productive of truly stable security. These critics were the recent exponents of the Kantian tradition.

The practice of emancipation

Just as the Kantian tradition has been marginalised in mainstream international theory, so the practice of emancipation has been the least developed of the various traditions in postwar European security. Nevertheless it has been in evidence, even if particular governments and people have not always recognised that they were acting on the assumption that security is likely to be enhanced by meeting claims for justice and by privileging individuals rather than states. States are a means rather than an end for this school of thought, and benevolent processes are emphasised rather than the structures which characterise the other two traditions.

The emancipatory project has been advocated in its pure form by social movements rather than governments. The European Nuclear Disarmament (END) campaign through the 1980s, for example, was prominent in arguing that security in Europe would only develop after the blocs had been dismantled, democracy spread, and disarmament progressed. The Europe that emerged after the generally peaceful revolutions of 1989, and which lifted a forty-year cosmic threat, is seen by END supporters as the vindication of a decade of END consciousness-raising and campaigning (Thompson, 1991). The main agents of security conceived as a process of emancipation will be the 'civil societies' within the established state framework and the emerging pan-European civic culture. END was wound up with the dismantling of the Iron Curtain, but it metamorphosed, philosophically, into the Helsinki Citizens Assembly, a pan-European dialogue of non-state groups.

States are not the primary referent for emancipatory projects but they are key actors and must be taken into account. From the neo-Kantian perspective, the preference has been for postures of common security and non-provocative defence at the state level, while pursuing justice and democracy at the level of the individual. Civil society can help shape and sometimes carry out the political agenda, but some outcomes critically depend upon the agency of governments. A notable illustration of this was the way in which the spread of 'anti-politics' delegitimised communism in Eastern Europe; however, the successful (and peaceful) revolutions which finally toppled the old regimes required Gorbachev's permissive 'Sinatra doctrine' in place of the oppressive Brezhnev doctrine. Since we live in a world of states, there is an inevitable tension for supporters of emancipatory projects between the security of states and the security of people. The insecurity of states can, in some scenarios, be catastrophic – for both people and state. A balance of sorts must be struck. It makes sense to pursue common security between states: but can common security be built up between states while some social movements or even governments work for the demise of each other's values and political structures? Here again we see the tension between order and justice, a problem which extends far beyond Europe.

At the state level the Kantian tradition has been evident in some human rights policies (the search for justice) and in economic and political integration (community-building). One of the supposed lessons of the 1930s –

reflected in parts of the UN Charter – was that war grew in the fertile soil of dictatorship, instability, oppression and hyper-nationalism. The strengthening of individual human rights was thereby seen as one of the building blocks of world security. The Council of Europe was an early monument to such thinking, giving the individual citizens of its members the right to take cases directly to the Court of Human Rights. More notably, the CSCE process gave the expanded conception of Europe (from Vladivostok to Vancouver) a human rights agenda. An important piece of evidence that a human rights regime was beginning to take hold was the agreement of the CSCE signatories at the end of the 1970s that human rights were legitimate items on the international agenda and that debates about implementation did not represent 'intervention in internal affairs' (Ropers and Schlotter, 1990: 20).

CSCE as a whole has promoted a mixture of interstate and transnational interaction. The original conference and its continuing processes have had a significant role in the growth of civil society in Eastern Europe; these social movements were critical in helping emancipate the region from political oppression and Soviet control; this in turn helped emancipate Europe from the nuclear shadow. The CSCE as an organisation faces many obstacles in creating a pan-European consciousness, but world affairs since 1989 are a useful reminder of the way in which the politically possible can expand dramatically.

The most remarkable engine of postwar international communitybuilding (via economic integration and dense social interaction) has been the European Community itself; it has helped to revolutionise the long history of interstate warfare in Western Europe. The EC's success can be seen as a vindication of Kant's idea of republican states living in perpetual peace. With the collapse of the Soviet bloc after 1989 the opportunity was created to broaden the EC's membership, and so widen even further the benefits of living in an economic, political and moral community.

ORGANISATIONAL POTENTIALS

Security matters in Europe will be shaped for an indefinite future by several organisations, each of which represents a rather different perspective on the character of Europe's security problems and on the framework for handling them. There is a possibility that new organisational forms will be created, but for the moment most opinion favours building upon the complex institutionalisation which already exists, and which seems to meet the needs of different interests, rather than devising new 'architecture' from the ground upwards. From the perspective of individual governments, therefore, the present challenge is not to create new organisations but to shift the emphasis of those that exist (by adapting their functions or changing their membership). The key organisations to consider are as follows.

NATO

With the death of the WTO in 1991, following the collapse of Soviet power over its Eastern European members, NATO clearly emerged as the most successful structure of the traditional state-centric/military power conception of security. With the wish of several Eastern European states (some now seeing themselves as 'Central' European) to move closer to NATO, and with a much-reduced sense of a Soviet/Russian military threat (even a Soviet Union – of Sovereign or Socialist Republics – run by hardliners would not be able to turn the clock back to the Cold War eyeball-to-eyeball confrontation), NATO's traditional rationale has been seen as eroding, and its long-term future must be considered in doubt (though this might be mitigated, temporarily, by setbacks to the reform process in the post-communist Soviet state or states). Planning for force reductions and strategic reform during 1990–1 were obvious indicators of a change of era for NATO. Nevertheless, NATO still has strong supporters, and for some years at least it will provide its members (and some non-members) with a sense of military security while a perceived military threat remains from the fragmenting Soviet Union and the post-Cold War transition continues its bumpy path. Of special significance in this respect is the fact that NATO is the only organisation which seems capable of providing effective collective defence for the West, and the only organisational structure which ties US military power to European affairs.

As NATO soldiers on as well as it can, two worries persist. First, some concern has been expressed in Western Europe that with less to do to confront the residual Soviet threat, NATO will become an arm of President Bush's vague and US-centric 'new world order'. It may therefore involve the unwilling European members of the Alliance in the pursuit of essentially US-defined interests 'out-of-area'. Second, a Europe-wide fear has been voiced from centre and left-wing opinion that NATO, representing the rich Western nations, will help reinforce a new division across Europe, between the prosperous West and the poor East. At the same time there is some worry that the continuation of a narrow NATO will institutionalise new security fears. Mistrust will be perpetuated the more the Soviet/Russian state is excluded from the Western 'club', and the longer it is targeted as the main military threat. Equally the exclusion of the Eastern and Central European states from NATO will leave them feeling exposed to any revival of Soviet/Russian power and ambition. Without radical reconceptualisation, therefore, the continued existence of NATO may inhibit the emergence of a truly pan-European security system. As long as it remains a Western club, NATO's search for a more 'political role' will not overcome the problems created by the division of Europe into 'us' and varying shades of 'them'. However, the London Declaration of 1990, which looked to more transparency and military reassurance, was a significant sign of greater awareness among the NATO allies in this regard.

The WEU

The further development of the Western European Union (WEU) creates similar risks of dividing Europe. For some years there has been an attempt to revitalise the WEU, in order to strengthen the European pillar of NATO; but there remains an important division within its members as to what that means. Some (mainly France) want to see the WEU as the military arm of an ever-integrating EC; Britain, in contrast, wants to use the WEU as a bridge between European and American NATO, and sees the alternative approach as a threat to the future of the alliance. German opinion, less suspicious of NATO than France, and much more pro-EC than the British government, follows a complex balancing act between these extremes.

If the European pillar of NATO is not strengthened, with the Europeans 'pulling more weight' in their own defence, then US disenchantment with the organisation could grow significantly; if the European pillar is strengthened, however, it could create other political strains, as a result of greater European independence from the United States. Critics of the WEU argue that there is a danger that the organisation might be the embryo of a West European military superpower; this is seen by critics as threatening the growth of a continent-wide peace order while contributing another major military player to the global scene and thereby helping further to militarise international relations. If the WEU did clearly emerge as the military arm of the EC, the possibility then arises that it could be used for peacekeeping operations in the complex disputes which exist in East-Central Europe and the Balkans.

The EC

Whatever the disagreements which arise from time to time among its members, the evidence suggests that a community of peoples as well as of states has evolved out of the original Common Market. The EC has become an increasingly important actor in the affairs of its members and in the business of the world. It has helped to create a stable security community in Western Europe, and in its present stage necessity and ideals are driving it in the direction of deepening existing integration while broadening its membership. Whether both of these objectives can be achieved at the same time remains to be seen.

There is a risk that the EC could become excessively inward-looking, and so further divide Europe economically between West and East, and the world generally between North and South. Alternatively, the EC's resources, wealth, expertise and market-potential give it the scope to play a key role in the recovery of the economies of the post-communist countries of Eastern Europe and the former Soviet Union. By contributing to the economic development of these countries, the EC would be increasing the prospects for political, economic and military security throughout the continent. But the influence of the EC has not been confined, and will not be, to economic matters only. As the Yugoslav crisis of 1991 showed, it will also seek to exercise political influence in the interest of security more widely across the continent. Furthermore, as will be suggested later, the EC will be an essential engine for the spread of security communities in other continents. Such arguments are rejected from the realist perspective. The latter, in contrast, argue that the Western European security community, focused on the EC, is likely to prove a temporary phenomenon. Realists argue that the 'community' was created in a mould made by US hegemony and Soviet military power, and that with the decline of these factors there is every possibility that the member states will at some time revert to their old conflictual ways (Mearsheimer, 1990).

CSCE

The CSCE, with its pan-European framework and comprehensive conception of security, is for some the rational forum for pursuing an expanded security agenda. Its broad remit includes: mutual security in interstate relations; military confidence-building and arms control; economic, scientific, technological and environmental cooperation; humanitarian cooperation, including human rights and fundamental freedoms; and provisions for a continuing CSCE process. It thus encompasses – if not in equal portions – aspects of the concerns of power, order and emancipation.

At present the CSCE's organisational development is limited, though it is developing; even so it offers a unique framework for communication and the raising of continent-wide consciousness in terms of the development of common norms, rules and decision-making structures. However, it will not be able to make a more significant practical contribution to security in Europe until governments give it effective power. But it is its very lack of power and structure, together with its broad remit, which has led some Western governments to prefer to rest their security future on NATO.

The attraction and the weakness of the CSCE is that it is based on the principle of one state one vote. If weighted voting were to be employed, the CSCE would largely become the instrument of the powerful, but as long as the unanimity principle operates the success of whatever conciliation and mediation services can be organised under the CSCE will depend upon general consent. The limitations caused by the latter were exposed by the Soviet veto over CSCE involvement in Moscow's problems with the Baltic Republics in 1990, and Yugoslavia's veto in 1991 over a proposed CSCE conference on the future of the country. If such episodes disappointed CSCE idealists, it only confirmed the beliefs of the CSCE sceptics. Middle-of-the-road Western opinion, however, tends to see NATO and CSCE as somewhat complementary, with the CSCE seeking slowly to create the foundations for a pan-European security order while NATO remains as a vital insurance against failure. Furthermore, mechanisms which prevent international organisations like CSCE becoming embroiled in complex and violent 'internal' affairs can be seen as safeguards rather than shortcomings.

The United Nations

The UN had no role in Europe during the Cold War. Since the late 1980s, however, the organisation has had a certain revival, and this has had growing implications for European security. At first this seemed likely to be confined to Europe's relationship with the wider world rather than within Europe itself. By its contribution to settling conflicts in the South, and by providing a framework for cooperative international military action, a revived UN could be a significant factor in European calculations when contemplating the use of force 'out-of-area'. European states (through NATO or the WEU) might well be more positive towards such activities if a proposed operation is UN-mandated, or even UN-led. Alternatively, some European states would be very reluctant to have important issues determined by the Security Council. Much will depend on the fate of Bush's controversial 'new world order', and the nature and extent of the role given to the UN. Some European states – in the West as well as the East – would be reluctant to subscribe to a military role in support of a 'new world order' which was merely a cloak for unilateral US interests. The 1991 crisis in Yugoslavia, however, has focused attention on the UN's possible role as crisis manager and peacekeeper within Europe itself. The unwillingness of most European governments to contemplate referring the issue to the UN Security Council probably reflects their belief that the latter would not wish to become embroiled in the internal affairs of a member state (Yugoslavia). Were Croatia and Slovenia to be recognised as independent states by the international community, the problem would be transformed into an interstate and not an intra-state conflict (a step which might or might not escalate the violence). Even without a formal recognition of the new states, a more adventurous interpretation of Chapter 7 of the UN Charter (as it relates to threats to international peace and security) would allow the Security Council to become involved in the crisis. This process might be stimulated by appeals from Republican leaders, Yugoslav Federal authorities, or concerned states such as Canada or France, for the dispatch of UN peacekeeping forces. In the absence of these possibilities involving the United Nations, regional solutions will be the main avenue available to European governments seeking to resolve the crisis (though 'regional' and UN initiatives will not necessarily be incompatible).

International non-governmental organisations

So far the actors discussed in this section have been states acting in concert. It is important to recognise that various non-states actors through the 1980s were important in shaping the agenda of European affairs (peace movements, opposition groups, environmental activists, consumers, religious organisations and refugees). Many of these movements developed transnational links. This was a European manifestation of a global phenomenon: there are now over 18,000 international non-governmental organisations (INGOs), creating what one writer has called a 'global civic culture' (Boulding, 1988). This process can be expected to flourish in Europe, where there is relative cultural homogeneity and ease of communications. The most interesting new INGO is the Helsinki Citizens Assembly, with its twofold aim of: first, creating permanent pressure for a pan-European security system to supplant the blocs and find ways of solving conflicts without reliance on military force; and second, the creation of a trans-European civil society, which will help integrate Europe 'from below' (Kaldor, 1991: 199–215).

In the Soviet Union in August 1991 the importance of 'people power' at this stage of world politics was seen yet again. Without doubt the victory of reformist forces over the communist junta owed a debt to the demonstration effect of the 1989 revolutions in Eastern Europe. The absence of 'another Tiananmen Square' confirmed that Moscow belonged to the European political tradition. As the post-communist system evolves it will again underlie the importance of the interplay between domestic political change and international politics. In the immediate aftermath of the failed coup there was cause for optimism, but it is as well to remember that the programmes of some non-state actors (for example, aggressive nationalist movements) are not necessarily benevolent, either at home or abroad.

SECURITY CHALLENGES

As the preceding discussion has made clear, the security issues which individuals and groups will want to place on the European agenda in the years ahead will be shaped by their philosophical assumptions about the nature and potential of humanity and how the latter can be appropriately managed. But the agenda will also be shaped by the urgency of the challenges which threaten important values. Three main issue areas can be identified:

Military threats

Although the pervasive fears of the past forty-five years have evaporated, post-Cold War Europe is not entirely free of a sense of military threats. Three persistent anxieties have been expressed since the revolutions of 1989 and the collapse of the Warsaw Pact: first, the need for caution towards the still powerful 'Soviet' military machine; second, the possibility of violence arising out of instability in East and Central Europe; and third, historic fears about an over-powerful Germany. Of these three putative military threats the second has been the cause of most concern, with the third being the least significant.

While the surviving fears of a united, nationalistic and revanchist Germany (perhaps armed with nuclear weapons) are understandable among those Europeans who suffered directly or indirectly from German ambition in the first half of the century, there is good reason to have confidence that German power will never again be expressed in the same brutal fashion. The apparent strength of German democracy, the lessons learned from a disastrous past, the general desire within Germany for its integration within a wider European framework, and the disutility of massive military force in a highly industrialised and interdependent continent such as Europe, all warn against facile historical analogies.

All agree – even 'hawks' – that the 'Soviet' military threat, both in intentions and capabilities, has been dramatically reduced as a result of the demise of the Warsaw Pact, the signing of the first Conventional Forces in Europe Treaty (CFE I) and the continuing domestic preoccupations of the increasingly fragmented Soviet empire. While the attempted coup against Gorbachev in 1991 revived fears in some circles of a Soviet military threat looming over Europe, it was difficult for the majority of Western opinion to take at all seriously the proposition of some scaremongers that the clock could be turned back in a military sense. The countries of East and Central Europe have shared the general sense of the lifting of the Soviet military threat, but they remain the most exposed to its residual capabilities, and given their recent histories are naturally the most concerned that a post-Gorbachev regime in Moscow might revert to pre-Gorbachev habits. It will still possess the greatest military power on the Euro-Asian continent, and as a result, NATO planners will continue to be concerned about its military capabilities. Indeed, at a time when they have no clear benchmark against which to judge force-planning, Soviet military capabilities will provide the standard against which further Western reductions can (or cannot) be made. In the longer term, as the relationship between the centre in Moscow and the republics unfolds, it is not inconceivable that the traditional 'juggernaut' of the Soviet/Russian armed forces will disappear, to be replaced by a proliferation of smaller national militias and professional forces. At this point NATO military planning will have completed a metamorphosis from Cold War nightmare to post-Cold War daydream.

Although Western military planners today have virtually no fears of a surprise blitzkrieg westwards – the determining scenario for nearly half-a-century – there are other anxieties. Of these the most urgent is the risk of the former Soviet Union breaking up into civil war. If this were to occur – and there are powerful reasons encouraging the leaders of the republics to ensure it does not – it might not present the countries to the west with a direct military threat, but it would create several security concerns. There would, for example, be the problem of what would happen to the approximately 30,000 strategic, theatre and tactical nuclear weapons now possessed by the central Soviet authorities but located in the republics. The problem of nuclear inheritance will exist, even if civil war is avoided as the Soviet state is decentralised and fragmented. Mitigating the fears of proliferation and accidents are the safety devices which exist on Soviet nuclear weapons, and Moscow's awareness of the dangers of nuclear irresponsibility. A second security concern for the rest of Europe which might arise out of conflict within the former USSR is the prospect of a massive exodus of refugees from the troubles, fleeing into East and Central Europe, and then further west. Even without civil conflict there are already some fears that with the poor state of the Soviet economy and the loosening of its emigration laws, large population movements from the east will pose problems for the rest of Europe. If the numbers seeking refuge or a better life in the west were very high, they would pose a risk to the cohesion of national societies – some of which are already struggling to cope with immigration from other parts of the world. Uncontrollable population movement is a growing anxiety in the prosperous parts of Europe.

At the root of the problems just mentioned is the distintegration of the centralised communist system and the uncertainty as to what type of relationship will develop between the central government in Moscow and the republics. This was a problem before the failed anti-Gorbachev coup in August 1991, but is even more acute in its aftermath. The possible futures for this huge geopolitical area are further complicated by the nationalities patchwork: the traditional Soviet empire consisted of 104 nationalities, with over 64 million people either living outside their home republic or being among the eighty-nine nationalities with no republic of their own (van Evera, 1990: 47–9). Of the twenty-three inter-republic borders in the USSR, only three are not contested (*Economist*, 13–19 July 1991: 20). Clearly, the potential for ethnic and national conflicts abound, with the brew of border disputes, hopes for self-determination, nationalist desires to reunite kith-and-kin living in other republics and the ever-present danger of minority rights being abused. It would be remarkable, in the dismantling of the Soviet Union, if the heady ethnic-nationalist-religious brew could avoid boiling over into violent conflict. While such violence would be unlikely to threaten the rest of Europe in a direct military sense, it would have a variety of security implications, as was mentioned earlier. Such disturbances would also raise the question as to whether other European states would wish (perhaps under the aegis of the UN, or WEU, but almost certainly with the consent of the newly independent republics) to become involved in peacekeeping. This is a question which has already arisen for Europeans in the context of the next category of potential military threats – instability in Eastern Europe – as a result of the crisis in Yugoslavia in the summer of 1991.

The fear of violence arising out of instability in East and Central Europe derives from two main possibilities: the breakup of multi-ethnic states in the face of nationalist demands for self-determination, and the emergence of one or more aggressive dictatorships as a result of economic and political collapse. The end of the Cold War created geopolitical space for the revival of several traditional enmities in the former communist states of Europe. Although East and Central Europe has reasonably settled international borders, historically speaking, and the ethnic inter-mixing is less complex than within the Soviet Union, nine potential border disputes do exist (van Evera, 1990: 48). Of these, the ones demanding most concern are Transylvania, with its large Hungarian population under Romanian sovereignty and the Balkan region which has all the intermingling of national groups which characterises the Soviet Union. The threatened break-up of Yugoslavia, arising out of the secessionist demands of Slovenia and Croatia in mid-1991, illustrates the dangers (see Chapter 3).

The risk that Balkan conflicts might escalate into a general European war, as in 1914, is so minuscule as to be irrelevant. Even so, the fear of some spillover is justified; it could take the form of large population movements, economic dislocation, or some military intervention by neighbouring countries on behalf of fellow nationals living as minorities in regions of conflict. All this means that any violence in East or Central Europe or the Balkans must be of general European concern. This was evident in the attention given by the EC towards the 1991 crisis in Yugoslavia; the EC offered mediation and sent a ceasefire observation force. Such actions could set a precedent for future West European involvement in local conflicts to the east.

The various threats just discussed, which contain at least some military overtones, have led traditional realist opinion in the West to argue in favour of maintaining substantial military capabilities; other viewpoints have argued that since the root causes of the problems are not fundamentally military, they can better be dealt with by alternative means. For example, a 'Marshall Plan' for Eastern Europe has been advocated as a means of reducing the dangers of instability arising out of economic causes; operative human rights regimes promise to ameliorate ethnic anxieties; the progressive incorporation of the Soviet Union (or what comes after it) into the mainstream of European affairs would reduce the sense of traditional Russian insecurity and hence its need for military preparedness; and a more-deeply integrated EC would make anachronistic historic fears about a united Germany. Realists have proved slow to recognise the significance of such approaches, and of the extent of change in international affairs; consequently much time has been lost since the mid-1980s.

While there is a growing appreciation of the limitations of military force in dealing with important security issues, even those advocating primarily non-military responses to present predicaments accept the continuing need for some military framework. Indeed, if the weapons of diplomatic isolation and economic sanctions fail, military intervention may be the only way of stopping interstate aggression or gross violations of human and minority rights in the new Europe. Securing a European consensus for military intervention into messy internal conflicts will not be easy, even if it is with the consent of the warring parties. It is too easy for those sent in as peacekeepers to become identified as partial to one side or the other, thereby becoming targets for attack. Despite this, if security in the new Europe depends upon increased protection for human and minority rights, European states may have to confront the prospect of backing up international conventions and rules with a range of coercive sanctions, including ultimately a willingness to deploy armed forces. There remains therefore a requirement for an accurate assessment of the security threats which might have a military dimension, and the need for the further exploration of ideas about those military postures (non-offensive defence versus rapid deployment forces for example) which offer the best promise of enhancing political stability.

Political and economic stability

In the immediate aftermath of the ending of the Cold War, and with the recognition of the problems of transition in Eastern Europe, Europeans everywhere became mindful of the interwar years, when internal political and economic collapse led to instabilities and dictatorships which had disastrous international implications. So far, the post-Cold War fear has been of a generalised 'instability' rather than the expectation of a specific 'aggression'.

As they attempt to emerge from their former Stalinist systems, the peoples and embryonic political systems of East and Central Europe are confronting severe difficulties. The novel problems of learning to operate democratic institutions are compounded by the dislocation involved in simultaneously moving towards market economies. In such circumstances there is the risk that the reform process will collapse, and with it social tolerance. This in turn could lead to the rise of authoritarian élites, whose policies might be characterised by the oppression of minorities and by more militant policies towards neighbours over disputed borders or dispersed nationals. Again, there is the danger that a wave of emigration could drive westwards. This problem in itself might drag Western European states into complex internal conflicts further east. Containment by military power is widely seen as having relatively small significance in controlling these problems. Instead, confidence-building, extending community, deepening cooperation and promoting economic development everywhere are thought more pertinent, though it is less clear how these aims should be operationalised, or where the money is coming from to improve their prospects. A greater sense of urgency was injected into the thinking of some Western governments about those matters as a result of the August 1991 coup in Moscow. The episode was a sharp shock about the way matters could suddenly become worse. There was also perhaps some recognition of earlier Western complacency in not acting with more energy and resources to assist in the political and economic transition of the Soviet Union from 1987 onwards, when it became generally clear that fundamental changes were taking place in the USSR.

There are also questions of political philosophy which need to be addressed. The crisis over Yugoslavia raises the question of whether the principles of legitimacy in whatever new European security order emerges should be based on the rights of states or the rights of individuals and peoples (including nations). When the former are given primacy, governments support the principle of the political and territorial integrity of states, and the idea that borders can only be changed with consent. If the latter are given primacy, issues of self-determination and human rights will come to the fore. Again, as we face the future we are confronted by the tension between the provision of order and the provision of justice as the bases for reducing Europe's security problems.

Environmental problems

The destruction of nature is most acute in Eastern Europe, but it is also an important issue in the west, both in terms of local problems and adverse global trends. Environmental decay in Europe is a cross-boundary problem not only because of, for example, shared air and water systems, but also because of the interrelationships between political and economic issues such as debt. Most environmental problems therefore require pan-European solutions.

Environmental issues and security, broadly defined, are interlinked. The degradation of nature will affect the physical and emotional wellbeing of populations and the effectiveness of societies; it threatens distress, economic under-achievement, instability and disputes within and between states as to how the many problems can best be settled. In Europe, and globally, environmental conservation and economic change are inextricably linked; consciousness of this is growing, but is slow in bearing fruit. As a result, across the globe, green rhetoric is more in evidence than green planning. Environmental degradation and development crises continue to be driven by the wants of the industrialised world. Which politician among the triumphant G7 capitalist countries dare tell his or her electorate that consumption must be reduced in the global interest?

EUROPE AND THE WIDER WORLD: THREE SCENARIOS

Few believe that Europe can achieve real security if there is serious and continued turmoil in the rest of the world. Equally, it is unlikely that the rest of the world can advance far towards greater security unless Europe plays a major role in the process of wider security-building. The security interests of Europe and the wider world are ever more closely linked. The spread of ballistic missiles to the Third World is a powerful symbol of the shrinking geopolitical space between North and South.

Turmoil in the Third World can take many forms: regional wars, local imperialism, economic instability, poverty, social distress, nuclear proliferation, mass migrations, arms races, human rights abuses and so on. These problems cannot always be localised, and as was just suggested, geopolitical space is shrinking. The South threatens to impinge upon security in Europe in a number of ways: the disruption of trade and resources (notably oil); the spread of weapons of mass destruction and their means of delivery (raising the prospect of a targeted Europe); the dangers of terrorism; and the possible interplay of Third World crises and domestic European politics because of religious and ethnic communities settled in Europe (notably the growing Muslim populations).

Consequently, even if Europe – however defined – creates a stable security order within its own boundaries, the question arises as to whether it will need recourse to the threat and use of force with the non-liberal South. Alternatively, can policies be developed which extend those non-violent mechanisms of conflict resolution which seem to exist between liberal-democratic states in the world? (Wheeler, 1991). Such issues as these will now be discussed in relation to three scenarios which highlight the problems, prospects and underlying philosophies of Europe's possible future relationships with the wider world. The scenarios offered below represent combinations of futures for 'Europe' (an EC superpower, a common security Europe and a European security community) and some possible futures for the international system in general (a multipolar world, a 'new world order' and a developing global civil society). What will emerge over the next decade is likely to be a changing mixture of outcomes, comprising elements of each pure type. The main aim of the scenarios offered below therefore is not to predict the future but to stimulate thinking about the key questions which need addressing about likely and desirable futures. At the same time the scenarios will underline the way in which different approaches reflect the various philosophical traditions discussed earlier.

An EC superpower in a multipolar world

The first scenario envisages a united Western Europe, with military and political as well as economic integration, and much greater independence from the United States; the international system will tend to split into yen, dollar and ECU blocs, leaving a sorry Third World as the object of the power politics of the main actors.

As West European integration has progressed, the question of a common defence policy has become more pressing. This in turn has raised the issue of whether an 'economic superpower' must necessarily become a military superpower, with a military role outside its own boundaries. Jacques Delors, the present President of the EC Commission, has been prominent in arguing the case that a common defence posture must follow a common market. He has painted a picture of an unstable world and expressed his conviction that Western Europe should play a role with others in shouldering the burden of future global policing. He favours, eventually, a merger of the EC and WEU, believing that political union requires a united policy on the threat and use of force (Delors, 1991).

The debate about Western Europe's future military posture became strained during and after the Gulf conflict of 1990–1 (Wheeler, 1991: 85–92). For some Europeans the 'lesson' of this experience was that there was little scope for developing a common European security policy. The British government's view was that the crisis should be a spur to greater efforts at European security cooperation, but that this should not lead to the development of the EC's supranational authority in the field of foreign policy, and that the 'security' discussed in EPC should be clearly distinguished from 'defence' (which had to remain the preserve of NATO). For other governments, notably those of France and Germany, the 'lesson' of the conflict for Western Europe was that greater cooperation was not only necessary, but that some evidence suggests it might be possible. The EC agreement about sanctions against Iraq and the WEU policing of the UN naval embargo were brought forward to support this case.

Early in the Gulf crisis Western Europe and the United States agreed on the broad objectives of upholding international order and protecting the free flow of oil. When it came to the threat or use of force, however, the European states pulled in different directions. All except Britain were reluctant to use force, although France did eventually provide significant support. The US Administration was disappointed at this response to what was seen as a basic threat to common values and interests. As US pressure on its allies to support a forceful response mounted, the West Europeans did agree to send some naval forces under the mechanism of the WEU.

Not for the first time, the NATO establishment and its supporters were encouraged to argue that NATO should extend its treaty remit to include collective action (as opposed to merely political consultation) in 'out-of-area' crises. But there are major obstacles to such a development. Germany is inhibited by its constitution and postwar experience from taking on distant military roles, and there is no prospect of an early constitutional change; France is reluctant to work under the NATO umbrella, since to do so would imply a commitment to a structure of military integration dominated by the United States; and the British government, while favouring the WEU as the mechanism for any West European military contribution to US operations out-of-area, fears that 'Europeanising' defence might produce a barrier between Western Europe and the United States, and not a bridge.

Were there pressure for a West European 'defence pillar' to expand into a West European superpower in military terms, the potential criticisms would grow. First, the idea is dismissed in some circles as not being a practical proposition within a foreseeable timescale. The problem is not primarily institutional – NATO vs. the WEU vs. the EC – but the very diversity of the members, and so their potentially divergent interests and values on different issues. The membership of NATO, the WEU and the EC do not neatly match, and so a neat solution is not on offer, while the broader the membership of any interstate organisation becomes, the more difficult it will be to achieve consensus on sensitive issues. If the result of a common defence policy were to be a defence policy based upon the lowest common denominator, what value would it have in practice? Critics would point to the disagreement over how to deal with Saddam Hussein's blatant aggression in the Gulf, and would ask whether there was any reason to expect greater agreement about the use of force in more complex conflicts in less vital areas.

Second, there is the vexing problem of future relations between Western Europe and the United States. The British government's anxiety about the EC extending its supranational competence into defence, arms control and so on has already been mentioned. An important dimension of this is the fear that it will increase the distance between the two pillars of NATO. But even the British government has accepted that NATO will have to be 'Europeanised' to some degree. In terms of out-of-area responsibilities, the British Foreign Secretary, Douglas Hurd recommended that a future multinational rapid reaction force for the NATO area should perhaps be capable of operating under WEU control for areas beyond Europe (Hurd, 1990). Hurd seems to have accepted the worries of Delors that the United States might not always be willing or able to defend Europe's interests out-of-area, and that there should therefore be a European identity able to act independently. 'Identity' remains a matter of some disagreement between Delors and Hurd. Whether Europe could or would act independently of the United States is another unresolved matter. The worst outcome for the British government would be a US withdrawal from European security. Like the neo-realist bad dream neatly laid out by John Mearsheimer, Hurd seems unsure about the vitality of the West European security community in the absence of the United States. Between the French, British and German views – the loudest contributors to this debate – other European governments, such as the Dutch, favour a more substantial defence and security role for Europe, but wish to remain loyal to the wider Atlantic order.

Third, there are those who question the very rationale of greater military integration in Western Europe. An EC military entity, and still less an EC superpower, is seen as a regressive step. It risks diverting international affairs away from actual future needs towards old ways of thinking; it may thereby contribute to the evolution of inward-looking consumerist and militarised blocs in the North which will attempt to insulate themselves from the surrounding chaos of the Third World. On some issues these blocs may act in concert, thereby replacing the old East–West military confrontation with a tougher North–South divide. Critics of an EC superpower therefore hope that the countries of Western Europe will show that they have given up the traditional power politics game, and will instead attempt to spread their model of peaceful interstate relations to other parts of the world. Power projection forces are largely seen as incompatible with this.

The idea of a (West) European superpower contains many difficulties. Not least is the very uncertainty surrounding the meaning of the word 'superpower' these days. The era of pre-eminent powers, to the extent of the United States and Soviet Union during the Cold War, has passed. Power is diffusing so that we can expect a tripolar or multipolar arrangement alongside an evolving North–South divide. The extension to the South of democracy and development offers the only hope of minimising the impact of this divide.

A common security Europe in a new world order

This second scenario envisages a broader, but still statist Europe, with the Western states integrating but not federating and still largely identified with the United States; there would be general stability within this Europe, and constructive engagement between the West and the post-communist USSR. Europe's relationship with the South would largely be established by the framework of a 'new world order' defined and dominated by the United States. (With the collapse of the 74-year-old Soviet state in August 1991 the final pretence at Soviet 'superpower' status disappeared; the scope for assertions of US power in the 'new world order' grew accordingly.)

The wide ranging debate about the future of security in Europe as a result of the Gulf conflict raised questions about the 'new world order' but did not get very far in providing answers. In large part this was because President Bush himself remained vague about the meaning of his capitalised New World Order, while at the same time milking its rhetorical value. Within Europe, most opinion was sceptical about both the ability and willingness of the United States to asssume again the role of global sheriff, on whose behalf they would be cast as a more or less willing posse. What the Gulf crisis did unambiguously underline was the importance for the Europeans in paying attention to the dangerous sparks in the Third World, of which the Middle East remains the most dangerous. Consequently, European eyes have been cast towards such matters as exercising mutual restraint on arms transfers to the Third World, and searching for the settlement of regional conflicts. Operationalising such ideas is likely to prove difficult. Furthermore President Bush has warned Europeans of the danger of developing a security role independent of NATO, and he does not want to see a bloc emerging independent of the United States.

Few European states have shown any enthusiasm for an active military role outside Europe. Consequently, a Europe which had achieved a high level of common security within its borders might primarily seek to extend its influence by political and economic means. In this respect its CSCE experience and framework would be an important asset. While some might argue that many regional issues in the Third World are not ready for a CSCE-type process to be organised, it should be remembered that the original CSCE had its origins in a bipolar Europe, and grew up against the background of the decline of détente in the second half of the 1970s and the second Cold War in the first half of the 1980s. Harmony is not a precondition for success; indeed, if there were harmony there would be no need for a CSCE-type process. Thus the contribution of a CSCE-type framework to regional security may be more generalisable than is sometimes thought. As long as there is a desire to avoid war, even though the level of confrontation might be high, CSCE processes can help further the growth of international society between states. Encouraged by the European example, the Italian government has already been prominent in calling for the setting up of a CSCE process for the Middle East, North Africa and the Mediterranean.

A growing worry for the industrialised states of the North is the threat to international society represented by the arms trade, and especially long-range systems and chemical and nuclear weapons. There have been efforts to grapple with the problem over the years, but the record of controlling the flow of arms from European countries to the Third World is poor. Iraq's behaviour in 1990–1 provided a salutary warning. After supplying Saddam Hussein's regime with modern arms for years, the governments of the major arms suppliers finally understood the dangers of such a policy and expressed a willingness to try to develop coordinated responses aimed at limiting weapons proliferation. One small step, initiated at the G7 summit of July 1991, was the proposal for a UN register of arms deals. The obstacles to the success of a significant curb on the arms trade are enormous; as with the problem of developing common policies on the use of force, different states have different and sometimes competing interests; and immediate economic pressures for some countries may clash with long-term security interests. These economic pressures are felt by the relatively prosperous Western states, and so it is not surprising that some of the struggling economies of Eastern Europe find the arms trade one of the easiest sources of foreign currency. Controlling the arms trade, as in controlling armaments more generally in chronically tense regions like the Middle East, is an outcome which Europeans increasingly recognise as desirable, but one in which few practical agreements have been secured. In the attempt to control arms, as in other respects, will the opportunity be lost for peace-building in the aftermath of the recent Gulf war? Were the fine words of Western leaders early in 1991 cant rather than Kant? Admittedly the problems of the Middle East are daunting, notably the conundrum of satisfying the demands for security and justice of both the Israelis and the Palestinians. A CSCE-type framework would be a start for building the security of the region, but nobody can be confident of an entirely satisfactory outcome.

The EC has sought to engage in a limited dialogue with the South, but its scope has been limited, with no attempt to address the whole security agenda. The immediate prospects of a concerted and committed EC approach do not appear promising. If the Western powers as a whole hesitated over a Marshall Plan for Eastern Europe in 1989, proved obdurate in the 1990 GATT talks in defending the EC's heavily subsidised farmers, and made negligible progress on the problems of African debt and the deteriorating environment at the 1991 G7 summit, is it likely that they – and specifically the EC – will soon adopt a positive attitude towards creating a new economic and political order in their relations with the struggling states and people of the Third World?

In the near term, a common security Europe looks the most likely of the three European scenarios to develop. Since the mid-1980s Europe has made enormous strides in the achievement of common security values (manifest, for example, in the emphasis in CFE on reducing particularly provocative systems). The 'new world order' dimension of this scenario, however, is more problematic. As conceived by the Bush Administration it looks likely to be less new and orderly than worldly; that is, it will be characterised by an American attempt to restore some of the primacy of the past, against a background of a significant level of disorder in various parts of the world. In this respect one danger for Europe is that instead of seeing itself as bridge between old and new ways of thinking and acting on North/South issues, it will drift and be coopted into playing an increasingly neo-imperialist role, and so exacerbating a bitter and exploitative divide between the rich and the poor. Realists would retort that this is how it must be, because no lasting accommodation is possible between states, and still less between North and South. Indeed, Robert Tucker has argued that lasting inequality between North and South is the key to international order, not the obstacle (Tucker, 1977). Tucker's controversial argument brings us back to one of the oldest and most fundamental questions: could a world, characterised by injustice for the majority, be a place of lasting order? Even if common security can be achieved at the level of states, regionally or even globally, can it survive if justice is not strengthened at the level of peoples? And how, practically, can moral progress be made in a world of states?

A European security community in a developing global civil society

The final scenario envisages a new Europe, characterised by a pan-European security community, a vibrant civil society, and a commitment to a comprehensive security agenda. Its relations with the outside world would reflect this posture. It would seek to expand such principles and policies as non-violent conflict resolution, democracy, economic welfare, environmental sensitivity, arms reduction, and respect for human rights (Kaldor, 1991: 199–200, 213–15). Openness to the outside would stem from the belief that Europe would see itself as one set of communities in a wider world community. The political and moral community, for those who define security in terms of emancipation, does not stop at the boundaries of one's own nation or state or even continent. Theories of the good life should be universal: indeed, they must be, since none are truly emancipated until all are. Ethical considerations aside, self-interest also requires a wider sense of obligation in an interdependent and shrinking planet. Security in Europe is a global project.

The commitment to security as a process of emancipation requires attention not just to the symptoms of the problems, but also to their causes. Consequently security-building in Europe must involve serious attention being paid to both the most dangerous extra-regional sparks, of which the Middle East is the most pressing, and to the general problem of those states whose political and economic systems are so inadequate that interstate tensions are threatened (by the movement of peoples for example). The cause of this sort of tension lies at the level of people as well as states. In this respect the CSCE concept is particularly helpful, since it bridges, to some extent, both the state and individual levels of security in its different 'baskets'. Within the CSCE process is the idea that there is a relationship between how a government behaves internally and its external behaviour. This sort of issue was urgently raised in the aftermath of the Gulf War, particularly as a result of the problem of how to handle the Kurdish tragedy. The latter led to some talk in French official circles, for example, of modifying the UN Charter to allow for humanitarian intervention. Stanley Hoffmann, whose opinions represent much Western liberal thinking on this matter, has written that no state should be able to claim that the way it treats its citizens is a sovereign right, if this is likely to cause international tension (Hoffmann, 1991). This was an opinion which was echoed by governments in the G7 summit in July 1991 (Helm, 1991). Further confirmation of the spread to offical circles of ideas previously advocated by radical opinion occurred during the crisis in Moscow in August 1991. The old END theme about the relationship between democracy, disarmament and human rights on the one hand, and peace on the other, was an implicit and sometimes explicit position on the part of Western governments.

The notion of a European civil society, as Mary Kaldor has written, seeks to tackle the roots of violent conflict and proposes state forms where sovereignty is based on *fields of activity* (the EC in certain economic fields, for example, and the Council of Europe in human rights matters) rather than on the traditional *control of territory* (Kaldor, 1990b). This viewpoint also sees Europe as having a major responsibility in constructing a comprehensive engagement with the South, to attempt to spread elsewhere its model of peaceful relations, democracy and economic justice. In this sense Europe is being advised to give up the traditional game of power politics. Such an argument raises an immediate question: does this mean that there are no circumstances in which a peaceful and democratic Europe would use force in defence of its interests outside Europe? If we are to build a solidarist international community should not the liberal democratic states occasionally be prepared to act with the sanction of force? Those cases justifying the latter might include flagrant breaches of international law and human rights abuses, as well as support of more traditional vital state interests (such as the free flow of oil). The use of force for community purposes raises difficult issues, in both theory and practice, including the broader question as to whether there can be a general consensus on international policing without there first having been created a global cosmopolitian culture.

Hedley Bull was prominent in arguing that 'global interdependence' requires states to develop a more cosmopolitan outlook – to see themselves as 'local agents of the world common good'. However, he was doubtful (in the early 1980s) whether it would be possible for states to reach agreement on the principles of justice that might underpin a universal political order. The best he could hope for was a global bargain to try to reconcile order and justice. In this grand bargain the North would agree to redistribute wealth more equitably while the South would agree to respect human rights and accept democracy (Bull, 1983: 14–18). Is such a revolution in attitudes feasible without there first having been fundamental changes in the domestic politics of most countries?

Clearly, the achievement of both main elements of this third scenario (a European security community and a global civil society) faces considerable obstacles; it is the most ambitious of the three packages discussed here. Nevertheless, there are sound arguments for taking this scenario seriously for what is 'politically possible' can change dramatically, and within the lifetime of individuals. Some historical perspectives are illuminating. Who, in the 1930s, would have seriously forecast a West European security community in the second half of the century? Radical surprises are possible in international politics, and ideas count. And if the static analyses of neo-realism are avoided, it is evident that, in an age of rapid and dense global interaction, history is not stopping; on the contrary, it is moving in fast-forward. Following the experience of 1989–91, who can rule out an eventual pan-European security community, or even a consolidating global cosmopolitan culture? Furthermore, it is becoming apparent to growing numbers of observers of world affairs, albeit patchily, that security threats are interrelated at the individual, domestic and international level. The approach must therefore be 'holistic' (Buzan, 1983: 245–58). In considering Europe's future relations with the wider world, a militarised posture will do little to overcome the roots of insecurity and instability in the South; for the most part these problems lie in politics, society, religion and economics.

34 *Security & the new European system*

CONCLUSION

The three scenarios just discussed are clearly simpler than the reality which will actually evolve; in practice a multi-faceted and shifting combination of different elements will emerge. One idea which unites the three scenarios, however, is the increasing recognition among the people of Europe – including governments – that European security is now inextricably linked with what happens in the world beyond. In this recognition, as with all political attitudes, there is a variable mixture of self-interest and ethics. There is the idea that European security and economic prosperity could be eroded by conflict elsewhere, and the idea that the privileges and wealth that go with being European carry with them obligations and responsibilities to others. When contemplating what is to be done, it should have become apparent that since world politics operate at a variety of levels, strategies of transition to a more secure Europe and wider world should also operate at a variety of levels. The rational way ahead is to adopt a mix of policies which attend to individual human beings, groups, states and the human collectivity as a whole; at the same time the needs of power, order and emancipation have to be juggled and agonised over, and decisions made. A simple formula cannot be offered, since the political world in its nature is a dynamic domain in which competing interests have constantly to be balanced and rebalanced. Power and order must be given their due, but so must emancipation. A strategy for world politics which excludes 'Utopia' will not succeed over the long term, just as a policy which neglects reality is bound to fail (Carr, 1966: 13, 93, 97, 172, 220, 223). A rational policy will be one of Utopian realism (Booth, 1991a).

The main conclusion we draw from this discussion is that, as within Western Europe itself, the ultimately most promising route to global security lies in community-building. There may be a limit to community-building on such a scale; but the people and governments of the world will never know what that limit is unless they seriously try to reach it; and they will not try unless they believe, philosophically and politically, that it is desirable and achievable. European security now needs a flexible response of the mind.

NOTES

1 The threefold distinction used below is that of Martin Wight (For his 'three R's' see Porter, 1978).
2 See also Chapter 7. In practice, policies overlap between the different traditions of thought; in a pragmatic political world made up of both states and people it is probably rational that they do. From a Grotian perspective common security is the best that can be achieved, and among its tactics will be some form of non-offensive defence. From a neo-Kantian perspective common security between states will also be an element, including more radical forms of non-offensive defence,

because states exist. However, the ultimate aim is to transcend the states system by the creation of a world community.

REFERENCES

Booth, K. (1990) 'A new security concept for Europe' in P. Eavis (ed.) *European Security: The New Agenda*, Bristol, Saferworld Report.

Booth, K. (1991a) 'Security in anarchy: utopian realism in theory and practice' *International Affairs*, **67**, 3: 527–45.

Booth, K. (1991b) 'Security and emancipation' *Review of International Studies*, **17**, 4: 313–26.

Boulding, E. (1988) *Building a Global Civic Culture*, Syracuse, N.Y.: Syracuse University Press.

Bull, H. (1977) *The Anarchical Society*, London: Macmillan.

Bull, H. (1983) 'Order and justice in international relations' *Hagey Lectures*, Waterloo, Ontario: University of Waterloo.

Buzan, B. (1983) *People, States and Fear: The National Security Problem in International Relations*, Brighton: Wheatsheaf.

Buzan, B. (1987) 'Common security, non-provocative defence, and the future of Western Europe' *Review of International Studies*, **13**, 4: 265–79.

Buzan, B. (1990) *People, States and Fear: Agenda for International Security Studies in the Post-Cold War Era*, Brighton: Wheatsheaf.

Buzan, B. Kelstrup, M., Lemaitre, P., Tromer, E. and Waever, O. (1990) *The European Security Order Recast: Scenarios for the Post-Cold War Era*, London: Pinter Publishers.

Carr, E. H. (1966) *The Twenty Years' Crisis, 1919–1939: An Introduction to the Study of International Relations*, London: Macmillan (first published in 1939).

Cox, R. W. (1981) 'Social forces, states and world orders: beyond international relations theory' *Millennium*, **10**: 126–55.

Delors, J. (1991) 'European integration and security' *Survival*, **33**, 2: 99–109.

Deutsch, K. (1957) *Political Community and the North Atlantic Area*, Princeton: Princeton University Press.

Falk, R. (1988) *The Promise of World Order*, Princeton, N. J.: Princeton University Press.

George, A., Farley, P. and Dallin, A. (1988) *US-Soviet Security Cooperation: Achievements, Failures, Lessons*, New York: Oxford University Press.

Helm, S. (1991) 'Seven seek a tougher United Nations' *Independent*, 16 July, p.8.

Hobbes, T. (1962) *Leviathan* (first published 1562, edited and abridged with an introduction by J. Plamenatz) London: Collins.

Hoffman, M. (1987) 'Critical Theory and the Inter-Paradigm Debate' *Millennium*, **16**: 231–49.

Hoffmann, S. (1991) 'A state's internal conditions are outsiders' business' *International Herald Tribune*, 27 February.

Hurd, D. (1990) 'European defence and security in the 1990s' unpublished speech delivered in Berlin, 10 December 1990.

Hurrell, A. (1990) 'Kant and the Kantian paradigm in international relations' *Review of International Studies*, **16**, 3: 183–206.

Jacobsen, C. (ed.) (1990) *Strategic Power: USA/USSR*, London: Macmillan.

Jervis, R. (1982) 'Security regimes' *International Organisation*, **36**, 2: 173–94.

Kaldor, M. (1990a) *The Imaginary War*, Oxford: Blackwell.

Kaldor, M. (1990b), 'Broader perspectives on security – Europe and the World' draft unpublished paper for the North–South Roundtable on the Economics of Peace, Costa Rica, 4–5 January.

Kaldor, M. (ed.) (1991) *Europe from Below: An East–West Dialogue*, London: Verso.

Kissinger, H. (1957) *Nuclear Weapons and Foreign Policy*, New York: Harper.

Linklater, A. (1990), *Beyond Realism and Marxism: Critical Theory and International Relations*, London: Macmillan.

Mearsheimer, J. (1990) 'Back to the future: instability in Europe after the Cold War' *International Security*, **15**, 1: 5–56.

Morgenthau, H. J. (1960) *Politics Among Nations: The Struggle for Power and Peace*, (3rd edn; 1st edn 1948), New York: Alfred A. Knopf.

Palme, O. (1982) *Common Security: A Programme for Disarmament*, London: Pan.

Porter, B. E. (1978) 'Patterns of thought and practice; Martin Wight's "international theory"' in M. Donelan (ed.) *The Reason of States*, London: Allen & Unwin.

Rapaport, A. (1964) *Strategy and Conscience*, New York: Harper & Row.

Roberts, A., Kingsbury, B. and Bull, H. (1991) *Hugo Grotius and International Relations*, Oxford: Clarendon Press.

Ropers, N. and Schlotter, P. (1990) *Regime Analysis and the CSCE Process*, Frankfurt: Peace Research Institute Report No.13.

Smith, M. (1986) *Realist Thought from Weber to Kissinger*, Baton Rouge: Louisiana State University Press.

Smoke, R., and Kortunov, A. (1991) *Mutual Security: A New Approach to Soviet-American Relations*, Houndmills: Macmillan.

Talbott, S. (1984) 'Social issues' in J. Nye (ed.) *The Making of America's Soviet Policy*, New Haven: Yale University Press.

Thompson, E. P. (1991) 'Ends and histories', in M. Kaldor (ed.) *Europe from Below: An East–West Dialogue*, London: Verso.

Tucker, R. (1977) *The Inequality of Nations*, New York: Basic Books.

van Evera, S. (1990) 'Primed for Peace: Europe After the Cold War' *International Security*, **15**, 3: 7–57.

Waltz, K. (1979) *Theory of International Politics*, Reading, Massachusetts: Addison-Wesley.

Wheeler, N. (1991) 'Europe's future security commitment', in S. Kirby and N. Hooper (eds) *The Cost of Peace: Assessing Europe's Security Options*, Reading: Hardwood, pp.81–107.

Wight, M. (1966) 'Western values in international relations', in H. Butterfield and M. Wight (eds) *Diplomatic Investigations: Essays in the Theory of International Politics*, London: Allen & Unwin.

Wight, M. (1977) *System of States*, Leicester: Leicester University Press.

Wilson, P. (1989) 'The English School of International Relations: a reply to Sheila Grader' *Review of International Studies*, **15**: 49–58.

2   Future security systems for Europe

Adrian Hyde-Price

This chapter is concerned with the future evolution of the European security system, and outlines four possible security systems for Europe in the early twenty-first century. The concept of a 'security system' refers to the overall pattern of overlapping and interlocking security relations, commitments and institutional structures in a specific security area.[1] It suggests that a degree of predictability and relative stability exists in this security area, at least in terms of its core relationships. A security system is more than just the sum of its parts, and our concern in this chapter is therefore not with the specific national security strategies of individual states, nor with the security problems of any particular military alliance in the European security area. Rather, it is with the interaction between the institutional structures and the patterns of bi- and multilateral relationships in Europe, and the implications of this for the future development of the European security system.

THE END OF THE POSTWAR EUROPEAN SECURITY SYSTEM

For over four decades, postwar Europe experienced a security system which was as stable and predictable as it was iniquitous and unacceptable. This security system was built on the bipolar division of Europe (with the *Spaltung* of Germany at its centre) and the hegemony of the two superpowers within their respective alliance systems. This bipolar division did not, it should be noted, produce a symmetrical arrangement between two comparable 'blocs'. While the transatlantic community developed upon the principles of pluralist democracy and welfare capitalism, the 'socialist community' was constructed upon the basis of authoritarian communism and command economies. This resulted in a bitter ideological and systemic conflict, which in turn generated a costly arms race and a massive concentration of conventional and nuclear weaponry in Europe.

The collapse of this Cold War security system came about as a result of a series of secular trends which had fatally weakened its underlying foundations. These trends included the systematic failure of Soviet-style socialism, the growing prosperity and integration of Western Europe, and the changing power relationship within the Atlantic community.[2] The catalyst for change was provided by the reform programme of Mikhail Gorbachev in the Soviet Union. It was the changes in Soviet domestic and foreign policies from the mid-1980s onwards which made possible the remarkable events of the Autumn of 1989, when the Berlin Wall was breached and communist power in Eastern Europe imploded.

The dramatic and largely unexpected events of 1989–91 constitute an irreversible watershed in European history. They shattered the comfortable assumptions of the bipolar Cold War era, and marked the end of the postwar European security system. The security situation in Europe has been greatly improved as a result of the changes in Germany, Eastern Europe and the Soviet Union, and the prospects for new forms of cooperation have been enormously expanded. Nevertheless, the collapse of communism has released a number of pent-up and deeply-rooted historical animosities – primarily of a national, ethnic or religious character. The disintegration of postwar certainties has also rekindled older worries in other parts of Europe, particularly those associated with German power. There is, therefore, the need for a new system of security which can manage, contain and hopefully resolve the new and emerging challenges to the security of the continent.

But the events of 1989–91, and the deeper processes of secular change which produced them, have still not worked themselves out. There is still enormous uncertainty as to the future institutional and political relationships in 'post Cold War Europe'. The biggest single source of uncertainty in Europe is the future of the former Soviet Union, but there are many others: can viable free-market democracies be built in Eastern Europe? Will the Balkans slide irretrievably into violent turmoil? What role will a united Germany play in the new Europe? Can the European Community combine 'widening' with 'deepening'? How will transatlantic relations evolve in Europe 'beyond containment'? The open nature of these fundamental questions means that it is extremely difficult to predict what the main features of the new security system in Europe will be.

Moreover, the very nature of security itself is changing in Europe. The contemporary security agenda is now very different from the Cold War security agenda which produced the bipolar division of Europe. To begin with, security can no longer be defined primarily in military terms. Economic, political, social and even environmental dimensions are now of growing importance, and hence we need an expanded concept of security. This reflects the changing nature of international relations in the late twentieth century, as a result of the impact of economic interdependence, regional integration and nuclear deterrence (Nye, 1989; O'Meara, 1984). Second, the nature of the security risks and challenges have changed. The postwar European security system was in large part the result of a perceived 'Soviet threat', and subsequently the overarching security concern was the management of the East–West conflict.

Today, however, there is a new European security agenda. On the one hand, there are a number of intra-European security concerns, such as the residual military capabilities of the former USSR; socio-economic instability in the former communist bloc; rising national, ethnic and religious tensions; and the growing influence of a united Germany. On the other hand, as the Gulf War has shown in dramatic fashion, there are a series of 'out-of-area' concerns. These include the proliferation of new weapons technologies; immigration; threats to supplies of raw materials and to sea-lines of communications; terrorism; and the instability generated by Third World poverty and the North–South divide (Eavis, 1990). The architecture and dynamics of the new security system in Europe will therefore be decisively influenced by this more diffuse, multi-faceted and variegated security agenda, and will reflect the changed nature of security in Europe in the closing decade of the twentieth century.

TOWARDS A NEW EUROPEAN SECURITY SYSTEM

The formal dissolution in early 1991 of the Warsaw Pact and the CMEA (Council of Mutual Economic Assistance) – the twin pillars of the former 'Socialist community' – constitutes the most visible outward expression of the fundamental change that has occurred in the European security system. But in the new conditions of the 'post-Cold War' era, all the remaining bodies in the European security area are facing enormous pressures to substantially change their functions, institutional relationships and composition. In the new Europe, it is already clear that three organisations will play a decisive role in shaping the contours of the evolving security system: the European Community, NATO and the Conference on Security and Cooperation in Europe. The precise nature of the new security system will depend to a large extent on what sort of relationships develop between these three key bodies. Within this triangular arrangement some other organisations will find their roles expanded and modified, most notably the Council of Europe, the Western European Union and possibly the Hexagonale.[3]

At the same time, the new security system in Europe will be determined not only by its institutional architecture, but also by the changing pattern of bi- and multilateral relationships in the continent. The political and economic dynamics of these relations are already very different from what they were in the Cold War years of rigid bipolarity. With the greater fluidity which now exists in European interstate relations, more traditional patterns of conflict and cooperation (determined by a mixture of geopolitics, cultural affinities and history) are manifesting themselves. However, this does not mean that European politics are simply reverting to older, pre-war behavioural norms. These traditional patterns of conflict and cooperation are emerging in the context of a continent substantially transformed by thickening networks of interdependence, radically new forms of supranational integration, higher levels of socio-economic development and a much more widespread acceptance of democratic values. The past can thus serve only as a partial guide to the future of European security. The Europe of the 1990s will certainly not be the Europe of the 1870s, 1930s, or 1950s.

Within the new Europe, there are a number of crucial bi- and multilateral relationships. Their future development will have a major impact on the evolution of the continent's new security system. The most important of these relations for the future of European security are as follows.

Intra-Western European

This includes the Scandinavian countries, but centres on the twelve members of the EC. In terms of changing patterns of security, relations between the 'Big Three' of Britain, France and Germany are particularly important, with the Franco-German relationship traditionally being seen as the most influential bilateral relationship in Western Europe.

US–West European

The emergence of the transatlantic community has been one of the defining features of the postwar era, and its future development is of crucial importance to European security.

Soviet–West European

Within this set of relations, the Soviet-German will undoubtedly be the most significant for the future of Europe (Sodaro, 1990).

Eastern Europe's relations with its neighbours

Eastern Europe – particularly East Central Europe – will be the area of greatest international realignment in the 1990s. These countries are currently forging new sets of relations with both the former Soviet Union (and its individual republics) and with the West (especially the EC).

The Balkans

Antagonistic relations between states in this region have on a number of previous occasions provided the spark which has ignited wider European conflicts. The end of the Cold War has brought renewed fluidity to Balkan politics. This has facilitated tentative steps towards limited regional cooperation, but it has also led to an increase in national and religious animosities, which have been fuelled by socioeconomic problems. At the heart of the Balkan conundrum is Yugoslavia, which in the summer of 1991 provided post-Cold War Europe with its first major internal crisis (see Chapter 3).

These sets of relations will have a decisive impact on the future European security system. They will both be shaped by the existing institutional structures of Europe (which provide a framework for interaction, and lay down common rules and norms of behaviour, which in turn help to mould expectations and actions), and at the same time, will shape the future development of this institutional architecture.

FOUR MODELS OF FUTURE EUROPEAN SECURITY SYSTEMS

As we have seen, the nature of the post-Cold War European security system will be determined by the changing security agenda, while its precise contours will be shaped by the interaction of its institutional architecture and with the evolving pattern of bi- and multilateral relationships in the European security area. Given the current fluidity in European politics, it is of course impossible to predict with any certainty the main features of the post-Cold War security system. But by extrapolating current trends, it is possible to suggest a number of likely models. These should be seen as 'ideal types' – their aim being to clarify some of the main issues and problems in European security, and to illustrate the longer-term implications of current policy proposals (Hyde-Price, 1991: 189–91). I would therefore like to sketch out four possible models of European security which could emerge in the next decade or so. These are an 'Atlanticist' Europe, based on a central role for a reformed NATO; a West European-based security system centred on a federated EC with a common foreign, security and defence policy; a pan-European collective security system within the CSCE framework; and more fluid and loosely structured 'Europe of Nation-States'.

NATO and an 'Atlanticist' Europe

The first Secretary-General of NATO, Lord Ismay, once defined the role of the Alliance as being 'to keep the Russians out, the Americans in, and the Germans down'. With the end of the Cold War and the far-reaching transformation of Central and Eastern Europe, it is not surprising that some now question the continuing need for the NATO Alliance. Nevertheless, for others, NATO's importance is now as great as ever before, even though they recognise that its precise structure and functions must change. This view is especially prevalent in official circles in the USA, the UK, Holland and Portugal, and among conservative and Christian-Democratic political forces elsewhere in Western Europe.[4] The reasons for this are fivefold.

First, NATO – it is argued – provides an irreplaceable mechanism for linking the USA to the defence of Western Europe. This transatlantic bond is seen by some as vital for preserving a security balance in Europe, and for ensuring the defence of common Western interests in an increasingly polycentric world.[5] Second, NATO provides a framework for military and defence cooperation, which reinforces feelings of solidarity and cooperation throughout the transatlantic community. This, it is argued, proved its value in the Gulf, even though NATO was not directly involved.[6] Third, NATO is a proven alliance of democratic nations which is politically incapable of offensive military action against peaceful neighbours. Such a tried and tested organisation should not be lightly given up.[7] Fourth, NATO provides a framework for the integration of German military power into broader, collective defence arrangements. Finally, NATO can be seen as an invaluable insurance policy against a recidivist Soviet Union, which remains the continent's only military superpower.

Those who wish to see NATO as the core of Europe's new security system recognise that the Alliance must evolve if it is to remain relevant and effective to the continent's changing security requirements. This process of evolution, it is argued, has already begun. The London Declaration, issued by the North Atlantic Council (NAC) in July 1990, was a landmark in this respect, and its main themes have been full elaborated by subsequent NATO documents. To begin with, as the Copenhagen NAC communiqué stated in June 1991, it is necessary 'to enhance the role and responsibility of the European members' within the Alliance.[8] This notion can be traced back to Kennedy's 1962 Independence Day speech in which he advocated an Atlantic Alliance based on two 'pillars'. To this end there have been a number of calls for Europeans to be given more senior commands within NATO, up to and including the suggestion that there should be a European Supreme Commander in Europe (SACEUR) (Eberle, 1990). It is also suggested that the WEU should be developed as the European pillar of NATO. In such ways, it is hoped, it may be possible to coax the French back into the substance, if not the structure, of NATO's integrated military command. But this project is politically very sensitive because there is a danger that a more pronouced European identity for NATO (including a distinctive European pillar based on the WEU) could lead the Americans to feel that their concerns were being marginalised in an Alliance dominated by a European caucus.[9]

Change is also required to NATO's strategy and military structures. The end of the Cold War and the unification of Germany have made the reform of NATO's strategic concepts of forward defence and flexible response an urgent necessity. The London Declaration initiated the search for a new strategic concept, based on a reduced reliance on nuclear weapons and smaller, more mobile conventional forces (see Chapter 6). In June 1991, the Copenhagen communiqué of the Defence Planning Committee (DPC) and Nuclear Planning Group (NPG) reiterated this call for a 'reduced reliance on and substantial reductions of nuclear weapons'. It also called for the Alliance's command structure to be streamlined and adapted to the new situation, and for its force structure to be remodelled on the basis of flexibility, mobility and multinationality. Among other changes, a new Rapid Reaction Corps (RRC) is to be established under UK command, despite French reservations.

NATO also needs to change its relations with the Soviet Union and the East European states if it is to become the core of a new security system. The London Declaration spoke of extending the 'hand of friendship' to former enemies in the Warsaw Pact, and this resulted in both the Joint Declaration of twenty-two States adopted at the CSCE Paris Summit in November 1990, and the establishment of 'regular diplomatic liaison' between NATO and former Warsaw Pact states. The Copenhagen NAC meeting subsequently issued a major statement on 'Partnership with the Countries of Central and Eastern Europe', in which it spoke of the Alliance's desire to foster 'new patterns of constructive dialogue and bonds of friendship', in order to 'promote both mutual reassurance and increasingly close ties'. In the spring of 1991, NATO came under strong pressure from East European states to offer them firm security guarantees and the eventual prospect of membership of the Alliance. This was resisted because of fears that such steps would antagonise the Soviet military and weaken the hand of reformist forces in the USSR. But proponents of a central security role for NATO in the new Europe have hoped to use this East European interest in the Alliance in order to strengthen NATO's role as a forum for security consultations and dialogue across the former East–West divide.

A final area for change in NATO concerns its out-of-area role. Commitments under Article 5 of the Treaty of Washington do not extend to so-called 'out-of-area' problems. Yet such problems are likely to figure prominently on the new security agenda. Although a formal extension of the NATO area is politically impossible at present, convinced Atlanticists argue that the Alliance can and should nevertheless play a vital role in protecting Western interests out-of-area. To begin with, they argue that the Alliance provides a vital forum for intensive consultation on security concerns at all levels – from heads of state to officials. Moreover, they point out that the military coalition in the Gulf benefited from years of joint training and cooperation within the NATO military command.[10] NATO's out-of-area utility could be further strengthened by giving NATO members involved in conflicts outside the North Atlantic area, either collectively or individually, the right to use the Alliance's logistical infrastructure. This includes the use of military bases; transport networks (in particular ports, airfields, and air traffic control facilities); equipment supplies, repairs and spare parts; ammunition transfers; and medical support. One interesting but controversial development which could be of great significance for the future of NATO's out-of-area role is the suggestion by some Turkish officials that the Allies' rapid reaction force in southern Turkey (deployed as part of Operation Poised Hammer) should come under the NATO umbrella.[11]

If NATO were able to change in the ways indicated above, then it might be able to remain relevant to the new security environment of Europe. In this case, it could provide the central bulwark of a new European security system, within a more diverse institutional architecture.[12] NATO would then provide the main guarantees for collective defence for its sixteen members, but would also act as a vital forum for pan-European security consultations and discussions. The EC would provide a complementary but distinct focus for economic integration and political cooperation, and would be loosely linked to NATO through the WEU (which would play a crucial 'bridging' role between the Alliance and the Community[13]). Finally, the CSCE would act as forum for pan-European discussions. It might also develop a mechanism for crisis management and the peaceful resolution of disputes (with particular reference to the problems of minority nationalism and ethnic clashes in Eastern Europe and the Balkans), but it would not pretend to be able to offer collective security guarantees to its thirty-five participating states.

This vision of an Atlanticist security system based on a rejuvenated NATO does not enjoy universal acclaim. It is strongly criticised on a number of counts. First, it is argued that NATO is a product of the Cold War and the bipolar division of Europe. It is thus not suited to the changed political realities of a Europe 'whole and free', and will only impede the construction of a 'common European house'. Moreover, it cannot really address the problems of ethnic and national conflict in the continent's east, which – as the Yugoslav crisis has demonstrated – are likely to be a major concern of the 1990s. Second, it preserves American hegemony over the affairs of Europe, and prevents the development of a more integrated and self-confident European Union. Third, NATO can never be a legitimate actor in out-of-area conflicts, and trying to extend its role is counterproductive. Its involvement in conflicts in the Middle East or elsewhere would only cause additional diplomatic complications with the former USSR and the developing world, and could undermine the political acceptability of the Alliance within NATO countries (particularly in Central Europe).

Such criticisms of NATO are frequently heard from the French Government, often supported by the Italians and Spanish. They argue that support for the Atlantic Alliance in its broadest sense does not mean support for NATO and its integrated military command structures. As President Mitterrand said at the Franco-German summit in Lille at the end of May 1991, 'NATO is not the whole of the Atlantic Alliance, and not all questions can be settled at that level... We are part of the Atlantic Alliance, but not of the integrated military arm of NATO'. He went on to say that:

> The question is not one of creating a defence organisation which would substitute for NATO, but of knowing the limits of the Atlantic Alliance, and of its military organisation, of its competence and of its geographic area, to know that Europe must not miss any opportunity to build itself a common policy and its own defence.[14]

A West European Defence Community

These French criticisms of NATO take us on to our next model of European security. This is a vision of a European security system constructed around a federated European Union which has acquired a common foreign, security and defence policy, and an effective capability for independent power projection and coordinated military action. This I have called a 'West European Defence Community' (WEDC). The word 'community' implies a degree of supranational integration going far beyond the current debate on the creation of a 'European defence identity'. It harks back to the failed Pleven Plan for a European Defence Community of 1952, but in a radically changed context. Such a defence community would no longer simply amount to a strengthened European pillar of the Atlantic Alliance within the context of the East–West conflict (as the Pleven Plan envisaged), but would constitute the key building-block of a new post-Cold War security system.

Incremental steps towards closer bi- and multilateral West European security cooperation were a significant feature of the 1980s (Gambles, 1989). The 1986 Single European Act and the events of 1989 gave an additional impetus to the European integration process, and resulted in two intergovernmental conferences (IGCs), one on economic and monetary union, and the other on political union. Current proposals in the IGC on political union include the creation of a common foreign and security policy (CFSP).[15] The Gulf War further fuelled the debate on a CFSP. For 'Euro-sceptics' like

Douglas Hurd, it exposed the gulf between the 'Europe of facts' and the 'Europe of words'. For pro-integrationists, however, it demonstrated the need to develop institutional mechanisms for the coordination of foreign and security policy, and ultimately of defence policy too.[16] More significantly, the crisis in Yugoslavia presented the EC with its first major test of the post-Cold War era. The Community played a key diplomatic and political role as the tragedy unfolded, given its economic clout and political influence. The EC 'troika' of foreign ministers was especially active, and, having helped to negotiate the Brioni Peace plan of 7 July 1991, agreed to send fifty EC observers to Slovenia. The Yugoslav tragedy thus increased the diplomatic standing of the Community, and boosted the hopes of those who wished to see the Community develop a common defence and security policy.

At the moment, the debate on the future security architecture of Europe has focused primarily on the WEU. Despite its inauspicious beginnings and chequered history, this body could end up playing a pivotal role in the new European security system. As we have seen, pro-NATO Atlanticists would like the WEU to be more closely associated with NATO, hoping that it will provide the basis for a European pillar within the Alliance. Others stress its potential as a bridge between NATO and the EC Twelve. A third group, which includes the French, Italians and Spanish, would like the WEU to be developed as the basis of a distinctive European defence entity, perhaps by merging it with the EPC (European Political Cooperation) and bringing it within the ambit of the Community. Agreement has now been reached on relocating WEU offices from London and Paris to Brussels, where it would be near both the EC and NATO (thus retaining a politically expedient element of ambiguity concerning its future role). But whereas the British would like Ambassadors to NATO to double up as ambassadors to the WEU, the French would like national permanent representatives to the EC to fulfil this role for the WEU (*Independent*, 1991). The Dutch have also proposed that the WEU be widened to include the non-EC NATO states of Norway and Turkey, while the French and Italians argue that WEU membership should be limited to Community members (*Financial Times*, 1991). Moreover, there are proposals for the 'double-hatting' of European forces in NATO; thus for example the NATO Rapid Reaction Corps could come under WEU command in the event of an out-of-area operation.[17] Debates on the WEU, therefore, are at the heart of debates on the future of the European security system.

Those who advocate the creation of a West European Defence Community do so for a number of reasons. To begin with, they argue that it would overcome the unnatural dichotomy in West European institutions between NATO and the EC, and constitute the logical culmination of the process of West European integration. The creation of a single market necessitated a common external trading policy, and this in turn generated pressures for foreign policy coordination (which was initiated through the intergovern-mental framework of the EPC, rather than through the Commission). This in turn has shown the necessity for a common foreign and security policy, which – some maintain – will ultimately necessitate the creation of common defence policy and an integrated military structure.

Second, Western Europe, it is argued, can and should no longer be dependent on the United States. A fundamental shift in power relationships within the transatlantic community is inevitable, given both the growing prosperity and cohesion of West European states, and more evident differen-ces in strategic, economic, and geopolitical interests between the USA and Western Europe. Advocates of a WEDC are not necessarily 'anti-American', or opposed to a continuing strategic alliance between the USA and Europe. However, they believe that a new partnership with the US cannot be built within the confines of NATO (which they see as an inevitably American-dominated structure), but only on the basis of independent and effective WEDC which can cooperate with the US as an equal.

Third, national procurement policies and national defence industries, it is argued, are becoming unsustainable given the spiralling cost of modern weapons, rising research and development costs, and higher production costs arising from lower production runs. Traditional efforts at multilateral colla-boration have also proved of limited success. Advocates of WEDC therefore argue that only the creation of such a body would make possible the establishment of a West European defence industry and collective procure-ment policies. This would have the additional benefit of freeing resources both for a 'peace dividend', and for more effective technological competition with the US, Japan and the non-industrialised countries (NICs). Thus the establishment of supranational integration in the defence industries and in procurement policies (along the lines of ESPRIT) has been proposed as the basis for a WEDC, rather than multinational collaboration based on voluntary inter-governmental agreements (as currently practised in the IEPG).[18]

Fourth, a WEDC would give Western Europe a capability for out-of-area power projection. This, it is claimed, is necessary in order to protect specifi-cally European interests, which might not always be identical to those of the USA. Furthermore, the UN cannot always be relied on to counter threats to European interests (given the possibility of a Soviet or Chinese veto), while NATO is limited to the North Atlantic area.

Fifth, a strong WEDC could provide a bulwark of a new European security system. The Yugoslav crisis has illustrated the growing importance of the EC in crisis management. Its efforts and authority would be greatly enhanced, it is suggested, if it also had a common foreign and security policy, including an integrated military force under supranational control.

Finally, a WEDC would integrate German power within wider West

European structures. This would provide reassurance to Germany's neighbours in the West, and might also make its growing economic influence in Eastern Europe and the Soviet Union more acceptable to the peoples of those countries.

For a viable and effective WEDC to be created, three major developments are necessary: the emergence of a federal European Union with a common defence policy; the creation of integrated conventional military forces; and the formation of a European nuclear deterrent. A federated European Union, based on the principle of subsidiarity, would have to incorporate qualified majority voting on issues of common foreign and security policy, including defence.[19] If a common defence policy were to have substance, it would need to have at its disposal an integrated European army under a unified command (as proposed in the 1952 Pleven Plan). At the same time, unless there is a major sea-change in European attitudes towards nuclear deterrence, a WEDC would have to include a minimum nuclear capability designed for war-prevention purposes. This could be based on close Anglo-French nuclear cooperation, combined with the creation of some form of collective political control (perhaps involving the creation of a WEDC Nuclear Planning Group).

Proposals for the creation of an autonomous West European security and defence organisation have come up against fierce criticism. Opponents of this *Kleineuropa* approach to European security (who come from a variety of different political and national perspectives) criticise it on six main grounds. To begin with, they question its very feasibility, given the entrenched national interests in Western Europe, and the substantial differences that exist on defence issues (such as the strategic relationship with the US, and the question of nuclear weapons) between the 'Big Three'.

Second, they charge that it would weaken US–West European security ties, and thereby imperil the wider security of the Western world. A strong US commitment to Europe, it is argued, is necessary to safeguard the strategic balance of Europe. Moreover, it is suggested that only by close cooperation and coordination with the USA can the West Europeans hope to have any substantial influence on developments in the Middle East and other areas of regional instability where European interests are at stake.

Third, the 'deepening' of West European security cooperation within the EC raises serious difficulties about the Community's 'widening' (Wallace, 1989). There are two dimensions to this problem: widening towards the East Europeans, and widening towards the neutral and non-aligned (NNA) members of EFTA. The East Europeans would dearly love to have security guarantees from the West, so this is not a major difficulty, although it might complicate the Community's relations with the Soviet Union (Dienstbier, 1991: 5). The NNAs constitute more of a problem. If they were to join the Community as it exists at the moment, they would probably oppose its evolution into a defence organisation. If the Community were to evolve into a WEDC, they would probably find it hard to join.[20]

Fourth, the replacement of NATO by a WEDC could weaken the security of Europe's peripheries, given that both Norway and Turkey are members of NATO but not the EC. Turkey in particular is of vital strategic importance to the West, both because of its border with the former USSR, and given its geographical proximity to the Middle East (Robins, 1991). The Turkish application for full membership of the Community was lodged in 1987, but has not received a favourable response to date. If it were excluded from the EC and the WEU, while NATO was superseded by a WEDC, this would damage Western interests and possibly undermine the domestic stability of Turkey.

Fifth, those who oppose the development of a common defence policy by the Community argue that such a move would antagonise the former Soviet Union, create a new security division in Europe, and harm prospects for pan-European cooperation and integration. The Community, they argue, would be better advised to concentrate on economic integration and political cooperation, while leaving security concerns to either NATO or the CSCE.

Finally, for many on the left, the idea of a WEDC is emerging as their new *bête noire*. They fear that a nuclear-armed WEDC could rekindle a 'nascent neo-imperialism in Western Europe', resulting in such a body 'dominating and looting weaker and poorer countries' (Kaldor *et al.*, 1989: 150; Smith, 1989: 23 and 149; Randle and Rogers, 1990: 93).

A CSCE-based pan-European collective security system

An Atlanticist Europe and a West European defence identity represent the two main competing visions of European security after the Cold War. But there are two further models of Europe which have their own rationale and advocates. The first of these is a CSCE-based system of collective security. The notion of a pan-European collective security system harks back to the interwar League of Nations, and draws on ideas that inspired the establishment of the United Nations. A European system of collective security has been the declaratory goal of the Soviet Union for most of the postwar period, and this goal was included in the 1955 Warsaw Treaty. After the democratic revolutions of 1989, the new post-communist leaderships in East Central Europe became enthusiastic advocates of a CSCE-based collective security system. Considerable sympathy for this sort of arrangement has also been expressed in Central Europe (notably by Hans-Dietrich Genscher, the German Foreign Minister), and by many centre-left political forces throughout Europe. With the conservative backlash in the Soviet Union in early 1991, the original enthusiasm of the new East European governments for the CSCE dimmed, and they subsequently began exploring the possibility of developing closer links with NATO and the WEU. None the less, this vision of a CSCE-based collective security system remains a powerful and, in many ways, an attractive vision of security in post-Cold War Europe.

The CSCE is one of the surprising success stories of modern diplomacy (Birnbaum and Ingo, 1990). Negotiations for the Conference on Security and Cooperation in Europe began in 1973, although the CSCE 'process' as such dates from the Helsinki Final Act of 1975. The Final Act served as a surrogate Second World War peace treaty, while the CSCE process subsequently provided a framework for the peaceful management of the East–West conflict (focusing primarily on human rights and security issues). With the ending of the bipolar division of Europe in late 1989, the character and potential of the CSCE has been fundamentally transformed. It is now widely seen as a fruitful forum of pan-European discussion and cooperation, and as an essential element of the new security order. The CSCE Summit in Paris in November 1991 was a landmark in this respect. It saw the adoption of the Paris Charter for a New Europe, and led to the institutionalisation of the CSCE process.

The CSCE now has a regular series of meetings at various levels, a permanent institutional structure, and a number of mechanisms for addressing problem issues on an *ad hoc* basis. Regular summits of heads of state and government are to be held at least every two years; foreign ministers are to meet biannually; and a Committee of Senior Officials (CSO) is to meet before ministerial meetings. As regards the CSCE's institutional structure, a Secretariat has been established in Prague; a Conflict Prevention Centre (CPC) set up in Vienna; an Office of Free Elections created in Prague; and an Assembly of Europe is being established (using the existing facilities of the Council of Europe). Moreover, there are also three main mechanisms for *ad hoc* meetings: the first was created by the Vienna Concluding Document of January 1989, and covers human rights issues; the second concerns 'unusual military activities' and involves the Vienna CPC; and the third is the 'Emergency Mechanism' agreed at the Berlin meeting of CSCE Foreign Ministers in June 1991, which was subsequently activitated to address the simmering civil war in Yugoslavia. Also on the CSCE agenda is a mechanism for the peaceful resolution of disputes, which would include the mandatory involvement of a third party. This was discussed at a meeting of experts in Valletta 15 January – 8 February 1991 (Lehne, 1991: 180–1).

Among proponents of an expanded role for the CSCE in the emerging European security order there are the 'maximalists' and the 'minimalists'. The former would like to see the CSCE absorb the responsibilities of the remaining military alliances, eventually replacing them by a pan-European collective security arrangement. This would include a wide range of sanctions against transgressors of the CSCE's commonly-agreed standards and normative values, from diplomatic ostracism and economic sanctions, up to and including the deployment of CSCE interventionary forces. The deployment of such forces would be the prerogative of a CSCE 'Security Council', modelled on the UN Security Council, with some permanent members and a system of weighted majority voting.[21]

The minimalists would also like to see the CSCE emerge as the overarching structure of a new pan-European security system, but recognise an enduring – albeit limited – role for both NATO and the EC/EPC/WEU. NATO, they suggest, will continue as a framework for transatlantic defence cooperation among the sixteen members, but with no wider security role in the rest of Europe. The Community, along with the WEU, will play an important role as the focus of economic and political integration in Europe, but will not assume responsibility for military security issues in the continent. The CSCE will therefore have a number of key roles to play: first, it will provide a framework for pan-European security dialogue and consultation; second, it will be the forum for further arms control and confidence building measures in Europe (with a strengthened role for the CPC); third, it will provide a series of mechanisms for conflict prevention, crisis management and the peaceful resolution of disputes, involving mandatory procedures for arbitration and conciliation, and the deployment of peacekeeping forces if necessary; finally, it will provide the institutional framework for shaping and deepening the networks of interdependence criss-crossing the continent.

This vision of a CSCE-based security system seems to correspond to the hopes for pan-European cooperation and integration which the end of the Cold War has encouraged. However, such a collective security system has been criticised on three main grounds. First, all decisions of substance in the CSCE take place on the basis of unanimity. This means that any state, however small, can block the work of the CSCE. Although there have been some proposals for adopting a system of weighted majority voting (either on the EC or UN Security Council model), it is hard to imagine this being acceptable to all CSCE participating states. The unanimity principle therefore means that the CSCE is prone to organisational paralysis at moments of crisis, and that it is too large and diverse to respond quickly and decisively to emergencies.

Second, an effective system of collective security requires a set of sanctions against aggressor states. The CSCE does not possess any instruments for enforcing its decisions, and given the unanimity principle upon which it is based, it does not seem likely to develop any. Moreover, the Helsinki Final Act and the various follow-up documents and agreements are not formal legal agreements under international law, but are only political commitments.

Third, many of the new security problems in Europe are not necessarily going to take the character of state-to-state disputes, but may be internal disputes involving human rights and minority nationalism. Yet most CSCE participating states have jealously guarded the principle of national sovereignty, and championed the concept of noninterference in the internal affairs of participating states. Although this principle has been partly modified by the Vienna Concluding Document's human rights review mechanism, the traditional understanding of national sovereignty remains a major impediment to the development of the CSCE into a viable collective security regime.

A Europe of nation-states

The preceding three models all share one feature in common. They all assume that the new security order in Europe will be built around a firm institutional structure in which either NATO, a WEDC or the CSCE will play a pivotal role. This final scenario, however, envisages a more fluid security arrangement, in which bi- and multilateral relations will be of far greater importance than the institutional architecture. Furthermore, if the last model of European security (based on the CSCE) reflected an 'idealist' approach, then this one is very much a 'realist' model; in other words, it assumes the continuing centrality of the nation-state – with its predominant concern with power-politics and national security – and the persistence of an underlying balance of power logic to international relations (see Chapter 1).

This model of a 'Europe of nation-states' is strongly influenced by De Gaulle's notion of *l'Europe de l'Atlantique a l'Oural*, which conceived of a Europe free of the bipolar hegemony of the two superpowers, and a new security order based on individual nation-states freely cooperating together. It finds its advocates among those opposed to supranational integration in Europe, and among those who believe in the continued vitality of the nation-state. But others have also suggested that this security system could emerge in Europe less by conscious design than by default. Such a diversified and polycentric Europe could emerge, it is argued, if the deepening process of EC integration stalls (particularly in terms of the development of a common foreign and security policy); if NATO withers away, perhaps spurred on by intensifying transatlantic trade disputes and a growing mood of German pacificism; and if the CSCE remains wedded to its consensus principle of operation.

Given the end of the bipolar division of Europe, and if existing European organisations prove unable to provide a firm institutional bulwark for a new security system, Europe may revert to older patterns of shifting multipolar alliances and polycentric 'checkerboard' politics (Christensen and Snyder, 1990). As the cohesion imposed on the European security area by the Cold

War evaporates, the European security system may become increasingly fragmented and polycentric. In this situation, security in Europe will become more and more 'divisible', particularly between the West European countries and the rest of Europe. Europe will consequently increasingly become a Europe of regions, with a West European 'core'; a Northern grouping seeking to preserve a distinctive 'Nordic balance'; a tripartite East Central European grouping (with close links to the EC); a more unstable and fragmented area of South-Eastern Europe and the Balkans; and a disintegrating Soviet Union. An organisation like the Hexagonale might assume greater importance, while new forms of cooperation may develop around the Baltic and the Black Sea, and among Southern European states bordering the Mediterranean.

In such a polycentric and pluralist Europe, the national security policies of the traditional European Great Powers will largely determine the political and security climate in the continent. Without robust institutional structures to shape their behaviour and expectations – and in a Europe of resurgent nationalisms – these states are likely to pursue a balance of power strategy. At the heart of this multipolar Europe of competing nation-states will be Germany. Germany, by virtue of its size, its geographical centrality and its prodigious economic strength, will be at the centre of this system of shifting alliances and checkerboard politics. German statesmen will have to balance their economic and political commitments to the West Europeans (particularly the French) with their growing interests in Eastern Europe and the Balkans. Close Soviet-German relations (which have become a key feature of post-Cold War Europe) will give rise to fears elsewhere in Europe of a 'new Rapallo'. At the same time, the French are likely to seek to reestablish close ties with East European states like Poland and Romania, and with the Soviet Union, in order to contain Germany.[22] Meanwhile Italy is likely to pursue its specific objectives in South-Eastern Europe and the Balkans, and to develop the Hexagonale as a counterweight to German influence in the region.

Security arrangements in such a Europe of nation-states would be based on national military capabilities and a multipolar system of defence agreements and non-aggression pacts. Collective defence alliances like NATO and the WEU might provide residual security guarantees for their West European members, although without the integrated military structures that NATO, for example, currently enjoys. It would be much harder negotiating comprehensive arms control agreements (such as the CFE Treaty) in a more polycentric Europe, but regional confidence-building measures would still be possible, along with bilateral military cooperation arrangements. The three European nuclear powers would undoubtedly attach considerable importance to nuclear deterrence, hoping that a multipolar nuclear stand-off might contribute to the overall stability of the continent. At the core of this multifaceted and loosely-knit structure, however, would be a series of defensive multipolar alliances, similiar to the Locarno Treaties of the inter-war years, guaranteeing the territorial integrity and security of Germany and its eastern neighbours (Snyder, 1990: 14).

For some, a security system based on *l'Europe des Etats* would be a natural and flexible arrangement corresponding to the enduring vitality of the nation-state in Western Europe and the break-up of multinational states such as Yugoslavia and the USSR. Others, however, are less sanguine. They argue, first, that such a multipolar Europe would leave the Soviet Union – or even the Russian Federation on its own – as the predominant military superpower on the continent. Second, they point out that it would rekindle modern Europe's most intractable security problem – namely, how to accommodate a country with the energy and ambition of Germany at the heart of a loosely-knit and polycentric Europe? Third, Europe is strewn with unresolved national, ethnic and religious rivalries, and a fragmented security system would simply lead to the 'Balkanisation' of Europe, with a return to the multipolar instabilities of the 1930s. Finally, critics of this vision of European security point out that its historical precedents are not encouraging: balance of power arrangements are notoriously unstable, and their breakdown in Europe has on two occasions led to devastating World Wars.

CONCLUSION

The discussion of these four alternative models of European security after the Cold War indicates the tremendous fluidity in Europe at the current time, and the wide range of options open to Europe's policy-makers. None the less, it is essential to realise that Europe's future security system may well be the product not of grand designs or bold architectural visions (such as Gorbachev's 'common European house' or Mitterrand's 'European Confederation'), but rather of a series of largely *ad hoc* responses to specific security problems. Since the collapse of the old bipolar security system in 1989–90, Europe's nascent security system has been evolving under the impact of three major crises: the Gulf War, the continued instability in the USSR, and the simmering civil war in Yugoslavia. The response of existing European organisations such as NATO, the EC and the CSCE – along with the policies of Europe's Great Powers – to these and future crises will therefore have a major impact on the contours of Europe's future security system.

NOTES

1 Barry Buzan has developed the concept of a 'security complex', which he

describes as 'a group of states whose primary security concerns link together sufficiently closely that their national securities cannot realistically be considered apart from one another' (Buzan, 1983: 106)

2 These secular trends are examined in greater detail in A. Hyde-Price and J. Roper, 'New directions in European security' (Booth, 1991: 248–55).

3 This body grew from a quadripartite agreement on limited regional and diplomatic cooperation between Italy, Austria, Hungary and Yugoslavia, signed on 11 November 1989. After the 'Velvet Revolution', Czechoslovakia joined, and on 27 April 1990, the 'Pentagonale Initiative' was formally launched. In May 1991, Poland became the sixth member, and the organisation became known as the Hexagonale.

4 The Dutch have emerged as particularly vociferous supporters of an Atlanticist approach to European security in the EC's Inter-Governmental Conference on Political Union. The Dutch Foreign Minister, Hans van den Broek, told his fellow EC foreign ministers in March 1991 that 'the European role in security and defence could be shaped in such a way that it not only contributes to further fulfilment of European integration, but preserves optimal security arrangements, including a continued North American political and military commitment to the security of Europe'. *Financial Times*, 27 March 1991.

5 This view is epitomised by the former Prime Minister Margaret Thatcher, who argued in Washington in March 1991 that the US 'should continue to play the dominant role in NATO to which we have become accustomed... Indeed, as was demonstrated in the Gulf, for all the asssistance which Britain and the other powers gave, only one nation really has the power to defend freedom and security in the world today – the US'. *Financial Times*, 9/10 March 1991.

6 This argument was clearly stated in the Final Communiqué of the Ministerial Meeting of the North Atlantic Council in Copenhagen (6/7 June 1991): 'Although NATO itself was not involved in the Gulf War, the long practice of cooperation, common procedures, collective defence arrangements and infrastructure developed by NATO provided valuable assistance to those Allies that chose to make use of them in their respective efforts in support of the UN Security Council resolutions on the Gulf' (NATO, 1991).

7 'We need NATO. It is tried by the West Europeans; it is trusted by the Americans; it is respected by the East Europeans' (Hurd, 1991).

8 At a two-day meeting of NATO foreign ministers in Brussels, NATO's Secretary General, Manfred Wörner, argued that 'The growing cooperation and unity of Europe in security and defence matters must lead to a strengthening of the Alliance and also, where necessary, to structural changes'. He added that 'Our goal must be a new transatlantic partnership of equals in which the Europeans share more responsibilities for Alliance security in Europe'. *Financial Times*, 18 December 1990.

9 William Taft, the US Ambassador to NATO, has said that 'The geography is tempting for us to think that we are in some way different from Europe... it is a fundamental principle of US partnership in NATO and support for NATO that this is not seen to be true. If it were to come about that the thing was set up so that constantly there was a Europe position and an American position, the idea would gain currency that our interests were not the same and we had to broker them each time'. He went on to state that the US favoured a European pillar, but 'where is the policy made that is executed by NATO? That is the key question... the Alliance

is not going to underwrite a security policy that is made somewhere else'. *Independent*, 9 March 1991.

10 'Years of joint training, equipping, exercising and developing common standards and procedures in NATO in peacetime made possible the efficient and coordinated military operations in the Gulf' (Taft, 1991: 8).

11 Reported in *Financial Times*, 2 July 1991. Placing the rapid reaction force under a NATO umbrella would mean that its deployment would not require legal sanction by the Turkish parliament, and that the force would come under Turkish command. But this could cause both domestic and international problems for the Turkish government, which is wary of being seen as a springboard for American operations in the region. It would also not be welcome to some West European NATO members.

12 The June 1991 Copenhagen NATO statement on 'Partnership with the Countries of Central and Eastern Europe' declared that 'Our common security can best be safeguarded through the further development of a network of interlocking institutions and relationships, constituting a comprehensive structure in which the Alliance, the process of European integration and the CSCE are key elements. Emerging frameworks of regional cooperation will also be important'.

13 John Major has argued that 'NATO should remain the focus for collective defence in Europe, because it provides the United States commitment to join us in the defence of Europe. We think that the Western European Union could sensibly be developed into the forum for a European defence identity, building a bridge between the Twelve and NATO' (*Independent*, 1 March 1991).

14 Quoted in the *Financial Times*, 3 June 1991.

15 The 132 page-long Draft Treaty on Political Union states that 'The policy of the Union aims at covering all areas of foreign and security policy... including, eventually, the framing of a defence policy'. The European Council would decide by consensus what areas of foreign and security policy should be conducted in common by the Twelve. Once an area was deemed 'common' by the Council, its implementation could be decided by weighted majority voting among the Twelve (the Rome European Council communiqué of December 1990 spoke of the 'possibility of recourse to qualified majority voting for the implementation of agreed policies'). The IGC will also consider merging the small Brussels-based EPC Secretariat into the Council of Ministers' larger one, and strengthening it with more diplomats seconded from national capitals. The Commission would have a limited role in foreign and security policy (limited to 'the non-exclusive right of initiation'), and the European Parliament almost none (although a mechanism for 'consulting and informing the European Parliament' is to be considered). The Rome communiqué also suggested that areas of foreign and security policy that might be conducted in common include arms control, disarmament and related issues; 'certain questions debated in the United Nations, including peacekeeping operations'; the CSCE; economic and technological cooperation in the armaments field; and the coordination of armaments export policy and non-proliferation (*Financial Times*, 17 December 1990).

16 Jacques Delors readily admitted that the Gulf War provided 'an object lesson on the limitations of the European Community' (*Financial Times*, 8 March 1991). But as Sir Leon Brittan (one of the British Commissioners) has pointed out, 'it is no use criticising the Community for not being what its member states have not so far wanted it to be' (*Financial Times*, 8 February 1991).

17 This has been proposed by Douglas Hurd (*Financial Times*, 15 April 1991), the

WEU Secretary-General Willem van Eekelen (*Financial Times*, 13/14 April 1991) and Manfred Wörner, the NATO Secretary-General (*Financial Times*, 7 May 1991).

18 This would require a revision of Article 223 of the Treaty of Rome, which states that 'any member may take such measures as it considers necessary for the protection of the essential interests of its security which are connected with the production of or trade in arms, munitions and war material'. Article 30 of the Single European Act modifies this by declaring a determination to 'maintain the technological and industrial conditions necessary for their security. [The signatories] shall work to that end both at the national level and, where appropriate, within the framework of the competent institutions and bodies'. The December 1990 Rome Summit communiqué also stated that it is 'in the common interest to bring defence equipment production and trade fully under the discipline of the Common Market', as proposed by the European Commission's draft Treaty on Political Union (*Financial Times*, 6 March 1991).

19 This could be created by merging the WEU with the EPC (after the WEU comes up for renewal in 1997), and bringing the resulting body under the umbrella of the Community (as the Italian Foreign Minister Gianni Di Michelis has already proposed). A first step in this direction was taken by the WEU Council of Minister's meeting on 22 February 1991 which approved an interim report suggesting that the EC Council should be empowered to issue guidelines for the work of the WEU. This however was opposed by the Dutch, and the US Administration also made clear its reservations in a letter to all WEU states (*Financial Times*, 23/24 February 1991).

20 The Swedish Prime Minister Ingvar Carlsson, whose Government formally applied for EC membership on 1 July 1991, told Swedish journalists in June 1991 that membership of the Community would not threaten the country's neutral security policy: 'It will be possible to avoid commitments which would compromise the credibility of Swedish security policy... Sweden cannot take part in a common defence policy or a mutual defence commitment within the EC framework' (*Financial Times*, 15/16 June 1991).

21 Hans-Dietrich Genscher has recently advocated the creation of a European Security Council and European 'green berets', both modelled on their UN counterparts. See *Financial Times*, 23 July 1991, p.2.

22 The crisis in Yugoslavia which erupted in June 1991 has already revealed deeply rooted French suspicions of German motives in Slovenia and Croatia.

REFERENCES

Birnbaum, K. and Ingo, P. (1990) 'The CSCE: a reassessment of its role in the 1980s', *Review of International Studies* **16**, 4: 305–19.

Booth, K. (ed.) (1991) *New Thinking About Strategy and International Security*, London: Harper Collins.

Buzan, B. (1983) *People, States and Fear: The National Security Problem in International Relations*, Brighton: Wheatsheaf.

Christensen, T. and Snyder, J. (1990) 'Chain gangs and passed bucks: predicting alliance patterns in multipolarity', *International Organization* **44**, 2: 137–68.

Dienstbier, J. (1991) 'The future of European security. Prague conference confirms agreement on basic ideas', *NATO Review* **39**, 3: 3–6.

Eavis, P. (ed.) (1990) *European Security: The New Agenda*, Bristol: Saferworld Foundation.

Eberle, J. (1990) 'NATO's higher command', in L. Freedman (ed.), *Military Power in Europe*, London: Macmillan.

Financial Times (1991) 27 March 1991.

Gambles, I. (1989) *Prospects For West European Security Cooperation*, Adelphi Paper 244, London: Macmillan.

Hurd, D. (1991) 'No European defence identity without NATO', *Financial Times*, 15 April 1991.

Hyde-Price, A. (1991) *European Security Beyond the Cold War: Four Scenarios for the Year 2010*, London: Sage

Independent (1991) 20 February 1991.

Kaldor, M., Holden, G. and Falk, R. (1989) *The New Détente: Rethinking East–West Relations*, London: Verso.

Lehne, S. (1991) *The Vienna Meeting of the Conference on Security and Cooperation in Europe, 1986–1989: A Turning Point in East–West Relations*, Oxford: Westview.

NATO (1991) 'Final communiqué of the ministerial meeting of the North Atlantic Council in Copenhagen, 6–7 June 1991', *NATO Review*, **39**, 1: 28–9.

Nye, J. (1989) 'The Contribution of Strategic Studies: Future Challenges', in IISS *The Changing Strategic Landscape, Part 1*, Adelphi Paper 235, London: Brassey's, 20–34.

O'Meara, R. (1984) 'Regimes and their implications for international theory', *Millenium*, **13**, 3: 245–64.

Randle, M. and Rogers, P. (1990) *Alternatives in European Security*, Aldershot: Dartmouth.

Robins, P. (1991) *Turkey and the Middle East*, London: Pinter.

Smith, D. (1989) *European Security in the 1990s*, London: Pluto.

Snyder, J. (1990) 'Averting anarchy in the new Europe', *International Security*, **14**, 4: 5–41.

Sodaro, M. (1990) *Moscow, Germany, and the West: From Khrushchev to Gorbachev*, Ithaca and London: Cornell University Press.

Taft, W. (1991) 'European security: lessons learned from the Gulf war', *NATO Review*, **39**, 3: 7–11.

Wallace, H. (1989) *Widening and Deepening: The European Community and the New European Agenda*, Chatham House Discussion Paper No. 23, London: RIIA.

3 Nationalism in Central and South-Eastern Europe

Stephen Iwan Griffiths [*]

We realised that the poetry was over and the prose was beginning.

(Václav Havel, in Linden, 1991)

Throughout 1990 and 1991, the number of nationalist problems in Central and South-Eastern Europe grew at an alarming rate. However, the problem of nationalism in Central and South-Eastern Europe is only just starting to receive serious attention in the European security community, though there is a general consensus developing that nationalism represents an important and potentially destructive force within the emerging European security system. The study of nationalism is one of the more challenging and trap-infested of academic pursuits; and attempting an analysis of nationalism and European security is an invitation to accusations of foolhardiness. In addition, the new European security debate is very fluid, and an analysis confidently made on one day can be overtaken by events and ideas within a week. Likewise, the debate is in a conceptual flux because few now know what European 'security' should be concerned with; the lines of demarcation between different areas of specialisation, especially between the study of domestic and international politics, seem increasingly absurd. Daniel Nelson has reinforced this sense of change by writing:

> Anything less than an unreserved Western investment in a new security concept may condemn Eastern Europe, and thereby the whole of the Continent, to recurrent trauma and national tragedy... Security after hegemony must be sought in this conceptually new world.
>
> (Nelson, 1991: 158)

In a sense, it is premature to write a study of the kind attempted here; Chairman Mao, when asked what he thought were the consequences of the French Revolution, replied that it was a little too early to say; the same, though even more appropriately, could be said of 1989 and subsequent

* Stephen Griffiths would like to acknowledge the invaluable advice given by Andreas Behnke during the writing of this chapter.

developments (Garton Ash, 1991). As a result, the analysis in this chapter is necessarily tentative, and no attempt is made to draw general conclusions. The chapter is divided into relatively self-contained sections: the first will consider the initial impact of events in 1989 on the study of nationalism and European security, and will address some of the problems associated with studying nationalism from a European security perspective; the second offers an appraisal of the development of nationalism in Europe; the third and fourth sections examine developments in Czechoslovakia and Yugoslavia respectively, being two of the major areas of nationalist instability in Central and South-Eastern Europe; and the final section consists of a brief overview of the developing debate on managing nationalist problems from a European security perspective.

1989 AND ALL THAT

In the wake of events in 1989, two substantial approaches have come to dominate the new European security debate. An obvious need for original ideas and approaches has humbled some scholars into a period of what could be termed 'Utopian introversion'. Their basic goal is to reassess research methods and capabilities, though from a 'conventional' standpoint. Those pursuing this approach see utility in the basic tenets of strategic thinking and a measure of 'realism', though they have developed a preoccupation with 'security architecture' (Booth, 1990; Clesse and Ruhl, 1990; Smoke, 1990; van Evera, 1990: 57–8). For those pursuing the second approach, 1989 signalled the need to consolidate 'realism's victory', though there has been a reassessment of threats and contingencies, and the debate on the inherent instability of multipolar security systems has been reopened; conventional security thinking remains in place, though it is now applied to new problems, most of which exist in the developing world and in Western Europe's 'backyard' – Central and South-Eastern Europe and to a certain extent the republics of the the Soviet Union. This group seems to be principally preoccupied with scenario-building, and constructing contingencies for those institutions, like NATO, that have come under threat of extinction as a consequence of the events of 1989 (Holst, 1990; Mearsheimer, 1990).

While these two approaches offer a relatively wide field of scholarly activity, only the latter approach, because of its preoccupation with discovering new threats, has allowed nationalism to enter the new European security debate (Mearsheimer, 1990: 33). One commentator has chosen to interpret the situation as: 'an ominous cloud is hanging over the young democracies of eastern Europe. It is called the past' – though this only brings to mind Garton Ash's warning to all 'cartographers of emancipation' that the popular rediscovery of the national past does not necessarily represent a resurgence of nationalism (Garton Ash, 1989: 242):

The lack of normal access to the national past was a form of deprivation; the recovery of it is a form of emancipation.

(Garton Ash, 1991)

While a number of scholars see only dangers in a world deprived of the sureties of the pre–1989 security landscape, others seem sure that a new European security order will be relatively free from the influence of pre-war style nationalism. For example, John Mearsheimer has concluded that, were it not for the Soviet presence in Eastern Europe, Hungary and Romania would have been to war over the Romanian treatment of the Hungarian minority in Transylvania. However, Jack Snyder, in one of the few major pieces to be written on nationalism and European security since 1989, has written that 'an outbreak of virulent nationalism in Eastern Europe and the Soviet Union seems possible, but not inevitable', though he balanced this by writing in the same piece 'the possibility of a rising tide of nationalism poses the greatest challenge to the security of the new Europe' (Snyder, 1990a: 58). Stephen van Evera has also pointed out that:

> the risk of a return to the warlike Europe of old is low... The nuclear revolution has dampened security motives for expansion, and the domestic orders of most European states have changed in ways that make renewed aggression unlikely. The most significant domestic changes include the waning of militarism and hyper-nationalism.
>
> (van Evera, 1990: 9)

Despite this, there is an emerging understanding in political and academic circles that nationalism in Central and South-Eastern Europe deserves to be a topic of study by European security specialists (Buchan, 1991a),[1] and there seems little doubt that a new debate on the possible impact of nationalism in the post-coup Soviet Union will emerge over the coming years. However, the study of nationalism by those concerned with security poses a number of problems, three of which will be discussed here: the first is concerned with what is best described as 'scholarly knowledge and historical priority'; the second, which is only briefly explored in this chapter is concerned with the domestic/international dichotomy in the study of European security; and the third is concerned with the problem of ascribing meaning to nationalism.

In the last forty years, the European security debate has not paid much attention to nationalist problems, despite the fact that nationalism was a determining factor in inter and intrastate policymaking in the former Eastern Europe (Gilberg, 1990; Glenny, 1990: 204–16; Simon and Gilberg, 1986). Before the Second World War, it would have been improbable that an analysis of security in Europe could have been undertaken without a sophisticated understanding of nationalist problems. However, it was safely assumed that the study of nationalism could become a subject worthy more of historical reflection than contemporary investigation. E. Hobsbawn has reinforced this view by claiming nationalism for the historians, though it would be fairer to say that it has also been the preserve of area specialists and social theorists (Giddens, 1987; Hobsbawn, 1990). This would suggest that a European security-oriented analysis of these problems would benefit from a revival of interest in pre-Cold War strategic scholarship, an examination of historical literature relating to nationalism, and a reappraisal of the role and function of nationalism in the former Eastern Europe during the period of communist rule.

Second, it can be argued that reintegrating the study of nationalism in Central and South-Eastern Europe is a fundamental challenge to traditional approaches to the study of European security. The most significant nationalist problems in Europe exist at the sub-state level. Studying this phenomenon, and offering remedies for it, requires an exploration of the 'borderland' between the international and domestic, something that most European security specialists have not had to do. In a sense, this means that new tools and methods of study will have to be adopted or developed in order 'to understand in a more profound way the processes by which the "realities" of contemporary life are made meaningful' (George and Campbell, 1990: 282).

Although it would be appropriate, in an effort to capture the diversity of developments in the former Eastern Europe, to consider the meaning of a great many concepts and ideas (including aspects of ethnic conflict and self-determination), nationalism forms the core of analysis, and it is therefore the only concept to be briefly explored. Nietzsche once noted that only that which has no history can be defined; unfortunately, nationalism, to adapt Bartelson's thesis, has a history of being a central concept in modern political discourse, and this has enabled it 'to soak up a multitude of divergent meanings' (Bartelson, 1990). The concept is in dire need of reevaluation, if only so that students of European security can demonstrate a degree of 'scholarly responsibility' when using the concept in their work; Neil Mac-Cormick has gone so far as to ask whether nationalism is philosophically credible (MacCormick, 1991). However, the historical significance of nationalism is beyond question. The American sociologist Feliks Gross has neatly summarised its importance:

> Nationalism... permeates every political philosophy, be it national, pan-national, imperialistic or international... It has taken on as complete a hold on modern thinking and attitudes as did religion and theology on the thinking of the Middle Ages.
>
> (Snyder, 1990b: ix)

However, this kind of statement merely illustrates the difficulty that social science has in providing definitions of concepts central to its task. Woodrow J. Kuhns has written, 'nationalism has involved different ideas to different people in different times', and much of the scholarship in the field serves more to confuse than clarify the issues of principle concern (Kuhns, 1986: 81). Louis L. Snyder has pointed out that the study of nationalism has taken on an interdisciplinary complexion, but specialists in the field approach the problem of definition from the point of view of their special interests (Snyder, L. 1990: ix-xxiii). It is not the intention of this author to add to the confusion by providing new definitions, only to present the most important and useful understandings of the concepts in the literature, and to indicate that new research needs to be done on the political and cultural characteristics of this much maligned concept. There is a general, though unsatisfactory consensus that nationalism is a phenomenon that is 'primarily psychological' (Giddens, 1987: 116). Hans Kohn has described it as 'that state of mind in which the supreme loyalty of the individual is felt to be due to the nation-state'. Karl W. Deutsch approached the problem of definition by studying communications theory. He proposed that the test of nationality be the ability to communicate more effectively with fellow members than outsiders (Snyder, L. 1990: 244–7). Snyder has also found it useful to characterise, as opposed to defining, nationalism as a force for unity, disruption, expansion, aggression, anti-colonialism and economic expansion (Snyder, L. 1990: x-xi).

NATIONALISM IN EUROPE

Ivo Lederer, in a now famous analogy, saw nationalism as one of the tributaries feeding in to the river that made up the Eastern European 'way of life'; he added that nationalism has run:

> so deep and strong that it has appeared to possess an elemental, almost gravitational, quality. Time, location, and circumstances have, of course, altered its flow, as have war, revolution, socio-economic transformation, ideology, perhaps even some of the brave attempts at emancipation from the bondage of historical fancy. Still, nationalism has been the fundamental fact of life for nearly two hundred years.
>
> (Lederer, 1969: 396)

Even during the years of communist rule, nationalism was an important determinant of policy within, and between, countries in Eastern Europe (Simon and Gilberg, 1986). The historical development of nationalism in Central and South-Eastern Europe is also best understood in contrast to its development in Western Europe (Sugar and Lederer, 1969: 3–54). Although nationalism, as a kind of philosophy of European history, has its origins in the Western enlightenment, the concept underwent important changes when it was transposed to Eastern Europe (Minogue, 1967: 19). Hans Kohn has written:

> So strong was the influence of ideas that, while the new nationalism in western Europe corresponded to changing social, economic, and political realities, it spread to central and eastern Europe long before a corresponding social and economic transformation... Nationalism in the west arose in an effort to build a nation in the political reality and struggle of the present without too much sentimental regard for the past; nationalists in central and eastern Europe created, often out of myths of the past and the dreams of the future, an ideal fatherland, closely linked with the past, devoid of any immediate connection with the present, and expected to become sometime a political reality.
>
> (Sugar and Lederer, 1969: 9–10)

An important reason for the difference lies in the relationship between homogeneity of populations and the development of the nation-state. In Western Europe, according to Kohn and others, the nation-state developed out of necessity. Of course, the task was made easier by the achievement of 'relative national homogeneity' in the eighteenth and nineteenth centuries (Okey, 1986: 59–83; Sugar and Lederer, 1969: 10). This happened as a result of two factors: large-scale migrations had ceased in Western Europe by the start of the nineteenth century; and the Roman Catholic church had acted as a funnel of assimilation in Western Europe since the early Middle Ages. By contrast, in Eastern Europe, nationalism appeared 'at a more backward stage of social and political development', the borders of eastern states were still fluid, migrations, sometimes forced, continued into the twentieth century. Likewise, ethnic distinctions were heightened by the clash between the Roman Catholic church and Byzantine culture. As a result:

> Nationalism grew in protest against and in conflict with the existing state pattern – not primarily to transform it into a people's state, but to redraw the political boundaries in conformity with ethnographic demands.
>
> (Sugar and Lederer, 1969: 10)

In this sense, nationalism became a tool of exclusiveness, and a justification for the Messianic mission of a chosen group.

By the summer of 1991, Bulgaria, Romania, Czechoslovakia, Hungary, Yugoslavia, Poland, Eastern Germany and all the Soviet republics of Eastern Europe were either experiencing, or had experienced in the months since 1989, nationalist troubles of one kind or another (Kusin, 1990). Of course, many of the problems in a number of these countries, notably Eastern Germany and Poland, have been minor, and the result of temporary local difficulties or the activities of small extremist groups. These problems are not the concern of this chapter. Other countries are beginning to demonstrate the potential for very great conflict, both internally and externally, in the future (Eyal, 1991b; Poulton, 1989). In Romania, for example, nationalist and ethnic problems are developing on four fronts – Moldavia, Transylvania, with the Yugoslavian minority, and with the officially-backed Romanian extremist grouping Vatra Romaneasca; and in Bulgaria, future economic difficulties could reopen difficulties with the country's Turkish minority (Andrejevich, 1990c; Deletant, 1991; Gallagher, 1991; Tchukov, 1990). Also, in the months following the failed coup attempt in the Soviet Union, most republics moved towards becoming sovereign entities, the Baltic states achieved their independence, and awareness of nationalist issues came to the fore. There is every possibility that nationalist problems in the former Soviet Union will join those in Central and South-East Europe as potential threats to European security, although (in the short term at least) interest in nationalist problems in the republics will be restricted to their direct impact on the future of the 'Soviet Union', and not necessarily their impact on European security. In addition, there is a widespread possibility of border tensions; van Evera has written:

> a tour of the map of Eastern Europe reveals at least nine potential border disputes, and at least thirteen significant ethnic pockets that may either seek independence or be claimed by other countries.
>
> (van Evera, 1990: 48)

However, in the absence of large-scale and state-threatening nationalist activity in these two countries, it is difficult to analyse, without large doses of conjecture, the possible impact of such conflicts. The most dangerous developments in Central and South-Eastern Europe have been in Yugoslavia and Czechoslovakia, though only in the latter case are the difficulties dependent on post–1989 developments. The rest of this section will be devoted to an analysis of the situation in these two countries.

CZECHOSLOVAKIA

Despite the perception, largely generated by President Václav Havel's huge popularity in Western Europe, that Czechoslovakia has been undergoing an enlightened transition from communist rule, the country has been facing increasing political and economic problems. For example, as the arguments between the advocate of 'slow reform' Deputy Prime Minister Valtr Komarek and the 'Thatcherite' Finance Minister Václav Klaus have deepened over the pace of economic reform, economic performance has deteriorated markedly (Robinson, 1991). In April 1991 it was reported that during 1990, Czechoslovakia underwent a 3.2 per cent decline in GNP, a 10.6 per cent decline in real earnings, a budget deficit of 24 billion koruna, and a foreign debt of $8.1 billion (*Eastern European Newsletter*, 1991; Economist Intelligence Unit, 1990). In addition, the programme of closures for bankrupt state enterprises, the 100 per cent plus rises in rents and fuel prices, the splitting of Civic Forum, political chaos in Public Against Violence (the Slovak partner of Civic Forum), the increasing inability of President Havel to offer workable solutions to the country's problems, the success of the communists in remaining a viable opposition, and the failure to resolve questions relating to the federal relationship between Czechs and Slovaks, as well as Moravians, Silesians and other minorities, have exacerbated social instability in the country.

Apart from the main economic problem, the key difficulty for Prague is resolving the aspiration for self-determination among Slovaks within a constitutional structure that allows for the continuation of a viable Czechoslovak nation-state.[2] These divisions are, of course, nothing new for Czechoslovakia. Joseph F. Zacek has written:

> It is unhappily apparent that a 'Czechoslovak nation', a single community composed of the majority of Czechs and Slovaks, sharing a 'Czechoslovak national consciousness' and asserting a 'Czechoslovak nationalism' has never really existed.
>
> (Zacek, 1969: 166)

The cultural differences between Czechs and Slovaks are minimal in terms of their common Slavic origins; only some eastern Slovak dialects produce comprehension difficulties for Czechs. However, substantial historical differences between Czechs and Slovaks have impaired the development of a unitary Czechoslovak state in the twentieth century. For example, Czech national consciousness has its origins in the late Middle Ages, and pre-dates that of Slovakia by nearly three hundred years.[3] For almost ten centuries after the fall of the Great Moravian Empire in the ninth century, Slovakia had no real independent history, and scholars have 'been reduced almost entirely to the use of linguistic and literary criteria in determining the origins of Slovak national consciousness' (Zacek, 1969: 186). In addition, in the late nineteenth century the Czechs developed a cosmopolitan and industrial society, while the Slovaks remained a largely agrarian society. Even after the establishment of the first Czechoslovak Republic in 1918, Czechs and Slovaks never really saw the necessity of ethnic unity in a single state, and the country has been affected by the demands of both Czech and Slovak nationalism ever since. If anything, Slovak nationalism was given a boost by the formation of a Czechoslovak state, and secessionist sentiments reached a peak with the formation of the Slovak Republic in 1939–45.

The current problems between Czechs and Slovaks have been further complicated by the legacy of communist dealings with the ethnic composition of Czechoslovakia. In the period from 1948–68, socio-economic development in Slovakia brought it close to Czech standards, and in the period after the Prague Spring of 1968, the Slovaks achieved 'full emancipation from Czech tutelage' (Krejci and Velimsky, 1981: 150–1). Whereas the Czech Socialist Republic came under the rule of the Communist Party of Czechoslovakia, the Slovak Socialist Republic had its own Communist Party, and this ensured a measure of Slovak participation in decision-making in Prague. Of course, if a Slovak also happened to be the First Secretary of the Communist Party of Czechoslovakia, then he was also President of the Republic.

One of the ironies of President Havel's Czechoslovakia is that it is something of a throwback to Tomas Masaryk's inter-war country; and the new leadership is in danger of making the same mistakes in relation to the handling of Czech-Slovak problems.[4] President Havel's December 1990 announcement that he would need direct presidential powers to handle the Slovak situation, and his denunciations of widespread racism and what he saw as Slovakia's romanticism over its Nazi past have enhanced his reputation in Western Europe, but his statements often exacerbate domestic difficulties (Simmons, 1990a, b). The three main sources of tension can be illustrated by reference to three incidents occurring in 1990 and 1991; one highlights the tension between Czechs and Slovaks over the details of constitutional matters; a second refers to the crucial nature of economic issues in the current Czech-Slovak political debate, the third incident raises important questions about the rights of Czechoslovakia's other minorities, and the possibility of minority problems becoming a source of cross-border tensions.

The incident which started the most recent phase of Slovak demands is now known as the 'hyphen controversy'. In April 1990, the Czechoslovak Federal Assembly decided to adopt a dual name for the country without incorporating a hyphen between 'Czech' and 'Slovak' (de Candole, 1991: 28; Martin, 1990: 1). This incident created suspicion of Czech intentions in Bratislava, and encouraged the rapid reawakening of nationalist and separatist tendencies. A new *ad hoc* organisation, the National Council for the Liberation of Slovakia, began organising demonstrations and calling for a nationwide referendum on Slovak independence. Second, in January 1991, Vladimir Meciar, the then Prime Minister of Slovakia unilaterally announced that Slovakia had decided to resume the production and export of heavy weapons, in direct contravention of President Havel's 1990 decision to wind down arms production and cease exports immediately. Although the decision was legal, coming a matter of days after Slovakia had gained new governmental powers, it represented a very severe personal blow to President Havel.

However, despite the fact that Slovak politicians never miss an opportunity to embarrass President Havel, this was not the reason for the decision. The primary motive seems to have been concern for the possible loss of up to 70,000 jobs, 10 per cent of the Slovak labour force, and an arms production capability (Colitt, 1991a, b). In this particular instance the needs of the Slovak economy were more important than the foreign policy initiatives of President Havel. Third, in October 1990, Public Against Violence proposed giving minorities in Slovakia the right to use their mother tongue in official business in those areas where they made up over 10 per cent of the population. The Slovak National Party (SNP), saw this proposal as a violation of Slovak national integrity, and advocated the banning of all languages other than Slovak in official business. After a heated debate, dominated by linguistic chauvinism, the government was forced to settle for a 25 per cent compromise instead of the originally planned 10 per cent, and guaranteed that relations between Slovaks and ethnic minorities, which comprise 13.3 per cent of the Slovak population, would worsen (de Candole, 1991: 28). More serious was the fact that 11 per cent of the Slovak population consists of Hungarians, and Hungary has made the treatment of its minorities outside its territory a major issue in its foreign policy (Jeszensky, 1991). The irony of the entire incident is that prior to Public Against Violence's proposal Slovakia had no restrictions on the use of minority languages in official business (Obrman, 1991a: 13–17).

Despite the fact that the SNP, the only group with parliamentary representation that advocates full independence for Slovakia, polled 12 and 14 per cent of the votes respectively in the federal and Slovak elections in 1990, and gained only 3.2 per cent of the seats in the Slovak municipal elections, its influence grew throughout 1991. For example, as it became clear that resolving the constitutional issues dividing the Czechs and Slovaks would be more difficult than first hoped for, the Slovak Christian Democratic Movement began to adopt SNP ideas, and began advocating the idea of a looser form of coexistence with the Czechs (Pehe, 1991). In March 1991, Public Against Violence began to fragment under nationalist pressure, and new radical nationalist groups issued a 'Declaration of the Sovereignty of Slovakia'. As a result, large demonstrations in support of Slovak independence began to occur throughout the spring and summer months (Simmons and Greenberg, 1991).

With increasing nationalist-inspired instability in Slovakia, and new demands for political autonomy coming from Moravia and Silesia, Prague's ability to manage developments across the country is under some strain (Obrman, 1991b). Nevertheless, Havel has sought to continue building on the 'Trencianske Teplice' initiative of August 1990 (when federal, Czech and Slovak leaders met behind closed doors to negotiate constitutional documents) by calling for a referendum to settle questions relating to the Czech–Slovak federal relationship (IISS, 1990: 158). Likewise, most polls continue to indicate a desire among the population of Czechoslovakia to construct a federal structure, though Slovak opinion is increasingly under the influence of separatists. As Slovenia declared its independence in June 1991, Vladimir Meciar declared that 'Slovenia is a model for Slovakia' (*Economist*, 1991). It would not be too much of an exaggeration to say that the future of the Czechoslovak nation-state is in some doubt.

YUGOSLAVIA

Despite the fact that Yugoslavia is the symbol of nationalism in Eastern Europe Lederer has written that 'nowhere in Europe can a more complex web of interactions be found... the territory of the Yugoslavs has unfolded as a microcosm of the region as a whole' (Sugar and Lederer, 1969: 396–7). Although the term 'Yugoslavia' did not come into official use until 1929, *Yugoslavism*, an overall nationalism, was a significant factor in the creation of a state of the southern Slavs in the wake of the collapse of the Habsburg Empire, and the defeat of the Central Powers in 1918. Despite the acute religious, social, cultural and political differences of the three main national groupings – the Slovenes, Croats and Serbs – they had come, since the end of the nineteenth century, to share certain geostrategic and economic interests, and had begun to see the advantages of collective security; and Yugoslavism, a theory of common cultural identity and a programme of liberation and unification for all the southern Slavs, was the force that made the creation of a state possible after the First World War.

However, Lederer has argued that even after 1918 it was:

difficult to ascertain how widely Yugoslavism engaged the popular imagination and to what extent it co-existed with or displaced the more particularistic loyalties of Serbism or Croatism... In the nineteenth and twentieth centuries, Yugoslavism was closely intertwined with Croatian, Serbian, and Slovene nationalisms. Immediately after the two world wars it overshadowed these particularistic nationalisms, but did not eliminate them.

(Sugar and Lederer, 1969: 398)

In the seventy years since the formation of a southern Slav state, Yugoslavism has proved to be a durable idea, especially when it was combined with Titoism in the second Yugoslav state after the Second World War. However, in the twenty years up to 1980, Yugoslavia's success became dependent on the charismatic leadership of Tito, and a ponderous and debt-ridden market socialist economic system.

Although the situation in Yugoslavia is extremely complex, the present troubles can be traced to four factors: the cumbersome power-sharing constitution created by Tito in 1974, the death of Tito himself in 1980, the rapid deterioration of the economy after the ending of IMF supervision in 1986, and the election of Slobodan Milosević as the new Serbian communist leader in 1987 (Milivojević, 1989; OECD, 1990).

The decentralised federal constitution of 1974 was designed to serve Yugoslavia's needs in the years after Tito's death. The constitution was seen as protection for Croatians, Slovenians and the Albanians of Kosovo, who 'were fearful of Serbian hegemonic ambitions' (Remington, 1990: 405–8, 429–31). However, after the death of Tito in 1980, effective power moved from the federal centre to regional party leaders. As the economy began to decline, these regional leaders started to take an interest in local ethnic problems, and in promoting division between the constituent nations. Unfortunately, as problems escalated, the complex system of power-sharing was shown to be inadequate to the task of brokering solutions among regional politicians. After 1987, economic catastrophe in the form of hyperinflation prompted Slovenia and Croatia to call for rapid market and political reforms, but their way was blocked by the election of Slobodan Milosević as the new Serbian communist leader. Milosević was determined to defend the interests of the Serbian minority in the Albanian-dominated autonomous province of Kosovo, an area sacred to Serbian nationalists because this was where the Serbs had been defeated by the Turks in 1389.[5] In post-Tito Yugoslavia the Albanians, who make up 90 per cent of Kosovo's population, had demanded a degree of self-determination. In Serbia these demands were considered a challenge to Serbian territorial integrity, and Milosević was thus determined to suppress Albanian demands. However, Milosević, a communist as well as a nationalist, also refused to give economic reform (as demanded by the western-oriented republics Slovenia and Croatia), any kind of priority until there was a solution to the situation in Kosovo on Serbian terms. As the situation in Kosovo deteriorated, and solutions seemed further away than ever, so the patience of Slovenia and Croatia also deteriorated (Lendvai, 1991; Scammell, 1990). By the autumn of 1989, Yugoslavia seemed in turmoil; Slovenia's decision to introduce a new constitution, guaranteeing the right to secede from Yugoslavia, caused widespread anti-Slovene demonstrations in Serbia and Montenegro, and in Kosovo violent demonstrations and riots were being ruthlessly suppressed by the Serbian military authorities (Dempsey, 1989; Tanner, 1990). It would not be too much of an exaggeration to say that the federal authorities were mostly powerless to defend the interests of Yugoslavia against those of individual republics; only the 1989 economic reform package of the federal Prime Minister Ante Marković made any headway in restoring a balance between federal and republic authorities.

In February 1990, the Slovene Communist Party followed its January decision to walk out of the federal party congress by voting to abolish itself, and in July the Slovenian National Assembly issued a declaration of sovereignty (Andrejevich, 1991; Chalupa, 1990; Tanner, 1990). The spring elections in Croatia and Slovenia confirmed support for the nationalists, as did the December referendum on independence in Slovenia, where 88 per cent of the electorate voted for independence. In Kosovo, Serbian suppression reached a new peak when the Serbian National Assembly announced the dissolution of Kosovo's government and provincial assembly, and introduced new censorship laws. This was the first time since 1946 that Serbia had assumed full administrative and executive power in the province, and represented another step towards the full reincorporation of Kosovo into Serbia (Andrejevich, 1990b). In Croatia, during August 1990, an incident occurred that highlighted another complication in Yugoslavia: the multinational character of nearly all the republics after 70 years of cohabitation. The Serb minority in Croatia, concentrated in the city of Knin, decided to hold a referendum over cultural autonomy. However, it turned into an armed insurrection, and the Croatian leadership rejected the referendum as unconstitutional (IISS, 1990: 167). By the end of 1990, all the Yugoslav republics had held successful multi-party elections, though in republics hitherto outside the arguments of Croatia, Slovenia and Serbia they served to revitalise local interests and radicalise the populations. In Macedonia for example, victory went to nationalists, which produced widespread worry that the Balkans was on the verge of a new pan-Macedonian nationalism; in Bosnia-Herzegovina, a close election produced victory to the Muslims (Andrejevich, 1990d); even in Serbia, where Milosević won an overwhelming victory, the first hints of opposition and discontent appeared in the form of a right-wing nationalist party, the Serbian National Renewal, under the leadership of Vuk Drasković. Indeed by March 1991, Milosević's authority in Serbia seemed under threat: in the biggest and most violent anti-communist demonstration in postwar Yugoslavia, 80–100,000 people clashed with police in Belgrade displaying the growing unrest in the republic over the political and economic policies of the communist authorities (Andrejevich, 1991). Both the Slovene and Croatian governments decided to invalidate federal laws on their territory in February 1991, and a series of crises between the army and the Croatian and Slovenian authorities (climaxing with the army's demand for the arrest of the Croatian Defence Minister General Martin Spegelj on charges of 'planning an armed insurrection' and threats of military intervention), marred attempts to find a peaceful solution to Yugoslavia's situation (Harden, 1991; Silber, 1991a; Tanner, 1991; Traynor, 1991).

In the last three years, a number of internal proposals have been made to solve the Yugoslav crisis. However, the main problem has been the dispute between federalists and confederalists, though there has also been strong pressure for an outright break-up of the country. In October 1990 for example, Croatia and Slovenia presented proposals for turning Yugoslavia into an alliance of sovereign states. Milosević however has stuck rigidly to the federal principle, and has warned that if Yugoslavia were to become a confederation he would consider the internal borders of the country 'an open political question'. The other poorer republics, and central authorities, have stuck close to the idea of a reformed and decentralised federal system (*International Herald Tribune*, 1991; Silber, 1991b). In June 1991, the presidents of the six republics held a final round of talks in an effort to devise a new governmental system for the country, but the talks served only to reinforce divisions. These meetings were prompted in part by the greater interest being shown by foreign governments and the European Community in Yugoslavia's internal crisis (although regional interest in the situation was becoming acute as the country moved rapidly to a state of near civil war, international interest had been minimal, and reserved to calls for the peaceful settlement of the Yugoslav situation, comment on particular incidents and the monitoring of the general situation) (Binder, 1990; Eyal, 1991a).

For some time, there has been a popular joke in Yugoslavia: 'how many states will there be in Europe in 1992? Seven: Europe, Croatia, Slovenia, Bosnia-Herzegovina, Macedonia, Serbia and Montenegro' (Bunce, 1990: 423). But with the independence declarations in June 1991 by Croatia and Slovenia this joke began to take on an air of reality. In essence, the Yugoslav crisis entered a new and deadlier phase, bringing swift federal and international reaction. Although Ante Marković had ruled out the use of force to prevent the break-up of the country, there seemed little chance of preventing armed conflict. In addition, the United States and most European countries, in an effort to encourage further negotiations, announced that they would not recognise the independence of Slovenia and Croatia. However, at the time of writing, and as the European Community's three-month agreement between federal and republic governments in Yugoslavia went into operation, it was already possible to say that the second Yugoslav state was at an end. Even if a third could be negotiated into existence, it would be of a different character to its immediate predecessor. More likely was that Slovenia, in particular, would become the first new state in Europe for forty years, and that the ethnic imbalance in Croatia would provoke further conflict and even war with Serbia.

NATIONALISM AND EUROPEAN SECURITY INSTITUTIONS

Of the three areas of analysis that form the basis of this chapter, this last one, because of its policy-orientation, might seem the most important and controversial. In academic terms, it is the least important because so much of the analysis relies on unsatisfactory conjecture. At present, acquiring an understanding of the course of developments in Central and South-Eastern Europe is by far the more crucial task for European security specialists. At the time of writing, the Yugoslavia crisis is producing a rapid evolution in thinking on the issues of nationalist conflict management and the division of labour among European security institutions. As a result, this section will briefly outline the parameters of the developing debate on 'management', and consider the function of peacekeeping forces.

The debate on 'management' can be considered controversial for three main reasons. First, it is not at all clear that any 'techniques' or 'practices' make the slightest difference to the course of events. Second, and only if one accepts the first reservation, there are few realistic ways of considering the issue without contemplating the use of military force, in one capacity or another. Third, and more importantly, there is a sense in which the debate is perceived in Central and South-Eastern Europe as a reformulation of the 'white man's burden'.

A small number of analysts in the former Eastern Europe are beginning to argue that the debate is simply a product of Western Europe's insecurity in relation to the changes in the region after 1989. They would argue that until Western Europe faces up to the very real 'ethno-territorial dilemma' in Central and South-Eastern Europe, cycles of nationalist crises will burden the European security system for generations. The logic of this argument allows for only one solution, and one that Western Europe could never contemplate: allowing the states and nations of the region to settle their own fate on their own terms, without the extension of western European 'solutions' or 'conflict management techniques'.[6] For politicians and interested academics in Western Europe a 'solution' of this kind produces unattractive visions of territorial disputes, state disintegrations, border revisions by un-peaceful means, and the return of unsavoury land wars to the European continent.

Despite this, the argument started to gain some currency as primary responsibility for brokering a peace settlement in Yugoslavia was taken by the EC, arguably the most important of the European security institutions to be, but one that has as yet no formal centralised foreign policy mechanisms, nor the means for consulting neighbouring countries in Central and South-Eastern Europe on issues that directly concern them. The CSCE, the organisation that most countries in the former Eastern Europe have devoted much effort to since 1989, managed to respond to the crisis only ponderously. As a result, there is now a developing debate concerning how the Yugoslavia crisis might be the 'architect' of the new European security system, and that the balance of power between the EC and the CSCE might have shifted towards the Community; something that few in Central and South-Eastern Europe look upon with much happiness (at least until they are themselves allowed to become members of the EC and so influence the course of the debate).[7]

All this would suggest that there is some room for the enhancement of independent regional cooperation initiatives that would ensure the involvement of states in Central and South-Eastern Europe in their own security. Since 1989, two sets of regional cooperation have come to the fore, the Visegrad Summit between the leaders of Czechoslovakia, Hungary and Poland in February 1991, and the Balkan Foreign Ministers Conference in October 1990. Neither forum has been used to initiate local ideas on security management however (de Weydenthal, 1991; Zanga, 1990). In addition, the Yugoslavia crisis might act as the catalyst for cooperation (or more serious crises) between on the one hand different sets of countries in the region and on the other Western European organisations, especially the EC. Cooperative initiatives might also be of help in defusing the developing tensions over the future of a European security system that is increasingly reliant on Western European organisations. It should however be added that the creation of 'little entente-style' conditions of 'EC-Visegrad' cooperation, for example, would be wholly inappropriate, and serve only to highlight instability.

Up until the declarations of independence by Slovenia and Croatia in June 1991, the debate on remedying or managing nationalist problems had centred on a broad agenda of abstract preventative methods. These relied on a wide definition of European security, encompassing cultural and economic factors, as well as the more traditional political and military factors. For example, Jack Snyder has put forward:

> a checklist of expedients to keep in mind in fashioning a policy on European nationalisms: (1) eliminate military threats to states' security; (2) provide economic resources so that states can legitimate their rule through economic growth; (3) encourage the spread of liberal, transnational, economic and cultural ties; (4) cushion the impact of market reforms on disadvantaged groups; (5) co-opt intellectuals; and (6) promote constructive dialogue between nationalities at the local level.
>
> (Snyder, J. 1990: 59)

Most of these are of obvious importance in tackling what seems to be the major reason for the resurgence of nationalism in Central and South-Eastern Europe – 'the discrepancy between the immensity of the reconstructive tasks facing the east Europeans and their political, economic and moral capacity to cope with them' (Brown, 1991). However, there remain few institutional mechanisms for implementing such a broad and abstract agenda at the present time.

In addition, work had begun on the creation of 'crisis' mechanisms within the CSCE. With the endorsement of the Valletta report on Peaceful Settlement of Disputes, and the development of the 'Mechanism for consultation and cooperation with regard to emergency situations', the Berlin CSCE Council meeting in June 1991 began the process of creating international political procedures to aid the management of potential nationalist conflicts in Central and South-Eastern Europe (USIS, 1991). The Berlin decisions came just days before the declarations of independence by Slovenia and Croatia, and were of little (if supportive) value during the initial phases of the crisis.[8]

As the first phase of what could be described as the EC's intervention in the Yugoslavia crisis illustrated, the institutional response was at best *ad hoc* and too late. The unarmed observer group that was initially deployed in Yugoslavia for example was treated with much disdain by the media (Freeman, 1991). Despite this, the EC can be complimented for preventing an initial rapid escalation of conflict and forcing a brief period of negotiation between the Yugoslav republics. In addition, and most importantly, the crisis put the EC firmly in the business of 'security' thinking.

The European Community has shown great reluctance to even consider the use of the military option to impose a peace settlement in Yugoslavia. However, as the prospect of civil war between Serbia and Croatia grew in August 1991, a number of countries and commentators began to advocate the use of at least peacekeeping forces, under the auspices of the Western European Union, to prevent a further escalation of violence (Gardner and Silber, 1991). At the time of writing, little consideration had been given to the uses of a rapid deployment force, such as the one under development in NATO, though this could represent the last 'unthinkable' stage of Western European involvement in the Yugoslavia crisis.[9]

Since 1989, there have been a number of academic analyses of the utility of peacekeeping forces in the new European context. For example, Phil Williams has written that an 'interposition force which would permit the disengagement of the hostile parties, and perhaps provide some time for conciliation processes' would be 'a necessary accompaniment to efforts at mediation and conciliation' in the new security system. In addition, he has written that the existence of 'even a modest capacity for peacekeeping activities would perhaps make it less likely that great powers would become involved in ethnic conflicts or nationalist rivalries in Central Europe.' (Williams, 1990: 283). However, while the principle of peacekeeping operations has been widely viewed as being of value (despite the reluctance of politicians to consider the use of military forces in volatile conflict situations) little consideration has been given to the record of peacekeeping operations in similar ethnic or nationalist situations. Although it is not always wise to draw parallels between similar situations in different parts of the world, the brief overview of peacekeeping operations that follows should serve as a warning that any such operations in Europe would be fraught with military, political and diplomatic dangers.

As Stephen Ryan points out, there have been three UN peacekeeping operations in multi-ethnic states: in Cyprus, Lebanon and the Belgian Congo. In addition there have been similar, non-UN operations carried out by the Organisation of African Unity (OAU) in Chad, the Arab League in Lebanon, the Multinational Force in Lebanon, and the Indian Peacekeeping Force in Sri Lanka. Only in the case of the UN operation in Cyprus can any of these be considered something of a success; and all those developed by other organisations have been near disasters (Ryan considered the OAU initiative in Chad a 'fiasco', and the Indian force in Sri Lanka a 'foreign policy blunder') (Ryan, 1990: 122–39).[10] Although the UN operations have been far from successful in most cases, all this would suggest that UN involvement and its moral authority is a prerequisite for any kind of success in this area of military activity.[11] As a result, there is much room for cooperation between the United Nations and European security institutions.

There is also considerable doubt about the possible nature of a European peacekeeping force, though the WEU would probably have primary responsibility for organising such a force. This, however, would not be without problems. One of the cardinal principles of peacekeeping operations is that the force is considered impartial. There would be something of a questionmark about the impartiality of a WEU-organised force operating in the former Eastern Europe. This is particularly true in terms of the Yugoslavia crisis, where the original diplomatic stances of some member countries would ensure distrust between different parties to the conflict. Under these circumstances, it would be useful to consider the involvement of those states that are traditionally 'neutral', such as Sweden. The use of forces from Central and South-Eastern Europe might also enhance the credibility of a force, and indirectly contribute to enhanced confidence in the European security system.

Despite this, it has to be said that the military option represents far from a panacea in such conflict situations. In many cases, the risks involved in conducting an operation would far outweigh the possible gains, and failure could impact throughout the system, ensuring the escalation of local violence, and directly undermining confidence in the European security institutions. In this way, 'management techniques' might exacerbate a conflict situation rather than help control it; and as such they should be used sparingly and carefully.

CONCLUSION

There is little doubt that nationalism is once again becoming a crucial security issue in Europe. The potential for violence and conflict is great, as the civil war in Yugoslavia has illustrated. For European security analysts there is much work to be done on the problems associated with nationalism. Four tasks though seem crucial: developing a rigorous understanding of the nature of nationalism in the new Europe; devoting more attention to the domestic sources of instability in Europe; acquiring a solid historical and sociological understanding of the course of developments in Central and South-Eastern Europe; and reconsidering the utility of testing security mechanisms against nationalist problems.

NOTES

1 The Christian-Democratic Party in the Netherlands is also conducting its own research into the possible impact of nationalism on European security.
2 The Slovaks represent one third of the country's population of 15.6 million.
3 There is some controversy over the origins of Slovak 'national consciousness'. Peter Brock has claimed that a 'consciousness of separate identity' in Slovakia pre-dates the use of a Slovak vernacular in the 1780s by a number of centuries (Brock, 1976: 1–19).
4 This has been a comparison also alluded to in IISS, 1990: 157.
5 There are approximately 200,000 Serbs in Kosovo.
6 I am grateful for Professor Hieronim Kubiak for providing me with a detailed explanation of developing security thinking in Central and South-Eastern Europe. These arguments are not attributable to him.
7 Jacques Delors, President of the European Commission, sees it as the EC's 'collective "duty" to get as involved in finding peace in Yugoslavia as the US is in the Middle East' (Buchan, 1991b).
8 This did not prevent use of the 'mechanisms'. Hans-Dietrich Genscher, the Foreign Minister responsible for managing the emergency mechanism, organised the first meeting of the committee of high level officials in Prague in July, and the Conflict Prevention Centre's Advisory Committee began examining 'unusual military activities on the part of the Yugoslav army'.
9 For a consideration of NATO's rapid reaction force see Palmer 1991.
10 Apart from the operations described here, the only other one of relevance to present developments in Europe is that of the UN Special Committee on the Balkans (UNSCOB), 1947–52, and the military observers of the Balkan sub-commission, 1952–4. See for example, Higgins, 1981.
11 For example, most UN operations lack resources, and most are in deficit. By the end of 1988, the Cyprus operation was over $164 million in deficit (Ryan, 1990: 140).

78 Security & the new European system

REFERENCES

Andrejevich, M. (1990a)'Kosovo and Slovenia declare their sovereignty', *Report on Eastern Europe* 1, 30: 45–8.
Andrejevich, M. (1990b) 'Serbia cracks down in Kosovo', *Report on Eastern Europe* 1, 30: 48–52.
Andrejevich, M. (1990c)'Illiescu's visit: the issue of Romania's Yugoslav minorities', *Report on Eastern Europe*, 1, 38: 29–31.
Andrejevich, M. (1990d) 'The election scorecard for Serbia, Montenegro and Macedonia', *Report on Eastern Europe*, 1, 51: 37–9.
Andrejevich, M. (1991) 'Unrest in Belgrade: a symptom of Serbia's crisis', *Report on Eastern Europe*, 2, 13: 12–18.
Bartelson, J. (1990) 'Deconstructing sovereignty', unpublished seminar paper presented to the University of Stockholm.
Binder, D. (1990) 'The withering of Yugoslavia', *International Herald Tribune*, 29 November 1990.
Booth, K. (1990) 'Steps towards stable peace in Europe: a theory and practice of coexistence', *International Affairs*, 66, 1: 17–45.
Brock, P. (1976) *The Slovak National Awakening: an Essay in the Intellectual History of East Central Europe*, Toronto: University of Toronto.
Brown, J. (1991) 'The resurgence of nationalism', *Report on Eastern Europe*, 2, 24: 36.
Buchan, D. (1991a) 'Havel warns of potential chaos', *Financial Times*, 21 March 1991.
Buchan, D. (1991b) 'The EC's very own visionary', *Financial Times*, 5 August 1991.
Bunce, V. (1990) 'The struggle for liberal democracy in Eastern Europe', *World Policy*, 7, 3: 396–430.
Chalupa, G. (1990) 'Threats of secession hang over every Belgrade manoeuvre', *The German Tribune*, 15 July 1990.
Clesse, A. and Ruhl, L. (eds) (1990) *Beyond East–West Confrontation: Searching for a New Security Structure in Europe*, Baden-Baden: Nomos.
Colitt, L. (1991a) 'Slovakia will defy Prague's arms exports ban to protect defence jobs', *Financial Times*, 10 January 1991.
Colitt, L. (1991b) 'Arms and the man in Slovakia', *Financial Times*, 22 January 1991.
de Candole, J. (1991) *Czechoslovakia: Too Velvet a Revolution?* European Security Study no. 11, London: IEDSS.
de Weydenthal (1991) 'The Visegrad summit', *Report on Eastern Europe*, 2, 9: 28–32.
Deletant, D. (1991) 'The role of Vatra Romaneasca in Transylvania', *Report on Eastern Europe*, 2, 5: 28–37.
Dempsey, J. (1989)'Kosovo army alert stepped up', *Financial Times* 5 November 1989.
Eastern European Newsletter (1991) 'Czechoslovakia crunch', 5, 8: 1.
Economist (1991) 'Czechoslovakia: compare and contrast', 13 July 1991.
Economist Intelligence Unit (1990) 'Czechoslovakia in transition', October 1990: 1–46.
Eyal, J. (1991a) 'Neighbours start planning for life after Yugoslavia', *Guardian*, 8 April 1991.
Eyal, J. (1991b) 'Balkan states crack on the rock of reality', *Guardian*, 10 May 1991.

Freeman, S. (1991) 'Tough realities of fighting for peace', *European*, 2–4 August 1991.

Gallagher, T. (1991) 'Common ground', *Planet*, 85: 70–5.

Gardner, D. and Silber, L. (1991) 'France seeks Yugoslav force', *Financial Times*, 6 August 1991.

Garton Ash, T. (1989) *The Uses of Adversity: Essays on the Fate of Central Europe*, Cambridge: Granta/Penguin.

Garton Ash, T. (1991) 'Poland after Solidarity', *New York Review of Books*, 13 June 1991.

George, J. and Campbell, D. (1990) 'Patterns of dissent and the celebration of difference: critical social theory and international relations', *International Studies Quarterly*, 34: 282.

Giddens, A. (1987) *The Nation-State and Violence*, Berkeley and Los Angeles: University of California.

Gilberg, T. (1990) *Nationalism and Communism in Romania: The Rise and Fall of Ceausescu's Personal Dictatorship*, Boulder: Westview.

Glenny, M. (1990) *The Rebirth of History: Eastern Europe in the Age of Democracy*, London: Penguin.

Harden, B. (1991) 'Croatia declares Yugoslav laws invalid', *International Herald Tribune*, 22 February 1991.

Higgins, R. (1981) *United Nations Peacekeeping: Documents and Commentary, vol IV: Europe, 1946–79*, Oxford: OUP.

Hobsbawn, E. (1990) *Nation and Nationalism since 1780: Programme, Myth and Reality*, Cambridge: Cambridge University Press.

Holst, J. (1990) *Exploring Europe's Future: Trends and Prospects Relating to Security*, Santa Monica: RAND.

IISS (1990) *Strategic Survey 1990–91*, London: Brassey's.

International Herald Tribune (1991) 'Macedonia offers proposals for unity', 23/24 February 1991.

Jeszenszky, G. (1991), unpublished address to Utrikespolitiska Institutet, Stockholm, 30 January 1991.

Krejci, J. and Velimsky, V. (1981) *Ethnic and Political Nations in Europe*, London: Croom Helm.

Kuhns, W. (1986) 'Political nationalism in contemporary Eastern Europe', in J. Simon and T. Gilberg (eds), *Security Implications of Nationalism in Eastern Europe*, Boulder: Westview.

Kusin, V. (1990) 'The ethnic factor', *Report on Eastern Europe*, 1, 44: 35–9.

Lederer, I. (1969) 'Nationalism and the Yugoslavs', in P. Sugar and I. Lederer (eds), *Nationalism in Eastern Europe*, Seattle: University of Washington.

Lendvai, P. (1991) 'Yugoslavia wihout the Yugoslavs: the roots of the crisis', *International Affairs*, 67, 2: 251–61.

Linden, R. (1991) 'The end of the beginning', *Report on Eastern Europe*, 2, 1: 1.

MacCormick, N. (1991) 'Is nationalism philosophically credible?', in W. Twining (ed.) *Issues of Self Determination*, Aberdeen: Aberdeen University.

Martin, P. (1990) 'The hyphen controversy', *Report on Eastern Europe*, 1, 36: 1.

Mearsheimer, J. (1990) 'Back to the future: instability in Europe after the Cold War', *International Security*, 15, 1: 5–56.

Milivojević, M. (1989) *Descent into Chaos: Yugoslavia's Worsening Crisis*, European Security Study no. 7, London: IEDSS.

Minogue, K. (1967) *Nationalism*, London: Methuen.

Nelson, D. (1991) 'Europe's unstable East', *Foreign Policy*, 82.

Obrman, J. (1991a) 'Language law stirs controversy in Slovakia' *Report on Eastern Europe*, **1**, 46: 13–17.

Obrman, J. (1991b) 'The issue of autonomy for Moravia and Silesia', *Report on Eastern Europe*, **2**, 5: 13–23.

OECD (1990), *Yugoslavia*, OECD economic survey, Paris: OECD.

Okey, R. (1986) *Eastern Europe, 1740–1985: Feudalism to Communism*, London: Unwin Hyman.

Palmer, J. (1991) 'NATO plans a rapid deployment force', *Guardian*, 13 April 1991.

Pehe, J. (1991) 'Growing Slovak demands seen as threat to federation', *Report on Eastern Europe*, **2**, 12: 2.

Poulton, H. (1989) *Minorities in the Balkans*, Report no. 82, London: The Minority Rights Group.

Remington, R. (1990) 'The federal dilemma in Yugoslavia', *Current History*, **89**, 551: 405–31.

Robinson, A. (1991) 'Czech minister says perestroika bars radical reforms', *Financial Times*, 26 March 1991.

Ryan, S. (1990), *Ethnic Conflict and International Relations*, Dartmouth: Aldershot.

Scammell, M. (1990) 'The new Yugoslavia', *New York Review of Books*, 19 July 1990, 37–42.

Silber, L. (1991a)'Slovenia moves further towards independence', *Financial Times*, 21 February 1991.

Silber, L. (1991b) 'Yugoslav premier stands firm on secession', *Financial Times*, 1/2 June 1991.

Simmons, M. (1990a) 'Havel attacks Czech racism', *Guardian*, 18 July 1990.

Simmons, M. (1990b) 'Prague Jews confront Havel over Slovak links to Nazis', *Guardian*, 23 August 1990.

Simmons, M. and Greenberg, S. (1991) 'Slovaks rally for independence', *Guardian*, 12 March 1991.

Simon, J. and Gilberg T. (eds) (1986) *Security Implications of Nationalism in Eastern Europe*, Boulder: Westview.

Smoke, R. (1990) *A Theory of Mutual Security*, Working Paper no. 11, Providence, N. J.: Brown University, Centre for Foreign Policy Development.

Snyder, J. (1990) 'Controlling nationalism in the new Europe', in A. Clesse and R. Ruhl (eds) *Beyond East–West Confrontation: Searching for a New Security Structure in Europe*, Baden-Baden: Nomos.

Snyder, L. (1990) *Encyclopedia of Nationalism*, Chicago: St James's.

Sugar, P. and Lederer, I. (eds) (1969) *Nationalism in Eastern Europe*, Seattle: University of Washington.

Tanner, M. (1990) 'Communists in Slovenia become "Renewal" party', *Independent*, 5 February 1990.

Tanner, M. (1991) 'Croats stage walkout at Belgrade summit', *Independent*, 1 February 1991.

Tchukov, V. (1990) *Still in the Queue: Bulgaria waits for Democracy*, European Security Study no.10, London: IEDSS.

Traynor, I. (1991) 'Croatian militia ready to resist Yugoslavian army', *Guardian*, 21 January 1991.

USIS (1991) 'Berlin CSCE Council issues summary of conclusions', USIS Information Sheet, Stockholm: US Embassy.

Williams, P. (1990) 'A conflict management centre for Europe' in A. Clesse and R.

Ruhl (eds) *Beyond East–West Confrontation: Searching for a New Security Structure in Europe*, Baden-Baden: Nomos.

van Evera, S. (1990) 'Primed for peace: Europe after the Cold War', *International Security*, **15**, 3: 7–57.

Zacek, J. (1969) 'Nationalism in Czechoslovakia', in Sugar and Lederer (eds) *Nationalism in Eastern Europe*, Seattle: University of Washington.

Zanga, L. (1990) 'The Balkan foreign ministers' conference in Tirana', *Report on Eastern Europe*, **1**, 49: 1–4.

4   The end of Eurocentrism and its consequences

*Peter Foot**

The net effect on Europe of the events of late 1989 has been dramatic. They marked the end of a remarkable period of almost exactly 500 years during which the continent of Europe, its peoples, ideas, culture and administrative systems, were the focus of global politics. From the opening of what Halford Mackinder liked to call the Columbian Era in the early sixteenth century, the affairs of Europe have been paramount in world history (Mackinder, 1904). Europe was important once because world power was wielded from that region; the postwar period saw the strength of two extra-European states, the United States and the Soviet Union, maintain the balance of power within it. The liberation of Central and Eastern European peoples from the domination of the Soviet Union, coupled with developments within the European Community, mean that the kinds of impulses that brought the United States into a security relationship with Western Europe in the late–1940s have been either satisfied or are no longer relevant (Foot, 1990: 82–94). The decolonisation process that also began in the late–1940s with the independence of Pakistan and India was a direct consequence of a decline in both relative and absolute European power. Geoffrey Barraclough has argued that the most significant aspect of the postwar world is not superpower confrontation but the decolonisation process (Barraclough, 1964: 153–98). What had subsequently kept Europe, if somewhat artificially, at the centre of affairs – superpower confrontation over a divided continent – already prefigured the larger issue that has now become clear. Eurocentrism, as a feature of international affairs, has come to an end.

This chapter explores the consequences of this. First, the general setting for discussing Europe's wider security interests and concerns is outlined. Second, constraints on both economic relations and military activity, interventionary and otherwise, are addressed. Finally, some suggestions are offered about opportunities that might characterise West Europeans' efforts

* The views contained in this chapter are those of the author and are not necessarily those of Her Majesty's Government.

to optimise their efforts to defend perceived political, economic and strategic interests beyond their own region.

THE SECURITY CONTEXT

It is natural that now as never before questions about European security priorities crowd in. States with experience of colonial possession and competition such as Britain, France and even Imperial Germany, have tended to focus on the balance of power in Europe – either to sustain or disrupt it – before considering dominion over pine and palm. British governments, representing the people seemingly with the greatest difficulty in coming to terms with the demise of Eurocentrism, have tended to:

> support those who, like Elizabeth I, William III, Marlborough, Chatham, Grey and others, argued the need for the British people to balance their natural wish for a 'maritime' way of life and strategy with a watchful concern for Europe and a determination to ensure that developments on that continent did not deleteriously affect their country's interests.
>
> (Kennedy, 1983: xxix)

Experiments with 'splendid isolation' have failed precisely because events on the European mainland are of more immediate concern than those further afield.

From the King of Spain's Armada to Brezhnev's Russia, the primary concern has been for the balance of power in Europe. The dismantling of the Warsaw Pact did nothing to undermine the validity of that remarkably consistent judgement. This is not to simply accept some of the more worrying prognostications about Eastern Europe: inevitable civil wars, massive dislocation, large refugee populations roaming Western Europe, and general turbulence. But nor is it to suggest that West European forces may be needed to sort out such difficulties. Apart from anything else, balance within Europe has been the goal, not general order in any particular part of it. Nevertheless, given the uncertainties surrounding political, social, economic and military developments in Central and Eastern Europe, it is no more than historical prudence to suggest that more rather than less attention should be paid to intra-European security matters. If nothing else, the shifting interests of the United States tend to confirm that judgement. The transpacific relationship with Japan has long concerned US economists; strategists have begun to note the significance only more recently (George, 1991; Huntington, 1991).

The second contextual issue is that of the nature of security itself. Clearly, the ending of the Cold War has made still more insistent those questions about the relationship between overall security and defence. Periods of war or high tension will see a closer connection between the two than in times of low risk and minimal tension. Adam Smith could safely say, in the context of eighteenth century Anglo-French rivalry, that the first duty of the sovereign was the defence of the realm; most of the participants in the Cold War also took as axiomatic the considerable overlap in security and defence matters. It is not merely the consequence of changes in Europe that little remains of that assumption. There is the argument that military power *per se* is of declining utility; that, as a means to achieve long-run objectives for states, armed force is less able now to deliver sustainable political and economic goals (Luard, 1988). Apart from the academic case, there is the example of the Soviet Union itself which, certainly since 1988, has accepted the logic of the point. Twenty years earlier the British, when deciding to withdraw from the Gulf by 1971, were not signalling the abandonment of their many interests in the region; rather it was that, given higher European priorities and economic difficulties, national interests further afield would have to be largely protected by non-military means. Today, there is a distinct return to that wider appreciation of what security means, that feeling secure involves acceptable levels of public health and welfare; stable economic conditions at home; open, international trading possibilities abroad; social cohesion under the rule of law equitably applied; attention to and respect for the environment; and a growing proportion of the population achieving high levels of broadly based education. With the passing of both the Cold War and the colonial epoch, specifically military contributions to security are harder to define.

The third contextual issue is the general complexity in the relationships that have emerged between Northern, industrial states and countries in the Third World since decolonisation.[1] The conditions that characterised independence; the subsequent quality of leadership; the availability of infrastructures capable of producing food, goods and services for consumption and trade; the level of industrial activity achieved; the extent to which the oil price shocks of the 1970s were overcome; the vulnerability of single-crop economies to unpredictable weather – all, and more, help shape the variety contained in the phrase North–South relations. These are not the kinds of issue which have always been most evident in the debate about security challenges to Western interests beyond the North Atlantic. For much of the 1970s and 1980s, for example, less developed countries (LDCs) were primarily looked at by Western (or Northern) states from the point of view of their orientation to the Soviet Union or the People's Republic of China. This was never the most reliable index of very much at all. But it did reflect the pervasive separation of specific defence matters from other, more general security issues that characterised Cold War assessments by the West. Much less attention was paid to issues closer to the day-to-day interests of developing states. Access to World Bank loans, support with balance of payments difficulties from the International Monetary Fund, and – above all – the ability to sell in North American or European markets were always more important to the LDCs.

Members of the Organisation for Economic Cooperation and Development (OECD) have only recently interested themselves in the plight of the LDCs, and then only with the difficulties created for their own perceived interests. The debt problem of the Third World becomes an issue only when North American and European banking institutions are undermined by the consequences of their own lending (Thomas, 1987). For example, the powerful players in the General Agreement on Tariffs and Trade, when conducting the Uruguay Round of negotiations (the focal point of world trade policy for the late 1980s and early 1990s and beyond) were not concerned with restructuring the system, despite the fact that, as Susan George has argued, the development model promoted by the World Bank and IMF has been disastrous for Third World countries.

> By any normal standards we ought to be able to affirm confidently that this model has failed, since it has plunged countries adopting it into a quagmire from which they show few signs of escaping and has caused immeasurable suffering for their people. Yet these same countries are now told, by those in a position to enforce their advice, that they must apply the same policies, only more so, in order to qualify for further loans and continuing membership in the international community. It is like prescribing cyanide as an antidote to arsenic.
>
> (George, 1988: 263–4)

For a scholarly community concerned for so long with deterrence and nuclear weapons in Europe, it is sobering and humbling to have it suggested that, in the Third World, something between 15 and 20 million people die each year as a consequence of present arrangements between North and South. That amounts to a death toll of Hiroshima equivalence every two days (George, 1988: 270).

MILITARY AND ECONOMIC CONSTRAINTS

The setting for any discussion of European security in the post-Cold War world thus imposes its own contradictory logic when the extra-European dimension is brought in. There is on the one hand the need to recognise the primacy of the demands which stem from the unification of Germany, and therefore of the continent. The definition of security itself, and that of the perhaps questionable utility of military force within it, requires prudent attention. But on the other hand the political, economic and social conditions of the Third World are in such a parlous state that to insist on the primacy of the European continent's demands is merely to perpetuate injustice in the wider world and, therefore, to sustain precisely the growing likelihood of challenges to Western interests which invite the despatch of military forces, ostensibly to 'solve' the problem.[2] Reflecting this set of contradictions, the debate about the use of Western armed forces has more than two positions. As with most debates, arguments tend to fall along a spectrum of views, with many instances of overlap.

At one end, there is the general proposition that, with the passing of bipolarity, the world is likely to become an even more turbulent place; that Eurocentric themes of balances of power need to be applied to specific regions where Western interests might be vulnerable to challenge; and that this cannot be achieved unless there is demonstrable military power, and the will to use it in support of economic and political interests. This proposition was powerfully strengthened, for some, by the outcome of the war in the Gulf occasioned by Iraq's invasion of Kuwait in 1990. The range of cited issues that could produce future challenges is wide: a hostile Islamic coalition on the southern Mediterranean littoral; desperation in sub-Saharan Africa; turmoil in southern Africa; expansionist tendencies on the Indian subcontinent; changes in Japan's defence policy; turbulence in South-East Asia. The list is a long one. According to this argument, military forces of a global, policing nature would have to be able to enforce stability as well as maintain it. Deployments should therefore not be solely reactive but be precautionary, thereby serving the purposes of deterrence wherever this was deemed desirable or necessary. The emergence of the Western Alliance, and particularly the United States as the overwhelmingly preponderant power in the world, naturally leads some to the conclusion that the kinds of inhibition born out of failure in Vietnam and elsewhere can be discarded. West Europeans may have a particularly valuable role to play by virtue of their long experience in Africa, the Middle East and Asia. If the international system is anarchic, then military power has a constructive and essential contribution to make to world order by supporting the economic and political status quo.

The argument at the other end of the spectrum shares the notion that the international system is anarchic but, in general, concludes that military power can do no more than manage chaos at the margins. The kind of predictability, allied to an arrangement consolidated by armed force, that has characterised Europe since 1945 is noteworthy because neither before that year in Europe, nor at any time anywhere else in the twentieth century, can it be said to have existed. Stasis is not a normal feature of dynamic systems. Consequently, it is counterproductive to think in terms of seeking to extend to the rest of the world mechanisms that applied to Europe for a particular period in unique circumstances. The outcome of the war waged against Iraq by the international coalition was held to support this position. Those who argued that the use of military power should be limited to enforcing an economic blockade against the aggressor were confirmed in their judgement by the fact that, despite being 'defeated', the Iraqi leadership would not concede. As one commentator remarked after the conflict:

The Iraqi dictator remains besieged by sanctions, containable by lesser military force as the result of the destruction of his own forces. But containment and sanctions were always the alternatives to war in the first place. We are told they will serve now. Perhaps, after all, they would have served then.

(Jenkins, 1991)

This is another way of saying that the wealthy, industrialised world will have to do what a good part of the rest of the world has always had to put up with: coping as best as maybe with an unpredictable environment and striving ever to satisfy that most basic of political criteria, namely not making the existing situation even worse.

Those at both ends of the spectrum, then, can accept that the possession of some armed force for use in Third World theatres is prudent. What separates them is the readiness to use such force. As Eberle has said, 'Ultimately the cost of taking military action has to be measured against the cost of not taking military action, when both these costs are extremely difficult to define' (Eberle, 1991: 34). For Europeans, that calculation is made more difficult still by the fact that some countries have constitutional or other inhibitions to taking military action, regardless of the outcome of such a balancing of advantage against disadvantage. Yet all perceive their interests to be at risk, albeit to a greater or lesser extent. Risks can range from the protection of nationals caught up in an area of crisis all the way to preserving regimes in power. Much will depend on circumstances as to whether the choice to deploy forces is taken (Taylor, 1984: 75).

In its narrowest focus, attention will naturally be given to the military 'lessons' of the 1991 Gulf War; the same happened following Arab–Israeli wars, as it did after the Falklands conflict.[3] A good deal of this will be either speculative or reflective of Service interests, defence industry needs, systems export potential or the protection of tactical practice and doctrine. The Gulf War certainly saw the results of many years' investment in high technology systems designed for deterrence and defence in Central Europe. Equally, the outcome of the war indicated the limitations of new technology in a number of ways. The population of a country where the infrastructure has been severely damaged for good military reasons, is not necessarily going to see the victors as wholly virtuous. The success of high technology weaponry in the Gulf could also be counterproductive in the longer run: it suggests the prospects of 'a clean, cost-free war' and therefore may encourage possessors of such hardware to rely unduly on the military instrument for the 'solution' of problems best dealt with in other ways, if only because of the casualties and damage inflicted on the other side as a consequence of success (Rochlin and Demchak, 1991: 260–70). More significantly, military technology does not exist in a political vacuum. The Gulf War, in which it was so evidently used, was the result of particular conditions: an old-fashioned attempt at territorial aggrandisement; an extraordinary consensus in both the United Nations' Security Council and General Assembly; and a fighting coalition of the Abrahamic peoples and their allies, led by the United States, partially paid for by Germany and Japan. If it was difficult to forecast such an event, it is even harder to see something like it happening again.

Where high technology is clearly going to be important in the 1990s is in the whole area of defence sales. The demand is undoubtedly there; the capacity to supply likewise (McCain, 1991). The obvious problem for the suppliers is the commercial need to find new markets for products no longer saleable in the context of the post-Cold War 'peace dividend'. For West European governments, the issue is one of keeping defence industries going, raising the old question of the delicate balance between defence expenditures being a burden to or a prop for the economy. For the Western Alliance, there are longer-term questions concerning the balance of power in a particular region. An area filled with high technology weapon systems is, by definition, more complex from the point of view of outside powers than one which is not. It may be simply too dangerous to become involved militarily, either because political leadership changes or other countries being supplied in the region feel threatened by the increase in weaponry and take destabilising action in response.

Governments thus see a need to harmonise on the one hand the interests of domestic military production and their natural wish to export, and on the other the overarching foreign policy and security interests. However, perhaps now it is not even the superpowers that can afford to let policy interfere with arms sales (Graves, 1991: 49). There is also the example of the Nixon Doctrine to be taken into account. That was an attempt to regulate the activities of strategically important regions through security assistance and arms sales, and through this support local balances of power favourable to the West without the physical presence of Western military forces. This was not just an American idea contingent upon getting out of the Vietnam imbroglio. Some Europeans also suggested the idea: in 1976, Giscard d'Estaing accepted the need to resist 'the local disequilibrium of forces' where difficulties created a sense of anxiety in the world (*US News and World Report*, 1976: 50–1). The revolution against the Shah of Iran raised serious questions about the viability of this policy however. Economic wellbeing, political stability, and pro-Western orientation – the essential elements behind the Marshall Plan for the recovery of the West in the 1940s – are not the automatic corollaries of aid, military or otherwise. Where local conditions are not receptive to what the West takes as natural goals towards which all are striving, such as liberal democracy in a secular state, the results can be counterproductive.

There is a wide literature now on the debate about the relative virtues of aid to the Third World. Both free market-Northern and Third World-Marxist analyses tend to the view that aid is, by definition, bad: for different reasons, both conclude that the results are counterproductive by creating permanent and debilitating degrees of dependency (Gilpin, 1987: 311–14; Strange, 1988: 214–25). The launching of the 'development decade' in the 1960s, with the rich nations committing themselves to giving 1 per cent of their national incomes to the poor countries, represented an international consensus that has long ago broken down. Even among those who are still in favour of aid as an essential way of moving the LDCs closer to reducing their dependence on the IMF, World Bank and non-governmental financial sources, there are deep divisions. Suppliers of aid monies are more than ever concerned with the borrowers' ability to service the debt; thus the general condition of international economic security is the dominant issue. Demanders of aid finance are less interested in a stable world economic order than they are in access to commodity export markets; their dominant concern is distributive justice. For bankers, the lender should control the loan; for the borrowers, such control impinges on political integrity and confirms the iniquitous status quo. Re-runs of the Marshall Plan idea, however comfortable to prescribe, belong to presumptions of another time, another place and another diagnosis (Strange, 1988: 214–22).

PREVENTING ALARMS AND EXCURSIONS

Faced with this level of complexity, it is easy to reach the conviction that nothing can be done to secure Europe's wider interests at all, or that which could achieve this (in military terms at least) is beyond budgetary realism. Most avenues of investigation end up with a recognition of the twin difficulties of the sheer scale of the problem of securing European interests in the wider world, and the inappropriateness of many of the instruments of power and influence that have been the stock in trade for so long. Such an attitude might indicate the acceptance of the end of Eurocentrism; but it would also suggest the abandonment of that confidence in rationalism which has characterised so many of Europe's contributions to civilisation and progress. The European strategic studies community need not follow the path taken by many economists over the past several years. Economic fashion has reflected a hopelessness in the face of what are taken to be vast, impersonal forces labelled 'the market': recessions are something approaching a Biblical curse, visited upon mankind by some external source of malevolence beyond control or modification. Gone, for the moment, is the notion that there can be actions other than reactive ones; few mainstream economists challenge this assumption. In so far as it is possible to speak of a grand strategy for Europe, it is evident that such passivity is both inappropriate and unnecessary.

With the end of the Cold War, European conditions have been irreversibly altered from features which characterised them for decades. What is now needed is a greater debate about the strategic consequences of these changes. Two areas in particular require attention. First, there is the intellectual problem of the relationship between a new definition of security and the concept of intervention. It is a moot point whether a new definition of security is the starting point for the assessment of the new Europe's interests, or whether interests are themselves the shaping device for the consideration of security and strategy. For Europeans, the old indications still apply: 'The criterion used to determine... interest in an interventionary situation is *comparative risk*: it is unwise to intervene where the the risk entails an even greater evil than the one the intervention is intended to prevent' (Beloff, 1970: 229). Such an approach implies that the risks should, where possible, be minimised. It makes no sense to worry about dependence on Middle East sources of energy supply for the Western economies without taking serious, high investment responses towards stockpiling, alternative suppliers and new energy sources.

Second, there are the practical and immediate issues of the diverse relationships between North and South. Most pressing in the short-term is the issue of arms control through the regulation of arms sales. It is unlikely to be in anyone's interest to continue the transfer of weaponry at the rate established during the 1970s and 1980s (Graves, 1991: 47–56; McCain, 1991: 79–80). This is particularly pressing given ballistic missile proliferation and the fear of nuclear and chemical weapons development (Nolan, 1991a, b). But the issue goes deeper than this. Over the longer run, it will again be necessary to address the questions of what is the best approach to the Third World including the matter of aid, its character and impact. The simplicities of the Cold War having come to an end would suggest that good globalism, as the phrase has it, amounts to the sum of good regionalism. Europeans should eschew the temptations to think about the 'out-of-area' problem; that is to impose an unwarranted uniformity upon a range of difficulties. Instead, the task is to be intelligently discriminatory with respect to interests as they exist in the wider world. What is right for French Polynesia is not automatically going to work in Central America or, even, Francophone Africa. What the British found to work in the South Atlantic in 1982 may never be usable again. If, as Kissinger has argued, 'America cannot police the world forever', the point is even more true of the Europeans (Kissinger, 1991).

With both of these, the skill will be in striking the right balance between becoming too negative about what might be achievable and over-confident that the United States and its allies can use their position of global pre-eminence at will within the international system.

An area that requires little attention is the one that has been widely discussed since the early 1980s, namely the institutional arrangements for policy making and coordination. There is a wide variety of international organisations whose members have degrees of interests beyond Europe. Frequently, economists, military personnel and academics, perhaps disliking bureaucratic untidiness, call for clarification: should NATO, WEU, OECD, the European Community, CSCE, the United Nations or, indeed, some new organisation be tasked with the responsibility? Precisely because individual nations have different interests in various parts of the world, it is prudent to avoid any one institution becoming the sole focus of Western or European policy. It is the case that there is considerable overlap between the international bodies listed. That is the strength of the system. It maximises flexibility for politicians to be part of a particular enterprise or not; it minimises, by that fact, the difficulties inherent in any multilateral initiative.

Such a plurality of organisations will be part of the new world order that is in the process of emerging. As Freedman has shown, this new order will not necessarily be the grand and elevated design suggested in some American rhetoric following the end of the Cold War and in the immediate aftermath of the Gulf War (Freedman, 1991: 195–209). For Europeans, it will probably be messy and unpredictable; certainly the rest of the world will not look to Europe as the foundation of the new order. Nor should it. Europe has considerable internal difficulties to overcome. They may have less glamour and interest than dealing with temporary crises in the Third World but, in general, they have a greater claim on Europeans' attention. Ironically, a world that remembers only too well that two world wars began in Europe is likely to be particularly grateful if the region from Portugal to the Urals, from Spitsbergen to Malta can be, at last, at peace with itself.

NOTES

1 For a justification of the use of the term 'Third World' see Thomas, 1987: 1–4.
2 The arguments against military action in the Gulf War need further scholarly attention. Brief treatments are Selbourne (1991) and Harris (1991).
3 These began to appear almost as soon as Kuwait was invaded (Copley, 1990; Meachem, 1991).

REFERENCES

Barraclough, G. (1964) *Introduction to Contemporary History*, London: Penguin.
Beloff, M. (1970) *The Intellectual in Politics and Other Essays*, London: Weidenfeld & Nicolson.
Copley, G. (1990) 'First lessons of the Gulf crisis', *Defense and Foreign Affairs*, November 1990: 7–15.
Eberle, J. (1991) 'The security interests of Western Europe', *The World Today*, February 1991: 33–5

Foot, P. (1990) 'The American origins of Europe: a reappraisal', in J. Smith (ed.), *The Origins of NATO*, Exeter: Exeter University Press.

Freedman, L. (1991) 'The Gulf War and the new world order', *Survival*, **23**, 3: 195–210.

George, A. (1991) 'Japan's America problem: the Japanese response to US pressure', *The Washington Quarterly*, **14**, 3: 5–19

George, S. (1988) *A Fate Worse than Debt*, London: Penguin.

Gilpin, R. (1987) *The Political Economy of International Relations*, Princeton: Princeton University Press.

Graves, E. (1991) 'The future of US security assistance and arms sales', *The Washington Quarterly*, **14**, 3: 47–60.

Harris, R. (1991) 'A quiet defeat for the dogs of peace', *Sunday Times*, 3 March 1991.

Huntington, S. (1991) 'America's changing strategic interests', *Survival*, **33**, 1: 3–17.

Jenkins, P. (1991) 'A victory parade without the victory', *Independent*, 23 June 1991.

Kennedy, P. (1983) *The Rise and Fall of British Naval Mastery*, London: Macmillan.

Kissinger, H. (1991) 'America cannot police the world forever', *Independent*, 12 March 1991.

Luard, E. (1988) *The Blunted Sword: The Erosion of Military Power in Modern World Politics*, London: Tauris.

McCain, J. (1991) 'Controlling arms sales to the Third World', *The Washington Quarterly*, **14**, 2: 79–89.

Mackinder, H. (1904) 'The geographical pivot of history', *Geographical Journal*, **23**, 4: 432–3.

Meacham, J. (1991) 'Lessons NOT to learn', *Defense and Diplomacy*, May/June 1991: 15.

Nolan, J. (1991a) *The Trappings of Power: Ballistic Missiles in the Third World*, Washington: Brookings.

Nolan, J. (1991b) 'The global arms market after the Gulf War: prospects for control', *Washington Quarterly*, **14**, 3: 125–38.

Rochlin, G. and Demchak, C. (1991) 'The Gulf War: technological and organisational implications', *Survival*, **23**, 3: 260–73.

Selbourne, D. (1991) 'The intellectual battle', *Sunday Times*, 27 January 1991.

Strange, S. (1988) *States and Markets: An Introduction to International Political Economy*, London: Pinter.

Taylor, T. (1984) *European Defence Cooperation*, London: RKP for RIIA.

Thomas, C. (1987) *In Search of Security: The Third World in International Relations*, Hemel Hempstead: Wheatsheaf.

US News and World Report (1976) 'Europe still needs the US', 17 May 1976.

Part II
Strategy after the Cold War

5   The evolution of NATO strategy 1949–90

John Baylis

The momentous events from 1989 to 1991 which brought about the collapse of communism in Eastern Europe and the Soviet Union, together with the demise of the Warsaw Pact, have resulted in a major transformation of the security environment in Europe. Unilateral Soviet troop withdrawals, major arms control agreements and the democratisation of Eastern European states have brought about an end to the Cold War and a significant erosion of the Soviet threat to Western Europe. For NATO, an Alliance forged in the era of East–West confrontation, these events inevitably represent a major challenge. With many of the assumptions underpinning the organisation undermined it became necessary in the early 1990s to review the whole basis of Alliance strategy. While most of the contributions to this book deal with the significance of these contemporary events the focus of this chapter is on the legacy of the past and how the history of NATO strategic doctrine is likely to have a powerful impact on the debates about the future of its strategy. Looking back at the evolution of NATO strategy from 1949 to the early 1990s a number of significant features stand out which contemporary military planners will need to consider in their attempts to reform Alliance strategic doctrine in the post-Cold War era. These features include continuity as opposed to change in strategic planning; the importance of compromise in the formulation of strategic doctrine; and the ubiquity of nuclear weapons in Alliance strategy.

The first feature of note is the relative consistency and continuity in operational planning over the years compared with the public declarations of major changes in strategic doctrine at various times. It is true that Alliance strategy has been subject to periodic alterations (especially in 1954 and 1967), but invariably this has involved modifications of existing strategic ideas and shifts of emphasis rather than the major changes of direction implicit in the rhetoric of public pronouncements. Declaratory concepts have changed at times but strategic planning has remained remarkably consistent.

This underlying continuity reflects another characteristic feature of

Alliance strategy, that when changes have occurred they have usually been the product of hard fought compromises between member states. Govern- ments have been forced to take account of their own domestic economic, social and political circumstances and those of their allies when attempting to move Alliance strategy in a particular direction. As a result NATO strategy has tended to reflect 'the art of the possible' rather than the military ideal of strategic planners. Such compromise has had both good and bad features. On the one hand it has reflected consensus which has contributed to the cohesion of the Alliance and the credibility of Alliance strategy. On the other hand it has invariably resulted in a certain lack of clarity which has bedevilled NATO operational planning over the years. This has been reflected particularly in the lack of precision in Alliance planning to use tactical nuclear weapons.

This in turn has contributed to a third characteristic feature of Alliance strategy: the continuing emphasis (some would say overemphasis) on the central role of nuclear weapons in Alliance strategic doctrine. From the birth of the Alliance onwards there has been a tendency to see nuclear weapons as the predominant instruments of deterrence and defence, a tendency which has become the very heart of NATO strategy. Nuclear weapons have been seen not only as the ultimate strategic deterrent but also as a substitute for expensive conventional capabilities, to be used militarily to cope with a variety of conventional and nuclear threats. As a result the Alliance has faced a continuous dilemma: how to keep the peace through credible threats to use nuclear weapons without making the escalation to all-out nuclear war inevit- able in the event of deterrence breaking down. Nuclear weapons have been emphasised as cost-effective instruments of deterrence, but the fear has nevertheless remained that if such weapons ever had to be used the conse- quences would be disastrous. Indeed the Alliance has never clearly made up its mind whether nuclear weapons can in practice be used in a military role or whether their sole purpose is one of deterrence.

These characteristics of NATO strategy can be discerned in the debates and changes in strategic concepts which have taken place throughout the period since 1949. For the sake of analysis it is useful to divide the history of Alliance strategy into three main phases: the period of strategic ambiguity from 1949 to 1954; the period of massive retaliation and a tactical nuclear strategy from 1954 to 1967; and the period of flexible response from 1967 to the early 1990s.

THE PERIOD OF STRATEGIC AMBIGUITY 1949–54

In the period immediately after the Alliance was formed in 1949 NATO strategy reflected the confusion and uncertainty which characterised military planning in the key member states. This was particularly true of the leading member of the Alliance, the United States. As David Rosenberg has shown, American defence planners grappled with the revolutionary impact of nuclear weapons throughout the late 1940s (Rosenberg, 1983). In the Joint Chiefs of Staff (JCS) war plans produced from 1947 onwards the atomic air offensive took pride of place. Precisely what targets were to be hit remained vague but war plan BROILER and its successors FROLIC and HALFMOON, envisaged the prompt use of atomic weapons against an aggressor much in the same way that conventional weapons had been used in the strategic air offensives of the Second World War. Because of the central importance of the United States in the newly-formed Western Alliance, NATO strategy from the beginning closely reflected American strategic preoccupations. Given the conventional preponderance of the Soviet Union, if war broke out Allied forces would fall back across Europe as far as the Pyrenees while a strategic nuclear offensive was launched against largely civilian targets in the Soviet Union. Both Britain and the United States planned in this early phase to withdraw their forces from the mainland in 'Dunkirk-like' operations shortly after war broke out (Barker, 1983).

Not surprisingly the French government was strongly opposed to this early Alliance defence doctrine. The French Premier Henri Queuille argued in 1949 that the Anglo-Saxon idea of withdrawing from the continent in order to regroup along the lines of Second World War strategy would be disastrous in the new circumstances. He told an American reporter:

We know that once Western Europe was occupied, America would again come to our aid and eventually we would again be liberated. But the process would be terrible. The next time you probably would be liberating a corpse... The real frontier of Western Europe which must be defended must be moved well beyond the actual frontiers, because once the geographic frontiers of these countries are crossed it will be too late for America to save very much. Even fifteen days after the invasion will be too late.

(New York Times, 1949)

The French argued forcefully for a much greater commitment by the Alliance to 'forward defence'.

The idea of 'forward defence', requiring the peacetime deployment of much greater conventional forces on the continent to hold the Rhine, was reinforced by two developments. The first was the Soviet explosion of an atomic device in August 1949. The shock which this caused in the United States led the State Department's Policy Planning Staff to reassess American strategic requirements. Their conclusions were contained in the National Security Document NSC68 which was approved by President Truman early in 1950. According to this influential study 'Soviet nuclear power might reach such proportions by about 1954 as to create a serious danger of conventional aggression or of blackmail that depended on the threat of such aggression' (Osgood, 1962: 61). The only answer was for the West to substantially increase its ground forces. This message was reinforced by the second significant development which occurred in June 1950: the outbreak of the Korean War. A divided Korea and a divided Germany seemed to be a worrying parallel. If the Soviet Union could encourage and support a North Korean invasion of the South might it not launch a similar attack itself from East Germany to West Germany? Many Western statesmen felt that the Soviet's possession of nuclear weapons and massive conventional superiority (over 100 divisions in the East to about twelve in the West) might tempt them to use the distraction of the Asian war to invade the West. As Winston Churchill said at the time 'my eyes are focused on the hideous gap in Western Europe'. Every effort had to be made to undertake a major rearmament programme not only to fight the war in Korea but to redress the dangerous conventional imbalance in Western Europe.

The scale of the rearmament programme undertaken by the members of the Alliance is summed up by Robert Osgood:

> the United States, setting the pattern for her allies, oriented her military plans towards the target date, or 'year of maximum danger', of 1952 and launched an all-out rearmament programme, which quadrupled her defence expenditure within three years. Britain raised her conscription period to two years, announced plans to form three new divisions, promised to increase the British contingent in West Germany to five divisions by the end of 1951 and undertook an ambitious arms programme that would raise defence expenditures to 12 per cent of the national income. France increased her defence budget by 30 per cent and planned to add 15 new divisions in three years. All the other European allies, except Iceland and Portugal, announced parallel plans for increasing their defence forces, periods of military service and military expenditures.
>
> (Osgood, 1962: 70)

In almost all cases the rearmament programmes were undertaken despite serious economic difficulties. In the medium term they were to have a significant effect on the economies of member states. In the short term the Soviet atomic explosion and the Korean War had an important impact not only on defence expenditure but also on NATO strategy. At the North Atlantic Council meeting in New York in September 1950 the Alliance explicitly adopted a 'forward strategy' of defending Europe as far eastward as possible. It was also agreed to examine, as a matter of great urgency 'the methods by which Germany could most usefully make its contribution' to improve the conventional defence of Western Europe (Osgood, 1962: 72–3).[1]

At the same time, in December 1950, the Council appointed General Eisenhower as Supreme Commander in Europe (SACEUR) and authorised him to 'train national units assigned to his command and organise them into an effective, integrated defense force' (*New York Times*, 1950). This was followed in February 1951 by the establishment of the Supreme Headquarters of the Allied Powers in Europe (SHAPE). The Alliance was set on the road to establishing an effective integrated defence in peacetime.

The rearmament programme, a 'forward strategy' and integrated defence were all brought together in the 'Lisbon goals' accepted by the Alliance in February 1952. An overarching plan was produced which envisaged a major build-up of NATO conventional forces in three phases between 1952 and 1954. The Alliance committed itself to a force of 50 divisions and 4,000 combat aircraft in 1952, in 1953 there were to be 75 divisions and 6,500 aircraft, and by 1954 NATO was to have 96 divisions and 9,000 aircraft. Of these 96 divisions, 35 were to be ready for immediate combat and 25 were to be used to defend the Central Front, east of the Rhine. As such the Lisbon goals represented an attempt, if not to match the Soviet Union man for man, tank for tank, at least to provide a serious conventional defence against the Soviet Union.

In practice, however, the Lisbon goals were never achieved. This was largely the result of three factors. First, the immediacy of the threat soon declined. After initial anxieties over the global implications of the Korean War, it soon became clear that the War was a limited regional conflict which was unlikely to spread to Western Europe. The war continued, but with the growing stalemate in 1952 the fears which had been expressed in 1950 were increasingly forgotten. This in turn led to a reconsideration of the economic burdens of rearmament. In Britain the Labour government had lost office in 1951 largely as a result of the social effects of defence spending. The new government under Winston Churchill first indicated a 'long haul' to spread the burden of rearmament over a longer period, and then subsequently reduced defence expenditure. In Britain, as in other member states, the political will no longer existed to bear the sacrifices of a major conventional rearmament programme.

The changing perception of the threat together with the opportunity costs of high levels of defence expenditure led to a third reason why the Lisbon goals were never achieved. This centred on a reappraisal of nuclear strategy which had by 1954 clarified some of the ambiguities inherent in the prevailing NATO doctrine. Hitherto the Alliance had emphasised both nuclear and more recently conventional capabilities. By 1952, largely as a result of economic pressures, Western strategists were increasingly emphasising the importance of nuclear weapons as the central instruments of deterrence. Initially these ideas were given clearest expression in Britain where the 1952

Global Strategy Paper provided a strategic rationalisation for the cut backs in conventional forces and the need for greater priority to be given to cheaper nuclear capabilities. The Global Strategy Paper's main architect, Sir John Slessor (Chief of the Air Staff) was fond of selling his ideas of a 'massed destruction' policy by arguing that 'the dog we keep to take care of the cat can also take care of the kittens'. In other words, large conventional forces were unnecessary because a powerful nuclear capability could deter not only major aggression but also lower levels of aggression as well.

Initially these ideas were unacceptable to American defence planners. At a time when the Truman Administration was seeking to persuade its allies to build up conventional forces and accept West German rearmament, British arguments appeared to be counterproductive. It was not long, however, before a new Administration under President Eisenhower, faced with much the same kinds of problems as the European allies, began its own strategic reappraisal. With the 'New Look' of 1953–4, the United States changed direction and embraced the idea of 'a maximum deterrent at a bearable cost'.

THE PERIOD OF MASSIVE RETALIATION AND A TACTICAL NUCLEAR STRATEGY 1954–67

In October 1953 the Eisenhower Administration adopted NSC 162/2 as its basic national security policy. According to this policy the American Joint Chiefs of Staff were authorised to base their planning on the assumption that nuclear weapons would be used in the event of either general or local wars. As Jane Stromseth has shown, the military strategy to implement NSC 162/2 provided 'tactical atomic support for US or allied military forces in general war or in local aggression whenever the employment of atomic weapons would be militarily advantageous' (Stromseth, 1988: 13). Conventional forces still retained their importance, especially in the NATO context, but NSC 162/2 argued that 'the tactical atomic support which can be provided to our allies will become increasingly important in offsetting present deficiencies in conventional requirements' (Stromseth, 1988: 13). This had a major impact on both American and NATO strategy. Although an emphasis on nuclear weapons had characterised earlier war plans, the new defence strategy increased even further the size and nuclear capabilities of the US Air Force. In line with this new priority American conventional forces were reduced. As the US Secretary of State, John Foster Dulles, told the North Atlantic Council on 23 April 1954, the primary focus of American deterrence doctrine was now based on the 'great capacity to retaliate, instantly, by means and at places of our own choosing' (Stromseth, 1988: 13). This implied a threat to use nuclear weapons in the event of aggression even if the aggressor invaded with conventional forces. Dulles urged the Alliance to embrace this new doctrine of massive retaliation to deter aggression and to compensate for the inadequacies in NATO's conventional forces. The 'New Look' was accepted by NATO Ministers in December 1954 as the basis for Alliance defence planning and was formally adopted by the North Atlantic Council as a new strategic concept, Military Committee Document MC 14/2, in December 1956.

Despite the formal adoption of a new strategic concept, the changes introduced were more apparent than real. The emphasis on nuclear retaliation had been a feature of American war planning from 1947, and from 1951 tactical nuclear weapons had been seen as a convenient instrument to offset Western conventional inferiority. In a memorandum to the Chairman of the Joint Atomic Energy Committee in August 1951 the Chief of Special Projects had pointed out that:

> Atomic weapons used tactically are the natural armaments of numerically inferior but technologically superior nations. They are the natural answer to the armed hordes of the Soviet Union and its satellites. Their coming into being should immeasurably strengthen Western Europe's will to resist, since they will decisively help to shift the balance of military power toward the free world and against the slave world.
>
> (Mansfield, 1951)

In February 1952 Project Vista, a comprehensive study of the prospects of using tactical nuclear weapons to defend Western Europe, concluded that such weapons, with yields from one to fifty kilotons, offered 'outstanding promise' for the defence of West European territory. Atomic artillery pieces were first deployed with American troops in Europe in October 1953 and these were followed in 1954 by short and medium-range missiles. For the rest of the 1950s the number of small-yield nuclear weapons were rapidly built up in Western Europe as Alliance military planning increasingly focused on how to fight a tactical nuclear war. NATO's conventional forces were regarded as little more than a 'trip-wire' to delay an attack just long enough to trigger nuclear retaliation against the Soviet homeland.

Despite the commitment of allied governments to the massive retaliation doctrine, throughout the 1950s criticisms of the strategy were made, initially in private within the defence establishments but later more vociferously in public. In Britain early criticisms came from the Nobel-prize winning scientist P.M.S. Blackett, Captain Sir Basil Liddell Hart and the chief of Naval Intelligence, Admiral Sir Anthony Buzzard. For all three massive retaliation was immoral and highly dangerous. If implemented it raised the distinct possibility of all-out nuclear war which would destroy civilisation. The answer according to Buzzard was a more 'graduated deterrent posture' which would involve the use of tactical nuclear weapons against military targets on the battlefield but would only sanction the use of thermonuclear weapons in retaliation if such weapons were used against the West. Blackett and Liddell Hart both emphasised the need for more reliance on conventional capabilities (Baylis and Garnett, 1991).

Similar worries were expressed in the United States by Army Chief of Staff General Maxwell Taylor and an emerging group of civilian strategists which included William Kaufmann, Paul Nitze and Bernard Brodie. These critics argued that by relying on strategic nuclear weapons to deter all-out aggression the West was encouraging the Soviet Union to engage in lower-level aggression. In such limited conflicts the lack of a flexible conventional capability put the West at a considerable disadvantage. These arguments were reinforced in October 1957 by the surprise launching of the Soviet Sputnik satellite. This technical feat, achieved in advance of the United States, demonstrated that the Soviet Union would soon possess the capability to strike directly at the American homeland. The critics of massive retaliation argued that the threat to launch nuclear attacks on the Soviet Union in the event of limited aggression would become increasingly incredible. Western threats would be taken as bluff and would encourage the Soviet Union to pursue a more adventurous foreign policy. The Berlin crisis which continued off and on from 1958 to 1961 seemed to confirm the validity of this view. At the same time growing public anxiety, symbolised by the CND movement in Britain, encouraged defence planners to look once again at their strategic ideas.

In December 1957, faced with increasing criticism from both within the defence establishment and outside, NATO defence chiefs moved to modify Alliance strategy. Largely on the initiative of NATO's Supreme Commander, General Lauris Norstad, the NATO Military Committee adopted a five-year plan, MC70, designed to increase Alliance conventional forces to thirty combat-ready divisions. Norstad recognised that Alliance members were reluctant to foot the bill for massive conventional rearmament but he also accepted the argument that the Alliance was overly-dependent on nuclear weapons. His ideas therefore were more modest than the Lisbon goals. A thirty-division 'shield' was designed not to fight an extended conventional war but 'to force a pause' in order to test Soviet intentions and to encourage the Soviet leaders to reconsider the dangers of nuclear retaliation if conflict continued. Despite this attempt to improve the flexibility of Alliance strategy, Norstad continued to deny 'the possibility of a limited war or of a conventional response beyond a brief holding action' (Schwartz, 1983: 75–9). Massive retaliation remained the central component of NATO strategic doctrine.

For the critics of massive retaliation MC 70 did not go nearly far enough. The most influential of these critics was John F. Kennedy. As a Presidential candidate in 1960 he criticised the defence strategy of the Eisenhower Administration arguing that:

> Under every military budget submitted by this Administration, we have been preparing primarily to fight the one kind of war we least want to fight and are least likely to fight. We have been driving ourselves into a corner where the only choice is all or nothing at all, world devastation or submission – a choice that necessarily causes us to hesitate on the brink and leaves the initiative in the hands of our enemies.
>
> (Kennedy, 1960: 184)

Consequently when Kennedy became President in 1961 he set his Secretary of Defense, Robert McNamara, the task of reappraising American strategic doctrine. The basic direction of the new Administration's defence policy was spelled out in Kennedy's Special Presidential Message to Congress on 28 March 1961. Two key objectives were emphasised by the President. First, that there was a requirement for invulnerable retaliatory forces which could survive a first strike and inflict unacceptable damage on an aggressor. Such forces, it was argued, would help to create greater stability in the new era of mutual deterrence caused by Soviet technological advances. Second, the United States and its allies required a wide range of flexible conventional forces which would allow the West to respond to threats at all levels, from guerrilla warfare to major conventional conflict (Stromseth, 1988: 27).

Having laid down the new direction of American defence policy McNamara engaged in 'a concerted effort to obtain agreement in NATO on an updated political directive and strategic concept which emphasised the need for flexible response capabilities, especially non-nuclear ones' (Stromseth, 1988: 26). McNamara's aim was to concentrate nuclear capabilities in the hands of the United States and to encourage a division of labour in the Alliance designed to improve conventional capabilities. The task of persuading the Allies to accept a flexible response strategy, however, proved much more difficult than McNamara envisaged. Despite the military logic of what became known as the McNamara doctrine, strong political and economic (and some strategic) objections from the Western European allies prevented the acceptance of the American changes for a further six years. In a bruising debate within the Alliance the British, French and the West Germans refused to accept the need for the major increases in defence expenditure which the McNamara doctrine seemed to involve. For the British and the French McNamara's aim of concentrating nuclear weapons under American control was unacceptable. In the aftermath of Suez they remained determined to continue the development of their own national deterrent forces. There was also a general concern in Western Europe that the renewed emphasis on conventional capabilities would undermine deterrence. By downgrading the nuclear response it was felt that the credibility of the Alliance deterrent force would be undermined.

The controversy over flexible response was only resolved in May 1967 when the most vociferous of the Western European allies, France, withdrew from the military command structure of the Alliance. For de Gaulle American proposals were 'incompatible with his commitment to construct a nationally-controlled nuclear force as the foundation for an independent foreign policy' (Stromseth, 1988: 119). More fundamentally, de Gaulle rejected American leadership of the Alliance and offered a profoundly different vision of the future of Europe in which France would play a central role in achieving an historic reconciliation between the Soviet Union and Germany. With French withdrawal from the military integrated structure of the Alliance the opportunity emerged for a compromise between the British and West Germans on the one side, and the United States on the other. The result of this compromise was the strategy of flexible response.

THE PERIOD OF FLEXIBLE RESPONSE 1967–90

On 9 May 1967 NATO officially adopted the strategy of flexible response. This required the Alliance to develop the capability of responding to any Warsaw Pact military action with an appropriate level and kind of response. Threats of less than all-out attack were to be deterred by the capacity to offer an effective, but less than all-out response. If the Alliance failed to achieve its objectives at any particular level of response, then the strategy was designed to provide NATO with the option to escalate, if need be, through the use of nuclear weapons. Put another way flexible response:

> seeks to be able to respond to any aggression at a level commensurate with the assault and, through the threat of escalation seeks to persuade the adversary of the very great risks and costs of continued violence.
>
> (NATO, 1975)

The credibility of the strategy depended on the ability of the Alliance to provide a wide range of military options, both conventional and nuclear, and to link them together in an escalatory chain that included (at the ultimate level) the strategic forces of the United States. The operational details of the new strategy took six months to work out and were included in Military Committee document MC 14/3, *Overall Strategic Concept for the Defence of the NATO Area*, which was accepted by the NATO Defence Planning Group on 16 January 1968. After more than ten years of criticism, massive retaliation enshrined in MC 14/2 had been finally replaced by what appeared to be a wholly new strategy.

Once again, however, appearances were deceptive. Various officials who were involved in the drafting of MC 14/3 have described it as 'a sandpapering operation' and 'as delicate as a wasps' nest' (Stromseth, 1988: 175–6). One of the British drafters of the Ministerial Guidance for MC 14/3, Arthur Hockaday, has argued that:

> flexible response was so flexible that it could be interpreted in any way – it had to be or it wouldn't have been adopted. It was a considerable achievement to produce a text which people could agree to as a foundation for the development of operational concepts and force structure.
>
> (Stromseth, 1988: 176)

Hockaday's comments reveal the fundamental difficulty of getting an alliance like NATO, with a large number of independent sovereign states, each with varying perceptions and interests, to agree to a new strategic concept. New concepts are possible but political reality dictates that evolutionary rather than revolutionary changes of direction are most likely. Flexible response was essentially a compromise in both military and political terms.

> Militarily, it was a compromise between a full-scale conventional defence and a 'trip-wire' strategy. In contrast to massive retaliation, flexible response provided for an initial non-nuclear response in a broader range of circumstances. Beyond this basic agreement, however, the operational implications of the new strategy were ambiguous, allowing for divergent interpretations. For example, it was not clear how long a conventional defence would be designed to last before resort to tactical nuclear weapons would be deemed necessary, nor was the precise role of tactical nuclear weapons in NATO defence clearly defined. Politically, flexible response was a compromise between the initial American goal of building conventional forces capable of responding to a major Warsaw Pact attack without resort to nuclear weapons, and the European preference for a more modest conventional capability. The German and British governments recognised the need to provide for a conventional response in certain limited circumstances, but they were not interested in building conventional forces capable of mounting a major conventional defence on the central front.
>
> (Stromseth, 1988: 176)

The adoption of flexible response therefore involved papering over the cracks which stemmed from continuing differences in perception between European and American governments.

The uneasy nature of the compromise was to be a key feature of Alliance debates about strategy for the following twenty years or more. The adoption of flexible response implied that the Alliance would significantly improve its conventional forces to provide the wide range of capabilities MC 14/3 required. For its part the US government interpreted flexible response as requiring ammunition stockpiles which would allow the Alliance to fight for ninety days at the conventional level. Given their reservations about flexible response, however, the Europeans interpreted it as requiring much more limited conventional capabilities. The result in reality was that they kept stockpiles for less than a week of non-nuclear combat. This meant that the strategy of flexible response pursued by the Alliance from 1967 onwards was very different from the concept envisaged by McNamara in the early 1960s. The inability of the Alliance to significantly improve its conventional capabilities meant that NATO strategy was more akin to 'flexible escalation' than 'flexible response' Not unlike Norstad's 'pause strategy' of the late 1950s, NATO maintained conventional forces capable of only a very limited non-nuclear defence. Throughout the 1970s and 1980s NATO commanders frequently referred to the need to use nuclear weapons at a very early stage of a conflict because of the inability of the Alliance to compete successfully for a prolonged period with the superior conventional forces of the Warsaw Pact.

The continuity in NATO strategic planning has also been evident in the continuing emphasis which has been given to strategic nuclear weapons. Despite the concern to move away from massive retaliation-style ideas, the difficulties of improving conventional capabilities has meant that in practice the ultimate sanction of strategic nuclear attack has remained a key component of Western strategy. As Soviet nuclear forces developed, especially in the aftermath of the Cuban missile crisis, McNamara increasingly emphasised the importance of what became known as 'mutual assured destruction' (MAD). McNamara argued that the United States must maintain a range of nuclear capabilities to be able to destroy a substantial proportion of the Soviet population and industrial infrastructure – in other words a capability for massive retaliation in the event of a Soviet attack upon the United States or its allies.

McNamara, however, recognised that the Soviet Union would develop similar capabilities of its own and therefore that some attempt had to be made to stabilise the mutual deterrent balance between them. This had to involve arms control agreements beneficial to both superpowers. In the aftermath of the Cuban crisis of October 1962, the first tentative steps in this direction were made with the Hot-Line agreement and the Partial Test Ban agreement. This was followed in 1968 with the Non-Proliferation Treaty and shortly afterwards the beginning of the Strategic Arms Limitation Talks (SALT) which produced the SALT I agreement in 1972 and the SALT II agreement (which was never ratified) in 1979. McNamara's objective was to achieve strategic stability by both superpowers limiting their strategic capabilities, and by emphasising invulnerable retaliatory forces rather than destabilising first-strike capabilities. According to this view, once each side had sufficient nuclear capability it did not need to go on building more and more nuclear forces. Such a version of stability, however, depended on both superpowers accepting American ideas of mutual assured destruction. In the 1970s, however, while the United States pursued its doctrine of sufficiency under Nixon and Kissinger the Soviet Union continued to build up its strategic forces in what appeared to the West to be a search for superiority.[2] This reflected the very different view of deterrence held by the Soviet leadership. According to the Soviet view, which was dominated by military not political calculations, deterrence required a range of conventional and nuclear capabilities which would enable the Soviet Union to convince an aggresssor that it could fight and if possible win a war at any level. This view rejected the American philosophy of mutual assured destruction and ideas of sufficiency, and emphasised instead deterrence through war-fighting.

Faced with this different view of deterrence McNamara's successors, James Schlesinger, Harold Brown and Caspar Weinberger began to shift American strategic doctrine to take account of Soviet military policies. If the Soviet Union was determined to go on building up its conventional and nuclear forces in the search for superiority the West would need to match them. In 1974 the Schlesinger doctrine was formulated to provide the United States with a wider variety of nuclear options, and in 1977 the Alliance adopted a Long Term Defence Programme (LTDP) designed once again to improve conventional forces. In 1979 the Carter Administration adopted Presidential Directive 59, shifting American strategy away from mutual assured destruction towards a countervailing or war-fighting strategy. This was extended further by a massive military build up introduced by the Reagan Administration which came to power in the early 1980s.[3] If the Soviet Union believed in the war-fighting conception of deterrence, then the United States felt that it had to go down the same road in order to provide capabilities which would appear credible to Soviet leaders. In the light of these developments the NATO members accepted a plan to increase defence spending by 3 per cent per annum in 1978. Apart from the LTDP a number of attempts were made in the late 1970s and early 1980s to improve the flexibility of Alliance conventional and nuclear forces. In particular a concerted effort was made in the early 1980s to improve the infrastructure and sustainability of Alliance forces to enable them to fight for a longer period at the conventional level. The overall impact of this concerted programme had two main effects, one military and one political. At the military level, although important deficiencies continued to exist in Alliance conventional forces (especially over reinforcements) the gap between the two alliances was narrowed during the 1980s. NATO commanders began to believe for the first time that a more sustained conventional defence was now a possibility. The Alliance continued to refuse to accept a 'no-first-use' approach to nuclear weapons, but a more optimistic assessment began to emerge which would allow NATO to pursue a 'no-early-use' policy. The decision by Alliance leaders at Montebello in 1983 to reduce NATO stockpiles of theatre nuclear weapons indicated a growing consensus that less emphasis should be given to such weapons.

At the political level, the deterioration of East–West relations and the military build-up on both sides which characterised the late 1970s and early 1980s led to a controversial debate in the West about NATO strategy. The catalyst for protest occurred with the decision in December 1979 by NATO leaders to deploy American Pershing II and Cruise missiles in Europe unless the Soviet Union agreed to eliminate its new SS 20 missiles targeted on Western European states. NATO planners argued that these weapons were necessary to maintain the link between short-range nuclear weapons and strategic nuclear weapons upon which the credibility of the threat to escalate to the highest level of nuclear war depended. For the vociferous opponents of the decision to deploy Cruise and Pershing II, NATO strategy was both dangerous and incredible. It was dangerous because the inability of the Alliance to build up its conventional forces to match those of the Soviet Union meant an undue reliance was placed on nuclear weapons. If deterrence broke down, as it might, a process of uncontrollable escalation would lead to Armageddon. The threat to start a war which would lead to the West's own destruction itself was incredible. These criticisms were summed up in Morton Halperin's vivid description of the threats implicit in NATO strategy.

> NATO doctrine is that we will fight with conventional weapons until we are losing, then we will fight with tactical nuclear weapons until we are losing and then we will blow up the world!
>
> (Baylis, 1988: 45)

It was in this atmosphere of public criticism that the Alliance moved to lessen its dependence on nuclear weapons. Large scale public demonstrations about NATO policy throughout Western Europe also strengthened the determination of Western leaders to find arms control agreements with the Soviet Union. In the early 1980s INF negotiations were undertaken but major differences between East and West precluded agreement. In 1985, however, Mikhail Gorbachev came to power in the Soviet Union and a new, much more positive era of East–West relations began. Gorbachev's 'new thinking' brought a withdrawal from Afghanistan, unilateral cuts in defence spending and a more constructive approach to arms control. In December 1987 the INF agreement was finally signed between the United States and the Soviet Union which for the first time eliminated categories of nuclear weapons. The agreement also signalled an unprecedented change in the Soviet approach to arms control through the Kremlin's acceptance of asymmetrical cuts and intrusive verification procedures. The INF agreement laid the foundations for a conventional force reduction (CFE) agreement in 1990 which transformed the military imbalance which has been at the heart of European insecurity since 1945.

Just as important as Soviet new thinking and developments in arms control for NATO strategy were the political developments in Eastern Europe in 1989. Gorbachev's renunciation of the Brezhnev doctrine and his tolerance of change led to a wave of people's revolutions throughout Eastern Europe which swept away the old communist regimes. In their place new democratic regimes emerged looking more to the West than to the East. As a result by 1990 the Warsaw Pact was no longer a credible military alliance and in 1991 it formally ceased to exist. This significant erosion of the Soviet threat brought a fundamental review of NATO strategy which was initiated by the sixteen NATO leaders at the July 1990 London summit. President Bush described the summit as signalling the start of a major transformation of the NATO Alliance. 'We see it', he said, 'as an historic turning point. The alliance has set a new path for peace'. The London Declaration which followed the summit, however, left the future of flexible response largely unresolved. On the one hand the Declaration stated that the Alliance would need to make radical changes to its military posture and revise its strategy so that 'nuclear weapons will truly become weapons of the last resort'. Forward defence was also seen as an anachronism given the changes in Eastern Europe. This suggested to many commentators that the Alliance was determined to move away from flexible response. At the insistence of the British Prime Minister, however, the Declaration also included a rather contradictory sentence saying that nuclear weapons would continue to fulfil an essential role in the overall strategy of the Alliance by ensuring that there are no circumstances in which nuclear retaliation in response to military action might be discounted. This suggested that, for Mrs Thatcher at least, flexible response remained a valid strategy. It might be reformed but given the uncertainties associated with the events in the Soviet Union a form of nuclear deterrence had to be maintained (*Guardian*, 1990; NATO, 1990).

The essence of this rather more cautious approach to Alliance strategy was spelled out in a remarkable address given by the top civil servant in the Ministry of Defence, Sir Michael Quinlan, to the Soviet General Staff in Moscow in November 1990. He expressed the view that, 'except perhaps in a future too remote and uncertain for the prospect of it to shape policy today – the retention of nuclear weapons in smaller but still significant numbers on each side, at both the strategic and non-strategic levels, will remain a prudent and positive element in the construction of a dependable international system for preserving peace among the countries of East and West'. He told the

Soviet Generals that NATO would have to retain a wide range of nuclear and conventional weapons for the purposes of war prevention. Despite the improvements in East–West relations, he argued, 'we are not yet at, or even perhaps very near, the point at which the military insurance element becomes entirely irrelevant between us'. It was therefore prudent for NATO to retain a wide range of different options – 'that is now, and has been since the late 1960s, the essence of NATO's defensive strategic concept'. This suggested a firm commitment by at least the British defence establishment to the essential elements of flexible response (Quinlan, 1991).

CONCLUSION

The dramatic effects of the changes in East–West relations since 1985, and particularly the events since 1989, provide the most significant challenge to NATO strategy since 1949. Ever since its foundation the Alliance has sought to defend its members against a Soviet Union which was ideologically hostile, well-armed and firmly entrenched in Eastern Europe. To achieve the security of its member states NATO has consistently relied on a strategy which has emphasised forward defence and nuclear deterrence. Despite the periodic changes in strategic concepts which have brought modifications to operational military planning, there has been considerable continuity in the way the Alliance has planned for its defence. The evolution of strategy has reflected the need for compromise and this in turn has encouraged the reliance on nuclear weapons as the cheapest form of deterrence.

With the erosion of the threat, the changes in Eastern Europe, the failed coup in the Soviet Union, and the impact of arms control agreements the Alliance has begun a careful review of its military strategy. The debate is likely to be fierce. For some forward defence is now meaningless and nuclear capabilities, already restricted by agreement, are likely to play a decreasing role in future Alliance strategy. This suggests the need for a wholly new strategic concept. For others the time is not ripe for a radical change. In modified form flexible response remains a sensible policy for NATO in a period of uncertainty. Past history suggests that, although changes can occur in NATO strategy in response to new circumstances, some form of compromise between these alternative positions is likely to emerge. It also suggests that such a compromise will involve a continuing (if reduced) role for nuclear weapons at least. Whether such a compromise is appropriate however when unprecedented changes have taken place in the European security environment is a moot point.

NOTES

1 This led to a major controversy within the Alliance over the form German rearmament should take. The French initially came up with the idea of a European Defence Community which submerged national units into a European Army. After this idea failed West Germany was brought into the Alliance in 1955 following the Paris agreements which imposed a number of restrictions on German rearmament.
2 US policy was not, however, quite as clear cut as this. Bureaucratic interests led to the development of weapon systems which the Soviet Union regarded as first-strike systems. MIRV warheads were a good example of this in the 1970s, and SDI in the 1980s led to similar worries in the Soviet Union.
3 For a time in the early 1980s it seemed that the US was seeking a 'prevailing' war strategy.

REFERENCES

Barker, E. (1983) *Britain between the Superpowers 1945–50*, London: Macmillan.
Baylis, J. (1988) 'The case for a new strategic concept for NATO', *International Affairs*, **64**, 1: 43–59.
Baylis, J. and Garnett, J. (eds) (1991) *Makers of Modern Nuclear Strategy*, London: Francis Pinter.
Guardian (1990) 7 July 1990.
Kennedy, J. (1960) *The Strategy of Peace*, (ed. A. Nevins), New York: Harper & Brothers.
Mansfield, J. (1951) 'Memorandum for the Chairman, 15 August 1951'. Papers of Harry S. Truman, President's Secretary's File, Subject File, NSC-Atomic, Box 202 – Atomic Weapons Stockpile, Harry S. Truman Library.
NATO (1975) 'Communiqué, ministerial meeting of the North Atlantic Council, 14 December 1967', *Texts of Final Communiqués, 1949–74*, Brussels: NATO Information Service.
NATO (1990) *London Declaration on a Transformed North Atlantic Alliance*, Brussels: NATO Information Service.
New York Times (1949) 4 March 1949.
New York Times (1950) 20 December 1950.
Osgood, R. (1962) *The Entangling Alliance*, Chicago: Chicago University Press.
Quinlan, M. (1991) 'Nuclear weapons and the abolition of war', *International Affairs*, **67**, 2: 293–301.
Rosenberg, D. (1983) 'The origins of overkill: nuclear weapons and American strategy', *International Security*, **7**, 4: 1–71.
Schwartz, D. (1983) *NATO's Nuclear Dilemmas*, Washington: Brookings.
Stromseth, J. (1988), *The Origins of Flexible Response: NATO's Debate over Strategy in the 1960s*, London: Macmillan.

6 NATO and nuclear strategy

Stuart Croft

INTRODUCTION

On 5 and 6 July 1990, NATO's heads of government and state met in London to consider the implications of the end of the Cold War for the Alliance. The resulting document issued by all parties – *The London Declaration on a Transformed North Atlantic Alliance* – was to set the parameters for the alterations in the nature of the organisation towards what was commonly referred to as 'a more political alliance'. The London Declaration appeared to be a very forward looking document. After congratulating NATO for having been 'the most successful defensive alliance in history', it recognised that 'the security of every state is inseparably linked to the security of its neighbours' and called for the Atlantic Community to 'reach out to the countries of the East which were our adversaries in the Cold War, and extend to them the hand of friendship'. (NATO, 1990: 1–2).

Inevitably, such rhetoric and new threat assessment led to an expectation that NATO's nuclear strategy would be transformed. Indeed, the London Declaration went out of its way to support those expectations. Stressing a desire for 'the lowest and most stable level of nuclear forces needed to secure the prevention of war', the Declaration called for arms control negotiations on short range nuclear forces recognising that 'there will be a significantly reduced role for sub-strategic nuclear systems of the shortest range';[1] further, that NATO would 'prepare a new Allied military strategy... modifying "flexible response" to reflect a reduced reliance on nuclear weapons'; above all, a call for the adoption of 'a new NATO strategy making nuclear forces truly weapons of last resort'. (NATO, 1990: 4–5)

The London Declaration set a very different tone from previous NATO communiqués. In May 1989, the 'Comprehensive Concept' was issued by NATO. The Comprehensive Concept was called for at the Reykjavik summit in June 1987 and was designed to produce a blueprint which all NATO countries could advocate, and which would support the unity of the Alliance.

As such, it was seen to be a very important document. There were, however, several points of contrast with the London Declaration. The latter stressed friendship to the East and common security; in contrast, the Comprehensive Concept noted that Soviet reform would take years to complete; that change in Eastern Europe was uneven; that 'the Soviet Union continues to deploy military forces and maintain a pace of military production in excess of legitimate defensive requirements'; and that 'it has long been an objective of the Soviet Union to weaken the links between the European and North American members of the Alliance'. (NATO, 1989a: 4) Indeed, in the communiqué that went with the launch of the Comprehensive Concept, despite the unilateral Soviet conventional reductions announced by Gorbachev at the United Nations some six months earlier, it was felt necessary 'to *challenge* the members of the Warsaw Pact to join us [NATO] in accelerating efforts to sign and implement an agreement which will enhance security and stability in Europe by reducing conventional armed forces'. (NATO, 1989b: 4)

In the nuclear sphere there were further contrasts. Whereas the London Declaration stressed the significantly reduced role of sub-strategic forces (SNF), the Comprehensive Concept noted that 'sub-strategic forces fulfil an essential role in Alliance deterrence strategy... Where nuclear forces are concerned, land-, sea-, and air-based systems, including ground-based missiles, in the present circumstances and as far as can be foreseen will be needed in Europe' (NATO, 1989b: 10). While the London Declaration could call for a modification of flexible response, the Comprehensive Concept noted that 'For the foreseeable future, there is no alternative strategy for the prevention of war. The implementation of this strategy will continue to ensure that the security interests of all Alliance members are fully safeguarded.' (NATO, 1989b: 6) Finally, the London Declaration called for nuclear weapons to be seen as weapons of last resort, whereas for the Comprehensive Concept 'For the foreseeable future, deterrence requires an appropriate mix of adequate and effective nuclear and conventional forces which will continue to be kept up to date where necessary; for it is only by their evident and perceived capability for effective use that such forces and weapons deter.' (NATO, 1989a: 5)

Of course, these differences between the Comprehensive Concept and the London Declaration are largely a reflection of the dramatic changes in East–West relations that took place in the twelve months separating the two meetings. The London Declaration, when compared to the Comprehensive Concept, illustrated how far NATO was apparently prepared to change. Yet, in sharp contrast to the rhetoric of the London Declaration, NATO's Strategic Concept has not produced a radical conceptual change in NATO's nuclear strategy. Rather, NATO's new nuclear strategy owes more to the approach outlined in the Comprehensive Concept. This chapter will seek to argue this by first outlining the pressure upon flexible response along with the scope of possible change in NATO's nuclear strategy. Second, an assessment of the actual changes in strategy will be made. Finally, an analysis will be made of why the changes in NATO's nuclear strategy have not lived up to the expectations generated by the London Declaration.

THE SCOPE FOR CHANGE IN NATO STRATEGY

Before examining the challenges faced by flexible response and the alternatives to it, it is important to attempt to be reasonably clear as to the meaning of flexible response in NATO strategy since 1967. There has been a broad baseline of doctrinal agreement. Under flexible response, NATO would seek to fight at the level of violence introduced by the enemy, but should the Alliance deem itself to be suffering defeat, NATO could escalate to higher levels of violence. Thus, the failure to successfully repel an attack and re-establish deterrence through direct defence would lead to nuclear use, possibly first use, in Europe; and should that be unsuccesful, there would be a move to general nuclear use. Thus flexible response couples the United States's strategic nuclear deterrent to the deterrence of conventional military aggression. Yet it should also be recognised that there is no unanimously accepted view as to the precise meaning of the doctrine (Daalder, 1988: Freedman, 1986; Stromseth, 1988). Indeed, NATO has never felt comfortable enough to be able to publish the document (MC 14/3) which outlines the doctrine. Broadly, while many Germans and Europeans have seen flexible response in terms of presenting the Soviets with the threat of almost immediate escalation from conventional to strategic nuclear conflict, some Americans – believing such an approach to lack credibility – have argued for war-fighting strategies at differing levels of violence. Thus, to an extent, it may be said that where one stands on the issue of the speed of escalation within flexible response has depended upon where one sits geographically within NATO.

Thus within NATO, flexible response has been an essentially contested doctrine. Yet this is not the reason why NATO has been faced with the dilemma of having to alter its nuclear strategy. Instead, two other major challenges have recently arisen: one political, and one strategic. It is of course the changes in the political relationships in Europe that has exacerbated the pressures upon strategy. Therefore it is the combination of these political and strategic challenges brought about by the tumultuous change in Europe that has led to the requirement for a change in NATO nuclear strategy.

In political terms it has been argued by some that flexible response damages the transition to a pan-European security order that should be the goal of all governments in post-Cold War Europe. Nuclear weapons, it is argued, should only deter nuclear weapons; another way of expressing this is to say that a nuclear no-first-use strategy would aid the build down of military forces in the post-Cold War world. This view, which has been associated with the German Foreign Ministry under Hans-Dietrich Genscher, has support elsewhere, for example in the Low Countries, the British Labour Party, and among certain analysts in the United States (Kaiser, 1990).[2] Given that conventional parity will be more than achieved through the implementation of the CFE Treaty,[3] and the need to support Gorbachev's position domestically in the Soviet Union, it was argued that it would be an important political gesture for NATO to renounce first use of nuclear weapons. Movement in this direction was read by some journalists and others in the London Declaration, with its phraseology of seeing nuclear forces as weapons of 'last resort'. Militarily this language seems to make little or no sense; although there was concern over *early* use, flexible response never allowed for 'first resort' to nuclear weapons; that is, before the use of conventional forces (although it did allow for first use). After all, the incredibility of such a strategy was one reason for the movement to flexible response from massive retaliation in the 1960s. Massive retaliation – the use of all nuclear forces in response to any level of attack – has no supporters within NATO as an explicit Alliance doctrine.

The strategic pressure on flexible response has come from the number and range of nuclear systems left in the Europe of the 1990s. Although many in NATO sought to maximise the number of systems deployed in Europe during the 1980s – notably the United States and the United Kingdom – in fact the reverse has been occurring. Both ground launched Cruise missiles (GLCMs) and Pershing missiles have been removed as a result of the INF Treaty; the Follow-on-to-Lance (FOTL) system has been abandoned (and the FOTL experience may well be repeated with the tactical air to surface missile, TASM); and battlefield systems will certainly be removed, either unilaterally or through arms control. After all, such systems can only strike democratic countries in East Central Europe that are no longer allied with the former Soviet Union; they are ageing, and there is no incentive for modernisation; while the Soviet military withdrawal from Eastern Europe means that Moscow has withdrawn its equivalent systems. The United States' nuclear commitment to Europe seems likely to be confined to nuclear capable aircraft and naval nuclear forces, both of which are highly mobile and hence susceptible to withdrawal. Thus, the United States may well be seen by some in Western Europe as slowly moving towards an 'existential' nuclear commitment to Europe.[4] These coming realities need to be taken into account if NATO is not to be seen by its electorates, in a period of *de facto* denuclearisation, to be suffering from a nuclear addiction.

Thus, NATO's governments have been forced to consider change to the Alliance's nuclear doctrine. Theoretically, the menu for choice is very wide. It may be argued that the only nuclear strategy for NATO in a legitimate pan-European security system is a non-nuclear one emphasising conven- ← tional deterrence. However, this chapter is concerned with smaller steps, and as such will examine two alternatives for NATO, selected for their immediate political salience. They are: minimum deterrence with no first use; and minimum deterrence with first use. Both will be examined in turn.

The first alternative could have been minimum deterrence and no first use: ← this would have been widely seen as a radical choice. Such a strategy would have allowed for the pursuit of a radical change in the conduct of European politics, the pursuit of a pan-European security community. The assumption would be that there is little chance of a 'relapse' of Soviet policy towards renewed hostility with the West, and that to worry about this is simply to miss historical opportunities to create a new peaceful order. Thus, the link between nuclear use and all other warfare must be broken; further, nuclear systems must be substantially reduced. This strategy would allow – unilaterally or through arms control – for the removal of all nuclear systems in Germany and the cancellation of TASM in the short term; for the radical disarming of the United States strategic arsenal; the removal of US nuclear bases throughout Europe; and to reassure the former Soviet Union about coming down to low numbers, moves towards the nuclear disarmament of the British and French (and Chinese?) along with tight restraints on strategic defences in the longer term.

This strategy would first break the link between nuclear and conventional forces, strategies, doctrines and deployments. In the longer term the process would lead to a break in the coupling of the United States and Western Europe. The argument would be that the politics of the new Europe require the elimination or at least major reduction of the nuclear element, and reliance on a new politics based on enlightened self-interest, economic aid and notions of common security (Booth, 1990). The strategy relies fundamentally upon a process analysis. Movement towards a pan-European structure would encourage more steps along the road to an eventual NATO policy of nuclear existentialism, should NATO survive that long. The danger is not of a Soviet relapse into hostility but of a nuclear relapse, for those who support this view in the main argued that before the revolutions of 1989 it was not the Soviet Union that threatened European security, but rather the danger was the threat of nuclear warfare.

The second alternative would have been a strategy of minimum deterrence and first use. Under such a strategy, there would be insufficient forces for a credible flexible response policy – it would be a minimum deterrence posture – for all the advantages outlined above. But the fear of Soviet relapse would lead to the taking out of insurance in the form of nuclear linkage to Soviet conventional aggression, and also the investment in accurate and penetrating nuclear systems, capable of being used against military rather than merely civilian targets. It would depend upon systems such as the Trident D–5 and MX/Peacekeeper, and on limited, accurate sub-strategic nuclear forces. The strategy would also retain a role for United States nuclear forces deployed in Western Europe. Thus, this strategy could be seen to offer the best of all worlds. It would allow progress to be made towards a new security community; while if the process goes wrong, it would allow for a ready-made system of credible and militarily operable deterrence.

Indeed, such a strategy could be made even more palatable politically by making an explicitly conditional no-first-use guarantee. For example, there could be a no-first-use commitment conditional upon the Soviet Union observing a CSBM regime; and/or implementing the CFE Treaty; and/or ensuring no Soviet forces on the territory of the former Warsaw Pact countries; and so on. Such a strategy would require an imaginative interaction between the governments of NATO; between the governments of NATO and NATO's military forces; and between NATO, East and Central Europe, and the Soviet Union.

Thus the menu for choice was fairly wide; yet NATO has finally adopted a conservative nuclear doctrine, one that maintains much of the ideology of flexible response. The next section will look at the actual changes to NATO doctrine to illustrate in the final section that, in contrast to the above strategies, NATO's new nuclear doctrine owes more to the underlying approach of the Comprehensive Concept than it does to the London Declaration.

NATO'S NEW DOCTRINE: THE RETURN OF FLEXIBLE RESPONSE

NATO's Strategic Review has produced a Strategic Concept that has brought about an end to flexible response, but brought into effect a strategy that in many ways resembles flexible response. This is because what has been rejected by NATO planners is the form of flexible response that has been in existence, that is to say MC 14/3, not the philosophy of flexible response itself. It is therefore important to make a distinction between the theory and the practice of flexible response. The practice of flexible response may have been invalidated by the political and strategic changes already discussed, but for NATO planners and strategic analysts, that does not necessarily mean that a new practice of flexible response should not be formulated. Indeed, it is clear from NATO's Strategic Concept that the philosophy of flexible response is deemed to be the perfect response to the uncertainties in European security in the 1990s.

What, then, are the underlying philosophical points that makes flexible response so attractive? There are perhaps three major advantages: it reassures the West in an unpredictable world that NATO can still defend itself; it reassures the Soviet Union and any other potential aggressors that NATO itself could not be an aggressor; and, in a nuclear world, it is the most morally acceptable strategy for the Western democracies. Theoretically, then, it is argued by the strategy's supporters that flexible response allows for security, prudence and morality. Each argument merits some development.

First, inherent in the theory of flexible response is an intrinsic flexibility designed to suit many diverse situations and scenarios. This may be seen to be ideal at a time when the major threat to NATO has receded, and when discussion is couched in terms of risks rather than threats (given that 'threat' has become a non-word in NATO lexicon) from a whole variety of sources. The multi-directional risks that NATO has decided that it needs to be able to respond to – from the remnants of Soviet power, instability and the danger of spillover from Central and Eastern Europe, out-of-area dangers (particularly from states adjoining Europe in possession of ballistic missiles) and 'indirect risks' – require that NATO operate a strategic concept that has at its core flexibility. This makes flexible response conceptually resistant to change, which could help to build military confidence and political reassurance in the West in a time of a transition in the nature of politics and security in Europe.

The second theoretical strength of flexible response is the stress on war termination rather than victory should a conflict occur. The purpose of the strategy, of course, is to re-establish deterrence at whatever level of violence is required. The strategy should therefore reassure any adversary – and it is the former Soviet Union that is still seen to be the most credible – that the West and NATO has no interest in any notion of 'victory' should a conflict occur. In the short term, it would assure the former Soviet Union that NATO did not seek to take advantage of the changes of 1989–91 to the detriment of the security of the former Soviet Union.[5] Thus, conceptually at least, flexible response could assure adversaries of the essential defensiveness of the NATO Alliance.

The third conceptual advantage of flexible response it is argued is that the strategy is morally acceptable, or at least less morally unacceptable than other credible military strategies, in that it relies on the principle of the minimum use of force in response to aggression. Thus, such a strategy is the only one both militarily credible and politically acceptable for Western liberal democracies.

Although all of these points are controversial in strategic, political and

moral terms, it is clearly felt by NATO planners that these three characteristics are ideal for the present situation. Conceptually, such a strategy
provides for the possibility of change while providing reassurance for both
East and West. Proponents of this view argue that it is the middle way
between two logical nuclear extremes: massive retaliation and nuclear war-
fighting. Minimum deterrence, it is argued, could in practice be
indistinguishable from massive retaliation. Under such circumstances, were
deterrence to be challenged there would be no options other than surrender
or all out suicidal response, the very dilemma that NATO's review in the
1960s sought to eliminate. Yet too many nuclear options could lead to ideas
regarding the feasibility of actually conducting a nuclear war, should deterrence be challenged. This in turn, it may be argued, would lead to crisis
instability and very likely arms race instability which would be a major
problem given the desirability of avoiding both outcomes in post-Cold War
Europe. For NATO planners, then, the concepts of the doctrine of flexible
response remain unchallenged by the changes in European security; further,
those changes actually reinforce the importance of the philosophy of flexible
response.

> Flexible Response does provide over-arching strategic principles which
> can accommodate any number of operational methods of employment to
> satisfy the security requirements of the Alliance... As a result, when
> changes occur in the strategic environment, it is possible to adapt methods
> of operations employment to the new circumstances without violating or
> requiring changes in the existing strategic principles.
>
> (Johnsen, 1990: 225)

It remains therefore to build a new practice of flexible response in the 1990s.

This new practice of flexible response at the nuclear level will rely on
more flexible assets than did the previous practice. Since the shorter range
ground-based systems in western continental Europe (excluding France)
have been or will shortly be withdrawn, NATO planners no longer face the
'use them or lose them' dilemma of the past, whereby such forces could have
been over-run by Soviet forces in the early stages of any conflict, thus giving
incentives for early nuclear use. But not only will those forces not be
deployed; the new political geography of Eastern Europe and the effective
disappearance of forward defence as a practical strategy in the area (although
it will remain as practice in Norway and Turkey) lead towards an obvious
emphasis on air- and sea-based assets. Thus, given the decrease in the threat
of Soviet attack, certainly after the implementation of the CFE Treaty and
the full Soviet withdrawal from Eastern Europe on which so much of this
change rests, a flexible response strategy could be fashioned in practice out

of American air- and sea-based nuclear systems continuing the linkage of Western European security to the US strategic deterrent.

If the concept of flexible response has not changed but the terminology has, how can this be explained? It is perhaps in part a reflection of a learning process. Past NATO actions and policies of Western governments have been littered with statements that can only be termed lazy at best, or as deliberately misleading at worst. For example, NATO INF systems were publicly justified in terms of the Soviet SS-20 deployment, when in reality the greater concern was with providing a greater degree of coupling.[6] Short range nuclear weapons were justified by Soviet conventional superiority, when their real purpose was to position the nuclear threshold at a level deemed appropriate to deter Soviet aggression. Discussion about a possible Comprehensive Test Ban Treaty was criticised on the grounds that it could not be verified, when in reality the concern was that such a treaty would forbid testing for modernisation, and thus undermine deterrence. In each of these examples, initial imprecision led to public embarrassment as widespread debate placed Western governments and NATO onto the political defensive. In the future, should there be a widespread public political debate over nuclear issues (over testing or deployments, for example) language will again be crucial, as in the past. However, unlike the past, there has been an attempt to get the language right in advance.

NATO's new practice of flexible response, then, will at the nuclear level be dependent upon air- and sea-launched nuclear systems. This makes some sense; in an era of 'risk' rather than 'threat', less rungs in the ladder of escalation or more seams in the web of deterrence – to use the NATO terminology – are required. However, such a strategy is vulnerable on five grounds. First, the deployment of TASM becomes central. Air-based deterrent systems have a political symbolism for West European governments that sea-based do not and cannot have. Since existing air-based assets are ageing, they will have to be modernised, and the TASM is the most credible system. Yet the funding of TASM, in general and in sufficient numbers, is by no means guaranteed in a US defence budget which has for some years been under great pressure. Deployment of TASM in united Germany may also not be taken for granted. Second, the significance of air- and sea-based nuclear assets means that they would therefore have to be strongly protected in any arms control negotiations. Thus, if pressure grew for nuclear arms control in Europe, perhaps as part of a decision to modernise its existing forces, NATO would be placed onto the defensive. Third, it is clear that the Strategic Concept is dependent upon the CFE regime; how could it respond to a potential collapse in that regime? Fourth, without floors being set in the levels of conventional forces, budget conscious nations may use the reliance on nuclear forces to dramatically reduce the level of their conventional forces.

(This may well be an argument for a no-first-use declaration.) Finally, the overall Strategic Concept, designed to be fully operational by the middle of the 1990s, is inherently vulnerable to changes in the strategic environment in the shorter term: perhaps to events in the former Soviet Union, Yugoslavia or elsewhere in Central and Eastern Europe; or perhaps to the process of federalism/confederalism in the European Community.

THE ESSENCE OF NATO'S NUCLEAR STRATEGY

It has been argued above that despite the wide menu for choice in strategic terms, NATO's new nuclear strategy in fact represents only a minimal shifting of ground. For NATO planners, the two alternatives outlined above have serious drawbacks. Minimum deterrence with no first use scores high on the political desire to build down nuclear forces in the post-Cold War world and on the opportunity to develop a more pan-European security process, but leaves little reassurance to those fearful of the process breaking down into hostility, a repetition of the past. In such circumstances, many could argue that minimum deterrence with no first use would be frightening; it would be nothing less than a return to massive retaliation at low force levels, leaving fears of pre-emption, first-strike instability and/or arms race instability. Given that scenario, it is clear that under such a strategy the only targets of Western nuclear forces would be cities. Indeed, by reducing the level of uncertainty in the mind of the aggressor, such a strategy it is argued could actually undermine deterrence. Minimum deterrence with first use can be criticised for moving towards a war-fighting strategy, at levels of force where – just possibly – a military leader in a crisis might believe that nuclear victory was possible. Further, it may actually undermine the political movement towards the creation of a pan-European security process as, by definition, it relies upon the most militarily threatening systems.

Strategically therefore, it is possible to argue in favour of the updated flexible response strategy. But importantly, NATO's move to remain wedded to flexible response is dependent upon politics. Strategy reviews are inherently controversial. During NATO's review from 1961–7 there was constant acrimony and argument between member states, eventually leading, after much bitterness, to a hardfought compromise between the original American view of flexible response and Europeans fears and desires. Even so, the compromise was not sufficient to prevent France from withdrawing from the integrated military command. Thus, the experience of the 1960s gives NATO decision makers a strong incentive not to hold a public debate over a wide range of strategic options. This is reinforced by the arguments and wrangling of the early 1980s which, from the perspective of NATO governments, were very damaging. For NATO governments and decision makers, therefore, there is a strong political motivation to minimise argument over nuclear forces, and in the Strategic Review of 1991 clearly nuclear forces were deliberately not discussed in controversial terms. This was facilitated of course by the argument that the nuclear issue was the one least affected by the changes of 1989–90 because the likelihood of nuclear conflict has in any case always been the most remote contingency. All of this gives a strong incentive to simply update flexible response rather than to repudiate the strategy altogether.

However, there is yet a third series of reasons for the survival of the flexible response philosophy, relating to underlying assumptions. It is a function of military planners to work on the basis of worst-case analysis in their threat assessment. As already seen, NATO's review has identified four 'risks' to the Alliance – from the remnants of Soviet power, instability and the danger of spillover from Central and Eastern Europe, out-of-area dangers and 'indirect risks'. Yet, although it is placed in a wider context, it is clear that the former Soviet Union is still seen as the major security 'risk' to the Alliance as a whole. Given economic, political and ethnic instability in the former Soviet Union, the growing discomfort of the military, rising nationalism:

> Intentions can change rapidly. An examination of the past for possible insights into the future would provide little comfort... although it may be difficult to discern future Soviet intentions, it is less difficult to identify future Soviet military capabilities... the Soviet Union will remain a nuclear superpower whose arsenal, while at numerical parity with the United States, will dwarf the European nuclear powers... the Soviets will retain formidable conventional capabilities... the Soviets are still in the midst of a massive and continuing modernisation programme.
>
> (Johnsen, 1990: 222–2)

Thus, for military planners, the desire to create a strategy that could move towards a more pan-European structure, one focusing on existential threats, has in fact been less of a priority than maintaining a strategy which could continue to deter one specific potential enemy.

These assumptions may or may not be the most realistic ones for the 1990s. One may argue that to continue to consider the Soviet Union in these terms is to miss the opportunity for moving beyond adversarial relationships. One may argue that to attempt to impose strategy in such fluid international circumstances is in any case doomed to failure. Yet what is clear is that these underlying assumptions owe much more to the rhetoric of the Comprehensive Concept than they do to that of the London Declaration.

The Comprehensive Concept stressed that deterrence and flexible response would have to remain 'for the foreseeable future'; in contrast, the

London Declaration emphasised 'extending the hand of friendship' and making nuclear forces 'weapons of last resort'. As seen from the above analysis, NATO's new strategic concept is still based upon deterrence, and 'last resort' still means flexible response. Last resort does not mean no first use, nor a strategy of massive retaliation, both of which might have been legitimate interpretations of the original statement. Instead, it merely means that nuclear weapons are less likely to be used because conventional war is less likely in post-Cold War Europe between NATO and any major state; while in a post-CFE world, conventional parity means that the need to resort to nuclear weapons would be less as the nuclear threshold has been raised. Last resort is the term for the new modalities of flexible response, not a dramatic change in strategy. It reflects the desire to use a term free from the associations of the past not only in the NATO–Soviet Union debate, but also in the NATO–France debate and the NATO–peace movement debate. The NATO view has been as predicted in the autumn of 1990 that:

> Undoubtedly, because of the new political climate in Europe, the names and labels of NATO strategy will change, but there is no need to alter the basic principles themselves.
>
> (Johnsen, 1990: 232)

Of course this line of argument is not meant to suggest that the Comprehensive Concept is a more important document than the London Declaration; the Comprehensive Concept was one of the first victims of the end of the Cold War. However, the argument here is that the spirit of the Comprehensive Concept tells the analyst a great deal about how to interpret NATO's new strategic concept, and indeed gives a greater indication of the continuity of thinking in NATO circles than the London Declaration would lead one to suspect. Admittedly, the London Declaration could be read as two documents: the first half, stressing the new cooperative approach; and the second half, emphasising the need for continued military preparedness. Yet the tone was clearly set by the first half. But the failure of the new strategic concept to live up to the rhetoric of the London Declaration does not illustrate a failure in the new concept; rather it says more about the international environment in the summer of 1990. With President Gorbachev under great domestic pressure, with the process of German unification and the inclusion of the united Germany in NATO yet to be concluded, NATO governments were prepared to go almost any distance to support the Kremlin leadership to achieve those ends.

It may well be that any new security process in Europe building new arrangements in the post-Cold War world will owe more to politics and economics than to military science. There may be a growing irrelevance of military force to the new post-Cold War Europe; it is interesting how few analysts put military/security relations and nuclear strategy at the heart of the debate over the new Europe (Hassner, 1990; Hoffmann, 1990; Howard, 1990; Waever, 1990).[7] This could lead to an argument that the debate over NATO nuclear strategy is now irrelevant: it no longer matters. However, it is unlikely that this can be the case. Without a secure security framework, few in the West will have the confidence to take the broad steps to seek to create some form of security community between East and West to which all are surely committed. And in this, the fate of nuclear weapons is central. Thus, choices made over nuclear strategy can have an important, albeit negative, impact upon the new security process in Europe. That is to say, choices over NATO nuclear strategy may provide no answers to the question: how can European security be improved? Rather, choices over strategy may be conditioned by the question: what damages the improvements in European security processes the least? (Booth, 1989: 204–7) It remains to be seen whether, in opting for caution, NATO's strategic choice will be able to make the maximum contribution to meeting that criterion.

NOTES

1   It is interesting to speculate on the origins of the term 'sub-strategic' in NATO parlance in the late 1980s. One view is that the change in terminology towards that used by the French was a manifestation of NATO's desire to move as close as possible to France to encourage French *de facto* if not *de jure* reintegration into the integrated military command. A second view is that the change in terminology reflected German *angst* about the term TNF or theatre nuclear forces, given the bitter arguments about Cruise and Pershing in the early 1980s. One might speculate that the change to the term sub-strategic in fact reflected both of these desires.

2   Although Kaiser argues against no first use 'since nuclear weapons would otherwise cease to be a war-preventing deterrent', he also argues that 'the dispute over "first use" will become more and more theoretical' (Kaiser, 1990: 491). However, Kaiser's emphasis on a movement from deterrence for NATO strategy, and his emphasis on limited nuclear deployments rather than on conceptions of nuclear use for deterrent purposes, put him very close to this group.

3   Given the collapse of the Warsaw Pact and the assumption that the ex-Warsaw Pact countries will not be military allies of the Soviet Union, the CFE Treaty – designed to produce parity between NATO and the Warsaw Pact – would actually produce, in some categories of weapons, a two-to-one NATO advantage over the Soviet Union, at least in terms of maximum allowable ceilings (in reality NATO may not reach all of its allowable ceilings).

4   Existentialism holds that deterrence exists merely through the possession of nuclear weapons, regardless of strategy and deployments (Freedman, 1988).

5   This was one of the messages carried to Moscow by Sir Michael Quinlan, Britain's chief civil servant on defence issues in November 1990. See his speech to the Soviet General Staff (Quinlan, 1991).

6   This has subsequently been accepted in official documents, for example 'NATO military planners were quick to point out that INF had been brought to Europe not

solely or even principally as a direct counterweight to the Soviet SS-20s, but as a political guarantee by the US to Western Europe.' (FCO, 1988: 1)
7 Compare these views with those of John Mearsheimer (1990).

REFERENCES

Booth, K. (1989) 'Alternative defence', in K. Booth and J. Baylis (eds) *Britain, NATO and Nuclear Weapons*, London: Macmillan.

Booth, K. (1990) 'Steps towards stable peace in Europe: a theory and practice of coexistence', *International Affairs*, 66, 1: 17–45.

Daalder, I. (1988) *NATO Strategy and Ballistic Missile Defence*, Adelphi Paper 233, London: IISS.

FCO (1988) *Briefing Paper 210*, London: Foreign and Commonwealth Office.

Freedman, L. (1986) 'Limited war, unlimited protest', in L. Freedman (ed.) *The Price of Peace: Living with the Nuclear Dilemma*, London: Firethorn.

Freedman, L. (1988) 'I exist: therefore I deter?', *International Security*, 13, 1: 177–95.

Hassner, P. (1990) 'Europe beyond partition and unity', *International Affairs*, 66, 3: 461–76.

Hoffmann, S. (1990) 'Reflections on the German question', *Survival*, 32, 4: 291–98.

Howard, M. (1990) 'The remaking of Europe', *Survival*, 32, 2: 99–106.

Johnsen, W. (1990) 'Is it time for a new NATO strategy?', in A. Clesse and L. Ruhl (eds) *Searching for a New Security Structure in Europe*, Baden-Baden: Nomos.

Kaiser, K. (1990) 'From nuclear deterrence to graduated conflict control', *Survival*, 32, 6: 483–96.

Mearsheimer, J. (1990) 'Back to the future: instability in Europe after the Cold War', *International Security*, 15, 1: 5–56.

NATO (1989a) *A Comprehensive Concept of Arms Control and Disarmament*, Brussels: NATO Information Service.

NATO (1989b) *Declaration of the Heads of States and Government Participating in the Meeting of the North Atlantic Council in Brussels 29 and 30 May 1989*, Press Communiqué M-1 (89) 21, Brussels: NATO Information Service.

NATO (1990) *London Declaration on a Transformed North Atlantic Alliance*, Brussells: NATO Information Service.

Quinlan, M. (1991) 'Nuclear weapons and the abolition of war', *International Affairs*, 67, 2: 293–301.

Slocombe, W. (1990) 'Strategic stability in a restructured world', *Survival*, 32, 4: 299–312.

Stromseth, J. (1988) *The Origins of Flexible Response: NATO's Debate over Strategy in the 1960s*, London: Macmillan.

Waever, O. (1990) 'Three competing Europes: German, French and Russian', *International Affairs*, 66, 3: 477–94.

7 Alternative defence

Colin McInnes

The debate over NATO strategy and security policy in the 1980s was not confined to the corridors of power and academic ivory towers, as had traditionally been the case since 1945. Rather it took to the streets, in both a literal and a metaphorical sense. In its most literal sense, the anti-nuclear protest marches of the early 1980s made the debate over INF deployment different in kind to previous NATO debates. But behind this was a more important metaphorical taking to the streets. The peace movement advocated a grassroots approach to strategic debate, a 'democratisation' of security policy which stemmed from a disillusionment with traditional strategic discourse. Thus the anti-nuclear protest was only part of a broader movement which challenged the fundamental basis upon which strategy had been thought about, talked about and formulated. It offered not a different strategy, but a different approach to security.

> The peace movement, which emerged in the early 1980s, appeared to be primarily an anti-nuclear movement... But the underlying concerns were more profound. They had to do with the role of the state in modern society and the issue of national self-determination. The Euromissile issue, in particular, was about the relationship of the USA to Western Europe, about national sovereignty in security matters, about who has the right to make decisions about life and death.
>
> (Kaldor, 1989: 61)

But the peace movement's success in mobilising public opinion was not matched in electoral terms. This led to interesting conclusions over the pattern of defence decision making, and over strategic discourse.

> Winning public opinion was not equivalent to prevailing over militarization... The lack of flexibility of democratic governments and their disregard for an adverse mass public opinion was a shock to many who had faith in Western democracy... The commitment and loyalty to a

military alliance took precedence over the implied accountability towards the citizenry in democratic states.

(Gerle, 1989: 371–2)

Alternative defence proposed a different sort of security to that developed by NATO, Western governments and academic strategists. This alternative view also conflicted sharply with that of the Soviet Union and its Warsaw Pact allies[1] – indeed in this respect there was more in common between NATO and the Warsaw Pact than between NATO and alternative defence. This difference of approach was reflected even in terms used: fundamental concepts such as peace and security began to mean very different things when used by alternative defence. As a consequence, when the Euromissile debate was ended by the 1987 INF treaty, alternative defence had emerged as something more than a single-issue protest movement. Rather it offered a different approach to security which is still of interest beyond the end of the Cold War. This chapter examines that approach, how it differs from the more traditional view of strategy pursued by NATO (and to a lesser extent the Warsaw Pact), and how it might be applied to the challenges of the new Europe.

NATO's STRATEGIC DISCOURSE

NATO strategy was – and to a large extent remains, despite the ending of the Cold War – based upon a number of assumptions. Some of these assumptions were shared by the Soviet Union and its Warsaw Pact allies, particularly those concerning the nature of security. These assumptions were sufficiently unchallenged both within official circles and by orthodox strategists that they served to define the parameters of the security debate. These assumptions did more than influence the way people thought about strategy; they conditioned those participants in strategic debates into a way of thinking about security, and provided the language for debates over strategy. Alternative defence was critical both of the assumptions made and of the language used. Thus two separate security discourses existed, that of NATO (which was, by and large, shared by the Warsaw Pact, and may therefore be termed 'traditional' or 'orthodox'), and that of alternative defence.

Some six assumptions can be identified as constituting the basis for NATO's strategic discourse. The first of these is that security is rooted in the state. Security is the concern of the state in the sense that it is the state which provides security (perhaps in alliance with other states). Moreover, security refers to the state and most particularly to its territorial integrity. Thus a security threat is defined as a threat to the state. The most important type of threat – and sometimes the only threat considered – is a military threat, which is best dealt with by military means. Therefore the provision of security is equated with the maintenance of military forces for the protection of the state – what is often termed 'national security'. The second assumption follows on from this: the threat to Western security was Soviet military power. It was an unquestioned assumption of NATO strategy and security policy that the Soviet Union was a threat, that the nature of the threat was military (as opposed to ideological, economic, etc.), and that Soviet policy was offensively orientated.

> The message to the West is clear. The Soviet Union continues to maintain massive military forces in Europe, both conventional and nuclear, well in excess of those required for its own defence. These forces are being constantly improved, particularly in their mobility and firepower. The Soviet leadership have demonstrated their willingness to use force to gain their own ends... While it remains the case that there is no evidence that the Soviet Union is planning any immediate attack upon the West, it is plain that we [the British government] and our NATO Allies cannot afford to base our defences on the assumption that the Soviet leadership are essentially benevolent and concerned only with the Soviet Union's security.
>
> *(Statement on the Defence Estimates*, 1983: 1)

Although recent events may have diminished this perception, it nevertheless remains central to NATO's thinking about threats (or what is now termed 'risks') to security (*Jane's Defence Weekly*, 1991).

The third element in this strategic discourse builds closely into the second: that the relationship between the Soviet Union and the West was competitive; that the Cold War was a clash of economic and political systems; and that the prevailing feature of the Cold War was tension and conflict. Détente reduced tension and conflict by addressing the military element of the relationship, but it did not change the nature of the relationship, which remained competitive (Kaldor, 1989: 64). Even revisionist historians held this view on the nature of the Cold War, merely reversing the roles of 'good guy' and 'bad guy' (Migone, 1989: 155). This competitive relationship enabled the widespread application of game theory to the Cold War, and particularly the tendency to see events in terms of a zero-sum game: that what was of advantage to one side was inevitably of disadvantage to the other. Thus the Soviet deployment of the SS 20 in the 1970s was seen as disadvantageous to NATO requiring the Alliance to deploy Cruise and Pershing II missiles to 'balance' this new development. This perspective led to the adoption of a policy of security through strength, a policy shared by the Soviet Union: 'the greater the Soviet military potential, the stronger the country' (Arbatov, 1990a: 12).

The first three elements of NATO's strategic discourse therefore concern the nature of security, of the threat and of the international system. The second set of three elements concerns NATO's response to this. It involves three linked assumptions: that security is best achieved by deterring war; that given Soviet conventional superiority and the need to deter war, NATO must rely on nuclear weapons for its security; and that stability is achieved by the threat of mutual devastation, the 'balance of terror'. As Hylke Tromp has argued:

> [NATO policy] is based on simple and convincing logic. Security depends on deterring a potential aggressor. Subsequently the deterrence posture is what really counts, and the final question is: what is enough for a credible deterrence?
>
> (Tromp, 1990: 169)

Within this policy of deterrence nuclear weapons play a central role, as was made clear in NATO's 1989 'Comprehensive Concept':

> Strategic nuclear forces provide the ultimate guarantee of deterrence for the Allies. They must be capable of inflicting unacceptable damage on an aggressor state even after it has carried out a first strike... The strategic nuclear forces of the United States provide the cornerstone of deterrence for the Alliance as a whole.
>
> (NATO, 1989: 6)

Within this deterrent framework, a high priority was placed on stability – indeed stability was sometimes interchangeable with security in NATO's strategic discourse. As the above also makes clear, stability did not rely on matching force for force, even conventional with nuclear. Rather stability depended upon the certainty of devastating retaliation, the 'balance of terror'.

> The Allies sub-strategic nuclear forces are not designed to compensate for conventional imbalances... Their role is to ensure that there are no circumstances in which a potential aggressor might discount the prospect of nuclear retaliation in response to military action. Nuclear forces below the strategic level thus make an essential contribution to deterrence.
>
> (NATO, 1989: 6)

NATO's security discourse was therefore state-centric, orientated almost exclusively towards a perceived military threat from the Soviet Union, in a competitive and confrontational international system. Its response was a deterrrent policy based on nuclear weapons which placed a high priority on stability as achieved through the threat of mutual destruction – the balance of terror.

ALTERNATIVE DEFENCE

Alternative defence was developed in the 1970s and particularly the 1980s (Dunn, 1991: 56–65), and was not merely critical of these assumptions but offered a different way of looking at, and a different language for security, even though some of the terms used were the same. In contrast with the traditional national security approach, which concentrated on security against military threats, alternative defence offered a holistic view of security with an expanded security agenda. For alternative defence, peace was 'more than just the absence of hot war' (Gerle, 1989: 379). Rather it involved security across a number of issues, and at a number of levels. In particular alternative defence became interested in security for the individual rather than that of the state, viewing threats to security as not merely external to the state, but within the state and its political and social structures.

> It became increasingly clear that getting rid of one or other weapons system would not solve problems associated with a militaristic world view... Peace has also to do with a deepening of democracy that is built on unconditional respect for human rights and the freedom to express other opinions than those held by people in control of state power.
>
> (Gerle, 1989: 374)

Threats to individual security clearly existed in the Eastern bloc (Fritzsche, 1989: 52–3). But alternative defence also argued that a more subtle threat to individual security existed in the West through the exclusion of citizens and parliamentary institutions from decision making over national security policy. Moreover these citizens were then used as hostages by the state in the nuclear balance of terror to preserve its own existence from external threats (Gerle, 1989: 376; Kaldor, 1989: 62–3). Thus the threat to security was not so much the Soviet Union (or from the Soviet perspective, NATO) as the repression of democracy and the pervasive nature of militarism (Fritzsche, 1989: 48). Because of this disillusionment with the state as a vehicle for promoting security – indeed for some alternative defence thinkers the state *was* the security problem – alternative defence emphasised links between non-governmental organisations and individual action at the grassroots level (what is sometimes called 'anti-politics' or 'pre-politics').

> Challenging the existence of nuclear weapons inevitably involved challenging the structures within which political power is currently exercised.
>
> (Kaldor and Falk, 1987: 13)

The experience of protesting against nuclear weapons created a reaction against the idea of security being defined simply in terms of *national* security. Rather individual security and human rights received considerable attention in writings on alternative defence and were talked of as a legitimate part of the security debate. But the widening of the security agenda did not stop there. The Greens were far from alone in identifying ecological and environmental dangers as being security issues (Buzan *et al*. 1990: 8). Environmental dangers threatened life, lifestyle and livelihood, and were therefore threats to security in the most basic of ways. But the Greens also went some way further by linking environmental concerns to militarism. There was an obvious link in that both anti-nuclear and environmental protest organisations were concerned with nuclear testing and the consequences of a nuclear war, but the Greens also argued that the structures of liberal-capitalism and authoritarian communism sidelined environmental concerns and allowed militarism to flourish (Ryle and Soper, 1989). Economic issues also began to figure in alternative defence's widened security agenda. Economic satisfaction and prosperity were considered stabilising, while the opposite could place individual security at risk (again by threatening lifestyle, livelihood and, *in extremis*, life). Economic and environmental concerns also threatened security at a more global level, a level above that of the state: the effects of an economic or environmental catastrophe could not be limited to one state and its citizens, but were likely to spill over into neighbouring states and perhaps the entire world. Security therefore began to be considered an issue at not merely the levels of the individual and the state, but at a global level (Buzan *et al*., 1990: 4). Therefore in place of the orthodox view of security as a national concern addressing military threats, alternative defence offered a holistic view of security which worked at the individual, state and global levels, and which involved a widened security agenda comprising economic, environmental and human rights issues as well as military.

It follows from this that alternative defence had a fundamentally different conception of the threat to (Western) security than did NATO. Whereas for NATO the threat was Soviet military power, for alternative defence it was a range of less tangible issues including repression of democracy and human rights, militarism, environmental dangers, and economic deprivation. On the specific issue of the Soviet threat, alternative defence thinkers argued that NATO had consistently exaggerated both the nature and extent of the threat. The Soviet challenge was considered a political rather than military challenge; the Soviet Union had proved itself to be a status quo power; its large armed forces were the product of a tradition of over-insurance, a reflection of the military's role and position in Soviet society, and to safeguard the Kremlin's empire; and Soviet military capabilities had been consistently exaggerated. Alternative defence, by and large, did not question the existence of a Soviet threat, but did argue that the nature of the threat to Western security was more complex than that of possible Soviet aggression, that

Soviet military capabilities had been exaggerated, and that Soviet interests were less belligerent and competitive than NATO believed them to be.

Alternative defence also questioned the nature of the Cold War. Gian Giacomo Migone, for example, has argued that the Cold War was marked more by agreement than by conflict, and in particular that it was distinguished by the superpowers' mutual interest in peace, and by their mutual satisfaction with the postwar settlement (Migone, 1989). Mary Kaldor has similarly argued that the Cold War was a tool to preserve social cohesion and superpower hegemony *within* the blocs, masking internal social divisions.

> Fear of the other, fear of war helps to ensure domestic cohesion. The Cold War was a way of prolonging the benefits of the Second World War – social cohesion, effective economic management, etc. – without the bloodshed.
>
> (Kaldor, 1989: 65)

Others accepted that the Cold War had been confrontational, but questioned whether competition was inevitable and whether security could be achieved by traditional unilateral attempts; after all, the Soviet unilateral deployment of the SS-20 had led to NATO's deployment of Cruise and Pershing II so that Europe was *less* secure than previously. Unilateral attempts at security were therefore increasingly criticised as merely fuelling the arms race, adding to fear and suspicion, and ultimately reducing security. Instead alternative defence promoted the idea of security being interdependent. Europe was distinguished by a shared insecurity arising from nuclear weapons and the division of the continent. This was exacerbated by the use of enemy images and the failure both to appreciate the other's security concerns and to pay adequate attention to threat perception. But the primary goal was *common* survival (Johanssen, 1989: 46–8 and 56; Podlesnyi, 1989: 73).

The answer offered to this interdependence of security was 'common security', as advocated by the Palme Commission in 1982 (Palme, 1982; Vayrynan, 1985). Common security involved an appreciation of security as a shared problem, and a commitment to work for common rather than national security. It encouraged processes which reassured both sides, which promoted trust and reduced suspicion, and which regulated threatening weapons developments. In particular it encouraged an appreciation of the other's legitimate security interests, and the manner in which that was related to one's own behaviour (McInnes, 1990: 21–9). In Ken Booth's words:

> The search for national security has a habit of being self-defeating. The interplay between national mistrust, the action–reaction phenomenon and the dynamics of weapons innovation, can produce greater national strength, but not necessarily greater national security. When one country

attempts to increase its security against another by accumulating military power, the insecurity of the targeted country grows. Neither national nor international security is enhanced if major powers feel edgy and vulnerable. The insecure in any society are not the easiest to handle. Because we have the destructive power to wipe out the Soviet Union as an effective industrial society, and they have the destructive power to wipe out us, and because neither of us has a defensive capability in sight, *national* security is ultimately impossible. There is only reciprocal security. Reciprocal behaviour means a relationship in which something is given by each of two parties; there is mutual and conscious interaction in a particular direction.

(Booth, 1985: 52)

Alternative defence therefore offered a radically different view of security. But it was also highly critical of NATO's military strategy – its policy of deterrence, its reliance on nuclear weapons, and its view of stability. Alternative defence rejected the 'spirit, logic and practice of deterrence' (Fritzsche, 1989: 46). Although some accepted that deterrence might work in certain circumstances, they argued that its negative side effects outweighed the positive gains: deterrence institutionalised the Cold War and inhibited the movement towards a more 'legitimate' international order; deterrence required an 'enemy image' for its own justification, which promoted a form of paranoia and a spirit of confrontation, thus creating a spiral of mutual distrust and hostility; and it risked escalation in a crisis by encouraging brinkmanship and through its enemy imaging which promoted confrontation, hostility and an unwillingness to compromise (Booth, 1985: 34; Boserup, 1990: 8; Fritzsche, 1989: 46 and 52). But alternative defence was also sceptical of whether deterrence would always work. Some questioned whether the deterrent threat was credible since it relied upon a disproportionate response to aggression (Boserup, 1990: 7). In order to restore deterrence's credibility, NATO had been forced into a policy of more limited responses, one of war-fighting rather than 'pure deterrence'. But this in turn was seen by alternative defence as highly dangerous since it was both threatening and reduced the war prevention element of deterrence (Johanssen, 1990: 48). Nor was deterrence considered proof against accidental war, war by miscalculation, or irrational acts of violence. Finally deterrence was considered vulnerable to technological advances, particularly the defensive technologies actively pursued by the Reagan Administration's Strategic Defense Initiative ('Star Wars'), but also to increased missile accuracy which created the possibility of a successful first strike (Booth, 1985: 33; Johanssen, 1990: 47).

Alternative defence's most prominent criticisms however concerned

NATO's reliance on nuclear weapons – as many commentators have pointed out, it was fear of nuclear war which was the key mobilising factor in the development of alternative defence, and which generated the large public protests of the early 1980s (Gerle, 1989: 370; Kaldor, 1989: 61). Although alternative defence is more than simple anti-nuclearism, the anti-nuclear stance holds a special position in its security discourse. The criticisms of nuclear weapons and of nuclear deterrence are well known, and need only be briefly identified here.[2] Alternative defence questioned the morality of using nuclear weapons, weapons of mass destruction whose effects would not only be felt by the citizens of the states involved (even in a counterforce strike millions of citizens might die), but by neutral third parties. Even to threaten the use of such weapons was considered immoral. Further, if such weapons were ever used the ill-effects would grossly outweigh any positive benefits; in other words the consequences of the failure of a deterrence policy based on nuclear weapons were too great to justify such a policy. The number of people killed and the damage to the environment would constitute an unprecedented catastrophe for humanity, one which it might not be able to survive. Attempts at limiting damage through war-fighting strategies were flawed however by the inability to control a nuclear war, while the development of such strategies actually reduced the deterrent effect by making nuclear war more 'thinkable'. Ultimately nuclear weapons reduced security by making the whole of humanity vulnerable – including one's own citizens. After all, what sort of a *defence* policy relies upon the *vulnerability* of the people whose security is supposedly being protected? As Elisabeth Gerle commented:

> Instead of increased security, people living near NATO military bases felt that they were being increasingly drawn into a risk zone and becoming prime targets in the event of an outbreak of war.
>
> (Gerle, 1989: 370)

Finally nuclear reliance meant a dependency upon the United States and decisions made in Washington. Security policy was therefore removed from the control of the people and their elected representatives, and placed instead in the hands of the United States.

Because of this anti-nuclear stance, and because of its criticisms of deterrence, alternative defence was bound to reject the balance of terror as a stabilising tool. The balance of terror was considered to be, if anything, *destabilising* because of its tendency to inflate threats, promote enemy imaging and support the arms race (Boserup, 1990: 10). Instead alternative defence promoted the idea of stability as resting upon defensive capabilities outweighing offensive.

It is generally assumed that military stability and some measure of security can be achieved through a balance of force. This has been a fundamental axiom in all disarmament negotiations to date. But it is utterly wrong. Stability does not arise from an equality of force but from an inequality: the superiority of defensive over offensive capabilities.

(Boserup, 1990: 9)

War would be prevented by the perceived disutility of aggression based upon the inability to win: a state would not attack because it would know that it could not win. If war did occur for some reason (accident, miscalculation, etc.) then the costs would be kept to a minimum by the maintenance of strong defensive forces rather than a reliance on nuclear escalation. Finally, forces which were structured in such a way as to maximise their defensive capabilities but minimise their offensive would be less threatening to other states, and would therefore fulfil one of the requirements of common security by taking into account the concerns of the other (Johanssen 1990: 48–9). This led alternative defence into developing a variety of defensive schemes falling under the general headings of non-provocative defence, defensive defence, or more commonly non-offensive defence.[3]

Non-offensive defence achieved prominence in the 1980s as alternative defence's preferred model for military security. It was based upon a number of principles which it is useful to identify at this stage. The first and central principle was that forces should be *structurally* defensive. It was insufficient for declaratory policy, strategy or doctrine to be defensive since this might in itself contain an offensive element (based upon the principle that the best form of defence is attack). More importantly these could all be changed relatively quickly into offensive strategies. Equally it was insufficient to attempt to limit those weapons which possessed offensive capabilities by arms control treaties, since almost any weapon could be used in an offensive manner. Therefore forces had to be made structurally incapable of offensive action, usually by limiting their mobility and modifying their organisation into small regionally based units which lacked the command structure to concentrate and move together (Unterseher, 1989). This would be both stabilising and reassuring, as well as exploiting the traditional superiority of the defensive over the offensive.

The second principle was to reduce and if possible eliminate pressures to pre-empt in a crisis, thus bolstering war prevention. By reducing both the advantages and the means of pre-emption, non-offensive defence hoped to promote stability, and particularly crisis stability. It identified both NATO and the Warsaw Pact as producing dangerous pre-emptive pressures in their conventional and nuclear doctrines and force structures. In particular the centralisation of logistics, nuclear warheads, command and control, and air power offered tempting targets for pre-emption, while long range high precision weapons, manoeuvre orientated doctrines, and a growing emphasis upon interdiction, provided the means for pre-emption. Non-offensive defence therefore addressed the means of pre-emption by advocating the removal of weapons with a pre-emptive capability (unilaterally or through arms control agreements) and the renunciation of doctrines based upon manoeuvre and interdiction. To counter the advantages of pre-emption it developed a 'no targets principle', whereby instead of concentrating assets and thus providing a few, tempting high value targets, forces would be structured in a highly decentralised manner to provide a large number of comparatively low value targets.

Third, non-offensive defence aimed at reducing and if possible eliminating the role of nuclear weapons, and replacing the policy of deterrence with one of defence. Deterrence was perceived as destabilising as it was based upon a system of threats and enemy imaging. In contrast a purely defensive system would be reassuring and promote stability. Similarly nuclear weapons were viewed as uniquely threatening systems, not just to the other but to one's own people. Non-offensive defence therefore favoured at the very least a policy of nuclear no first use, and at most unilateral nuclear disarmament. The variety of defensive schemes which were proposed by non-offensive defence to replace deterrence were characterised by an emphasis upon attrition. Since any aggression would probably take the form of an armour-heavy assault which emphasised speed, manoeuvrability and firepower (a latter-day 'blitzkrieg'), non-offensive defence proposed to trap such forces in a net primarily consisting of infantry armed with anti-tank weapons. An attack would therefore be steadily ground down, its momentum would be broken up, and the possibility of a quick victory denied. Forces which broke through this net would be dealt with by friendly armoured forces lying deep and organised into relatively small units (to minimise their own offensive capabilities). These forces might also be used to recapture territory lost in the initial assault.

Finally non-offensive defence sought to promote arms race stability by addressing the fear and suspicion which provided the important link in the spiral of competitive weapons procurement. By emphasising defensive capabilities and severely reducing, if not eliminating offensive potential, the perceived threat to the other would be reduced. This would reduce the pressure to continue the arms race, and therefore assist in the development of stability.

ALTERNATIVE DEFENCE IN THE 1990s

Since alternative defence rose to prominence with the nuclear protest movement of the early mid-1980s, there is a prima facie case that with the decline of nuclear controversy, alternative defence will similarly decline. Following from this is the conclusion that alternative defence has little to say about post-Cold War Europe since its main concern (reducing the nuclear threat) has been adequately dealt with by the 1987 INF treaty and the reduction in the Soviet threat. This though would be to misunderstand the concerns of alternative defence. Alternative defence was and is more than an anti-nuclear protest movement. Rather it offers a conception of security which is arguably more relevant to post-Cold War Europe than that of orthodox strategists – a Europe where the Soviet threat is seen to have diminished to the margins, where military issues are no longer seen as the only issues on the security agenda, and where security is no longer necessarily equated with stability. Indeed a case may be made that the end of the Cold War vindicated the concerns of alternative defence, and that from the mid- to late 1980s issues raised by alternative defence began to feature prominently in the mainstream European Security agenda: the 1987 INF treaty saw the removal of those weapons whose deployment alternative defence had campaigned against, campaigns which in many senses had forged alternative defence; in the Soviet Union President Gorbachev was refashioning the security debate by leaning heavily upon concepts developed by alternative defence, such as the interdependence of security, defensive defence, and the importance of nuclear disarmament; the ending of bloc confrontation and a breaking up of the blocs, issues ridiculed by alternative defence's critics, had become reality; and grassroots protest movements in Eastern Europe had shattered the edifices of existing power structures.

But where does alternative defence go from here? Part of the problem is that alternative defence is not a simple, coherent body of ideas with a clearly defined programme, but an umbrella covering sympathetic ideas and concerns. The unifying factor in the early mid-1980s was the anti-nuclear protest; but by the late 1980s this had become marginalised. As Mary Kaldor has noted, the problems for alternative defence began in the aftermath of the INF treaty. Although there was agreement upon the desirability of moving towards a new security system, there was no such agreement upon the nature of that security system, the defining issues of concern, or the means by which to achieve this. Kaldor identified three main areas of disagreement following on from the INF treaty: whether to focus on denuclearisation and demilitarisation, or whether to broaden the debate into wider issues of underlying political and social insecurities; whether to work closely with left wing political parties, and therefore be able to influence them when in power, or whether to aim at a more broad based support such that even right wing politicians might move towards accepting alternative defence's security agenda; and whether to attempt to influence governing élites, or to create 'détente from below' by building up grassroots support throughout Europe (Kaldor, 1989: 62–3). The point then is not so much that alternative defence had nothing to say, but that it had lost some of the cohesion over what it was saying once the INF issue was resolved.

How might it regain that cohesion? And what issues might alternative defence focus upon in the 1990s? There seem to be four issues which are of sufficient centrality, and upon which there is sufficient agreement within alternative defence, for them to offer a unifying core – to create an agenda upon which alternative defence can campaign and attempt to set the terms of the debate on European security. These are: a broadened security agenda; a policy of common security; continued denuclearisation; and defensive/non-offensive military strategies.

A broadened security agenda has long been a feature of alternative defence, though the focus has often been on the military component within that agenda. The end of the Cold War though has eroded that centrality for both alternative defence and more orthodox strategists. A security agenda which embraces economic, environmental and human rights issues, as well as military, now seems to be widely accepted. The difference between alternative defence and orthodoxy however lies in the relationship between these four elements. For orthodox strategists military security is likely to remain the central concern, and other security issues may be compromised to safeguard military security (Mearsheimer, 1990). An increased awareness of other security concerns is likely, but military security will remain the priority. For alternative defence, however, military security is less an answer than a problem. The emphasis on military security may create tension between and within societies, while failing to address (and potentially exacerbating) underlying insecurities arising from economic, environmental and human rights concerns. For alternative defence, these underlying insecurities are the important issues, and the pursuit of military security can all too easily compromise them. Rather security policy should address these concerns first, and be willing to reach compromises over military security in order to promote them.

Second, alternative defence might emphasise common security, not as a policy which once achieved would produce some measure of security, but rather as a *process* whereby trends which contribute towards mutual security are encouraged (Booth, 1990: 32–4). Common security would also seek to change the way in which security is perceived; away from a unilateral, self-help conception, and towards one where states are sensitised to the interdependence of security and to the consequences of their own actions. Specific policies might include: restraint in the deployment of new weapon technologies, and in particular new nuclear weapons; an emphasis upon arms control and disarmament; restructuring NATO into a looser, more broad-based security structure, one which might include the former Soviet Union and former Warsaw Pact states; confidence building and crisis prevention measures; rules and norms over the treatment of ethnic minorities; and finally the implementation of defensive military strategies, where threatening and potentially offensive components are reduced to a minimum. The aim of all this would be the development of a regime where behaviour is controlled by what is considered acceptable, and where acceptable behaviour is defined as non-threatening.

Third, denuclearisation is likely to remain high on alternative defence's agenda. Despite the INF and START treaties, and the series of unilateral initiatives of September/October 1991, Europe remains a nuclear battle-ground, both superpowers retain huge strategic arsenals, the British and French are both modernising their independent deterrents, and obsolete land-based systems in Europe might still be replaced by sophisticated air-launched weapons such as the tactical air-to-surface missile, TASM. In addition there is a growing fear of nuclear proliferation in the developing world, a fear which came all too close to reality with Iraq. Given alternative defence's historic concern over nuclear weapons, denuclearisation is likely to remain a priority. The emphasis however is likely to be on de-nuclearisation rather than disarmament, and on multilateralism rather than unilateralism. Marjorie Thompson, the chair of the Campaign for Nuclear Disarmament (CND), has talked of 'weaning' it off unilateralism, while the British Labour Party has abandoned its commitment to unilateral nuclear disarmament in favour of multilateralism. A new emphasis on non-proliferation is also likely, linked to a call for the nuclear powers to set an example by moving away from nuclear strategies.

Finally, alternative defence is likely to continue to advocate non-offensive defence as its preferred military strategy. Deterrence is likely to be seen as even more difficult to justify given the lack of a clearly identified enemy – indeed deterrence might be considered dangerously counterproductive by encouraging a search for potential enemies to deter, which then become real enemies through the workings of threats and enemy imaging. In contrast non-offensive defence creates security without threats; nor does it require a specific enemy, and therefore avoids the self-fulfilling dangers of enemy imaging. The non-offensive defence schemes which have been developed to date vary in their military credibility. Though some have been developed over a number of years and display considerable sophistication (Brauch 1989; Unterseher, 1989), none are totally convincing, and most share a number of major problems: the schemes proposed are inherently inflexible and overly reactive; they assume a single form of attack – an armoured 'blitzkrieg' – when others might be developed; the static nature of most schemes render them vulnerable to enemy concentration of firepower on a few key breakthrough sectors; non-offensive defence tends to rely on the mass mobilisation of reservists who may lack the necessary training and commitment for the demanding light infantry role they would be required to play; technology may have shifted the balance between offence and defence away from the defence and in favour of the offence; most schemes display an excessive faith in portable anti-tank guided missiles, and these schemes would therefore be vulnerable to a technological breakthrough rendering these weapons ineffective; some schemes may prove prohibitively expensive despite the comparatively low unit cost of the weapons used; non-offensive defence has little or no capability for protecting interests out of area; and there are major doubts as to whether such schemes have the sustainability necessary to fight to a draw and impose sufficient attrition upon an aggressor (Flanagan, 1988: 112–20; Gates, 1987; McInnes, 1990: 177–83). What is clear from this is that non-offensive defence has yet to prove itself as a practical strategy, despite the value of the principles which underlie it. The 1990s are therefore likely to see further work on non-offensive defence in order to improve its military credibility.

CONCLUSION

Alternative defence developed in the 1980s as more than a single-issue protest movement. Rather it offered a different conception of security to that traditionally pursued by both NATO and the Warsaw Pact. In particular it was critical of a series of assumptions which provided the foundation for NATO's strategic discourse: its state-centric approach; the nature and extent of the threat to security; the nature of the Cold War; the value of deterrence as a security policy; the reliance on nuclear weapons; and the nature of stability. Alternative defence promoted a holistic view of security, with a widened security agenda; it argued for a reduction in superpower hegemony, and for cooperation towards mutual rather than unilateral security; and it developed the concept of non-offensive defence as a more stabilising and secure strategy than deterrence and nuclear reliance. These elements are likely to remain central to alternative defence in the 1990s, and will govern its views concerning the future of European security. What is interesting though is that some of the ideas alternative defence developed in the early 1980s have, by the 1990s, moved into the mainstream of European security: nuclear disarmament, the disintegration of the blocs, a reduction in superpower hegemony, and a widening of the security agenda represent the new orthodoxy. What remains unclear is whether the debate on European security is moving decisively towards alternative defence's security discourse, or whether this represents a degree of synthesis in a dialectical process.

1   In the early 1980s alternative defence was a predominantly Western phenomenon. Within the West it was principally developed in the Federal Republic of Germany and Western Europe as a whole, and had comparatively little impact in the United States. One of the rare exceptions in the East was the Evangelical Church of the GDR (Fritzsche, 1989). By the late 1980s however alternative defence ideas were much more widespread in the East, including the Soviet Union, and were beginning to have an impact upon policy (Bluth, 1990; Holden 1989b: 115–46).

2   For more extensive and detailed criticisms see: Booth, 1985, 1987; Neild, 1981; Thompson and Smith, 1980.

3   For a more detailed examination of non-offensive defence see: Boserup and Neild, 1990; Gates, 1987; McInnes, 1990: 163–84; Unterseher, 1989.

REFERENCES

Arbatov, A. (1990a) 'Defence dilemmas', in A. Boserup and R. Neild (eds), *The Foundations of Defensive Defence*, London: Macmillan.

Arbatov, A. (1990b) 'Problems of defensive defence', in F. Cerutti and R. Ragionieri (eds), *Rethinking European Security*, London: Crane Russak.

Bluth, Christoph (1990) *New Thinking in Soviet Military Policy*, London: Pinter.

Booth, K. (1985) 'The case for non-nuclear defence', in J. Roper (ed.) *The Future of British Defence Policy*, Aldershot: Gower.

Booth, K. (1987) 'Nuclear deterrence and "World War III": how will history judge?', in R. Kolkowicz (ed.), *The Logic of Nuclear Terror*, London: Allen & Unwin.

Booth, K. (1990) 'Steps toward stable peace in Europe: a theory and practice of coexistence', *International Affairs*, **66**,1: 17–45.

Boserup, A. (1990) 'Deterrence and defence', in A. Boserup and R. Neild (eds), *The Foundations of Defensive Defence*, London: Macmillan.

Boserup, A. and Neild, R. (eds) (1990) *The Foundations of Defensive Defence*, London: Macmillan.

Brauch, H. (1989) 'West German approaches to alternative defense', unpublished paper delivered to the joint ISA/BISA annual conference, March–April 1989.

Buzan, B., Kelstrup, M., Lemaitre, P., Tromer, E. and Waever, O. (1990) *The European Security Order Recast: Scenarios for the Post-Cold War Era*, London: Pinter.

Cerutti, F. and Ragionieri, R. (eds) (1990) *Rethinking European Security*, London: Crane Russak.

Dunn, D. (1991) 'Peace research versus strategic studies' in Ken Booth (ed.), *New Thinking about Strategy and International Security*, London: HarperCollins.

Flanagan, S. (1988) *NATO's Conventional Forces: Options for the Central Region*, London: IISS/Macmillan.

Fritzsche, H. (1989) 'The security debate in the Evangelical Church of the GDR', in O. Waever, P. Lemaitre and G. Tromer (eds) *European Polyphony: Perspectives beyond East–West Confrontation*, London: Macmillan.

Gates, D. (1987) 'Area defence concepts: the West German debate', *Survival*, **29**, 4: 301–317.

Gerle, E. (1989) 'From anti-nuclearism to a new détente in the 1980s', in M. Kaldor, G. Holden and R. Falk (eds) *The New Détente: Rethinking East–West Relations*, London: Verso.

142   *Strategy after the Cold War*

Holden, G. (1989) *The Warsaw Pact: Soviet Security and Bloc Politics*, Oxford: Basil Blackwell.
Jane's Defence Weekly (1991) 'Soviets still NATO focus', 25 May 1991, 871.
Johanssen, M. (1990) 'Beyond deterrence through common security', in F. Cerutti and R. Ragionieri (eds) *Rethinking European Security*, London: Crane Russak.
Kaldor, M. (1989) 'The new peace movement and European security', in O. Waever, P. Lemaitre and E. Tromer (eds) *European Polyphony: Perspectives beyond East–West Confrontation*, London: Macmillan.
Kaldor, M. and Falk, R. (eds) (1987) *Dealignment: A New Foreign Policy Perspective*, Oxford: Basil Blackwell.
Kaldor, M., Holden, G. and Falk, R. (eds) (1989) *The New Détente: Rethinking East–West Relations*, London: Verso.
McInnes, C. (1990) *NATO's Changing Strategic Agenda: The Conventional Defence of Central Europe*, London: Unwin Hyman.
Mearsheimer, J. (1990) 'Back to the future: instability in Europe after the Cold War', *International Security*, 15, 1: 5–56.
Migone, G. (1989) 'The decline of the bipolar system, or a second look at the history of the Cold War', in M. Kaldor, G. Holden and R. Falk (eds) *The New Détente: Rethinking East–West Relations*, London: Verso.
NATO (1989) *A Comprehensive Concept of Arms Control and Disarmament*, Brussels: NATO Information Service.
Neild, R. (1981) *How to Make up Your Mind about the Bomb*, London: Andre Deutsch.
Palme, O. (1982) *Common Security: A Programme for Disarmament*, London: Pan.
Podlesnyi, P. (1989) 'Non-military aspects of security: the view of a Soviet scholar', in O. Waever, P. Lemaitre and G. Tromer (eds) *European Polyphony: Perspectives beyond East–West Confrontation*, London: Macmillan.
Ryle, M. and Soper, K. (1989) 'Ecology and the new détente', in M. Kaldor, G. Holden and R. Falk (eds) *The New Détente: Rethinking East–West Relations*, London: Verso.
Statement on the Defence Estimates 1983, vol. I (1983) London: HMSO.
Thompson, E. and Smith, D. (eds) (1980) *Protest and Survive*, London: Penguin.
Tromp, H. (1990) 'Nonoffensive defense and conventional stability in Europe: the wrong problem, the wrong solution', in F. Cerutti and R. Ragionieri (eds) *Rethinking European Security*, London: Crane Russak.
Unterseher, L. (1989) *The Spider and the Web: The Case for a Pragmatic Defence Alternative*, Bonn: SAS.
Vayrynan, R. (ed.) (1985) *Policies for Common Security*, London: SIPRI/Francis Taylor.
Waever, O., Lemaitre, P. and Tromer, E. (eds) (1989) *European Polyphony: Perspectives beyond East–West Confrontation*, London: Macmillan.

Part III

National concerns and perspectives

8 The United States and European security in the 1990s

Michael Brenner and Phil Williams

INTRODUCTION

The revolutions of 1989 in Eastern Europe ushered in a period of immense uncertainty about European security and the transatlantic relationship. The 'bonfire of the certainties', as it was described, created a whole new set of imponderables and ambiguities as the West European states attempted to define their relationship with each other, with the East Europeans, with the Soviet Union and with the United States. For the United States the questions were, if anything, even more formidable. Having defined its role and rationale in the world for over forty years in terms of containment of the Soviet threat, the US discovered that victory in the Cold War was not an unmitigated blessing. The beginning of the post-Cold War era is shaped not by familiar constellations of power but by a fluidity and unpredictability that defy old strategic formulas and structures. An immediate, compelling and direct threat has been replaced by unpredictable risks of contingent circumstances. Their diverse origin and character require a readiness to make discretionary responses to a wide range of contingencies. Although the nature of the challenge has therefore changed, the need to define and maintain a place for the US in the security of Europe remains. What this place is, however, remains elusive. Indeed, in some respects it appears that the US has lost an enemy and not yet found a role.

There are two broad approaches to defining America's role and responsibilities in the post-Cold War era. The first is the kind of holistic approach embodied in the concept of a 'new world order' enunciated by President Bush. This approach is based on a grand if somewhat elusive vision of a world operating in accordance with the precepts of the UN Charter under the benign direction of cooperative great powers. Partly because of the lack of conceptual clarity, and partly because of structural and political constraints, however, it is unlikely that it can provide the basis for a new US role in the world. The alternative is a more pragmatic approach which deals with issues and regions on a case-by-case basis, without an underlying all-embracing philosophy. The rhetoric may suggest that the former approach will prevail. However, the realities of international politics, the urgency of particular problems, and the unwillingness or inability of other states to accept the roles assigned to them by the United States, suggest that the order which develops in the post-Cold War world is unlikely to be that envisaged by President Bush.

This chapter sets out to highlight the main uncertainties hanging over the future of European security and to consider US attitudes towards security institutions in Europe and especially towards European defence cooperation. A concluding section of the chapter offers an assessment and highlights changes of attitude that are necessary in both the United States and Europe if they are to maintain their fruitful partnership.

THE UNCERTAINTIES

Contending with the uncertainties over the future of European security is compounded by the need to confront the wider issues related to the future terms of engagement between the United States and its European allies. The highly institutionalised postwar American defence commitment to Western Europe is likely to be superseded by a somewhat looser relationship. It is one in which the security guarantee *per se* remains, but acquires new shadings of meaning in reference to evolutionary changes in the economic institutions and the community of shared political values which have always been the ultimate foundation for Atlantic security cooperation. The fabric of cooperation itself is likely to change as one constituent element – security cooperation – is modified and rewoven into a different, albeit perhaps still recognisable, pattern.

A diminished security threat is only one of the new threads in what for so long looked a seamless tapestry. The loss of US economic supremacy, and the progress of the European Community towards political union, have raised new question marks over the future transatlantic relationship. Moreover, the mood in which this relationship has to be thrashed out has changed. In the first half of 1990 the mood was one of celebration. Reform was the dictate of success as the Atlantic nations were inspired by the beguiling vision of a world moving inexorably toward democracy and interstate cooperation. Security policy seemed to involve little more than dismantling the military structures and psychological bulwarks of the Cold War. By mid-1991 the prospects had dimmed somewhat. The West has been administered a heavy dose of realism by events not only in the Gulf, but also in Moscow, where the forces of regression and repression seemed to be making a strong comeback, and in the former Communist states of Eastern Europe, where forecasts for democratic consolidation and economic progress have proved overly optimistic.

No longer do we inhabit a political universe wherein anything seems possible – for Western cooperation, for Europe, for world order. The fluid conditions of 1990 encouraged some false hopes (a pan-European collective security system that would remove all concern for military confrontration, and need for military alliances) and some false fears (a powerful Germany carving out a zone of dominance for itself in *Mitteleuropa* at the expense of its Community and Atlantic affiliations). By mid-1991 it was easier to separate the merely conceivable from the plausible, and the visionary from the workable. Yet the uncertainties remain profound. They concern almost every aspect of the European security system – the roles of the former Soviet Union and the United States prominent among them.

The future of the former Soviet Union is particularly murky and of singular importance. One possibility is that its economy will go into freefall. Another is that ethnic and nationalist disputes will erupt into violence. Either could produce political and social disintegration whose effects would be felt well beyond the borders of what was the Soviet Union.

A second set of uncertainties surrounds the future United States role in Europe. US leaders are aware that the United States does not have the same measure of authority, or capabilities, that enabled Washington to direct affairs during an earlier period. Today, the US lacks the abundant economic resources needed to finance a policy of global activism; the world scene lacks a menacing enemy to activate the sense of national mission; and the Alliance is no longer characterised by the automatic deference of the European governments – the factors that together made American leadership seem natural or preordained. Moreover, the end of US supremacy has been accompanied by a growing introversion in the American body politic, and a preoccupation with its troubled domestic affairs. This mood expresses itself in a more parochial approach to international economic issues, and a questioning of what is widely felt to be excessively heavy burdens borne by the United States within the Alliance. The debate over national decline reflected this sense of weariness with leadership responsibilities, borne over the past fifty years, whose costs increasingly seemed to outweigh its privileges.

That national state of mind was relieved by the surrender of Soviet communism in the Cold War, while the demonstration of US military prowess in the Gulf was widely seen as a redemption for Vietnam. The robust response to Saddam Hussein's challenge did much to restore national self-confidence. But it also exposed serious discontinuities in American national strength (its financial weakness) and in the distribution of duties and responsibilities among the liberal democracies. Once the well-earned self-congratulation ends, a sober sense of proportion will return. There is unlikely to be a full revival of the optimism and the activism that were hallmarks of American thinking about foreign affairs a generation or two ago. The world in which America came of age as a superpower has changed too drastically for the keen desire to be the world's custodian of peace and master-builder to be rekindled.

The third set of uncertainties concerns the progress towards European defence cooperation. The attempt to create a European defence identity began in the early 1950s and has undergone a series of false starts since then. During the Cold War, when there seemed to be a clear and present danger, the Europeans were unable to move towards a more coherent and self-reliant stance on defence policy. There were several reasons for this, perhaps the most important of which was the belief that reliance on the United States was the only feasible option given the scale of the Soviet threat. Underlying much of the discussion about European self-reliance was a sense that the Europeans alone could not provide the kind of countervailing power that was necessary to deter the Soviet Union. Moreover, reliance on the United States was very comfortable. It meant that the European allies never had to provide sufficient military capabilities to keep the Russians out, but simply enough to keep the Americans in – by demonstrating that the allies were serious about their own defence. At the same time, there was a concern that if the Europeans did cooperate more fully this could encourage US disengagement – either because Washington would feel that the Europeans were defining their indentity in opposition to US preferences and policies, or because it might conclude that the allies no longer needed American protection. In these circumstances, the fundamental problem was a lack of incentive for serious moves towards greater self-reliance.

Compounding this problem were the differences among France, Britain and Germany. There was never really a triangle of cooperation partly because there was always an odd one out among the three: Germany was not a nuclear power, after 1966 France was outside NATO's integrated organisation, and Britain still regarded itself as an Atlantic rather than a European power and was opposed to many of the moves towards closer European cooperation on defence and security. These differences were reflected in divergent conceptions of a more self-reliant Europe. The French conception was of a European Europe, independent of the United States, acting as a third force in world politics; the British conception of Europe was as a second pillar in the Atlantic Alliance, working very closely with the United States (Lieber, 1973).

The other inhibition to greater European defence cooperation was the attitude of the United States itself. Kenneth Waltz once captured the essence of United States policy when he suggested that Washington wanted a Europe that was strong and independent enough to share burdens but docile and pliant about which burdens were to be shared (Waltz, 1964). Put slightly differently, the United States was always much more interested in burden-sharing than in responsibility sharing. Today, that remains, at least implicitly, the prevailing attitude within the Bush Administration. At the same time, Congressional sentiment leans towards a more drastic scaling-back of US defence commitments and welcomes moves by the European allies that promise to relieve the US of both burdens and responsibilities. There is understandable concern in the White House that the leadership on Capitol Hill will seize on evidence that a self-sufficient European defence entity is taking shape to push retrenchment further and faster than the Administration deems prudent. The net result is to make the Administration's defence planners all the more chary of any innovation that even appears to put in doubt NATO's keystone position.[1] This attitude, coupled with European concerns about continued American protection, has helped to stifle progress towards greater self-reliance.

In the aftermath of the revolutions of 1989 and the trend towards a reduced American military presence in Western Europe, there has been some revitalisation of the idea of West European defence cooperation. The decline of the Soviet Union, the disintegration of the Warsaw Pact, and the independence of Eastern Europe mean that the Soviet threat is no longer as formidable as in the past. This cuts both ways however. While the old sense of futility about European defence cooperation is no longer justified, the incentives for greater cooperation have diminished with the decline in the threat.

The familiar differences among the leading European states have also resurfaced. France, in arguing that the WEU should be integrated into the European Community is still pushing the idea of a European Europe. Britain, in contrast, sees the WEU as the basis for a European pillar in the Atlantic Alliance, and is still thinking in terms of Atlantic Europe. The situation has also been complicated by the tendency of the German Foreign Minister, Hans-Dietrich Genscher, to think in terms of a pan-European Europe. Although the aspirations for a pan-European security system have diminished somewhat through the first half of 1991, the idea of a united Europe is one which follows very logically from the existence of a united Germany. Official German policy supports both the retention of the Atlantic Alliance *and* the creation of a European defence entity, each visualised as a building-block of a continental security system. However, there is a noticeable difference in tone between the utterances of Chancellor Kohl, who stresses NATO, and Herr Genscher, who places the accent on the prospective security role of the European Community. As a consequence the German government has experienced internal stresses while being pulled in different directions by its American and French partners. The fear of Atlanticists, in Bonn as elsewhere, is that the civilian-minded German public may find 'Europeanisation' of the country's defence structures a more acceptable basis for maintaining a military establishment than a NATO tinged with Cold War imagery.

In short, there are no longer simply two competing conceptions of future Europe, instead there are three. The result is great uncertainty about the future direction of Western Europe.

There is even more uncertainty about the future of Eastern Europe. It would be surprising were Eastern Europe not to experience considerable turmoil and instability. The task of revitalising the East European economies is as formidable as it is compelling, and in the event that this does not succeed, the prospect for long-term democratisation and stability in Eastern Europe will be seriously compromised. Moreover, ethnic tensions and the re-emergence of what John Mearsheimer termed 'hyper-nationalism' could result in a series of conflicts in Eastern Europe that, even if they are insulated from great power intervention, could pose a serious challenge to stability on the continent (Mearsheimer, 1990).

These uncertainties yield a range of possible outcomes in Europe. At the optimistic end of the continuum, a best-case analysis foresees the extension of cooperative ventures in Western Europe into Eastern Europe, while a benign former Soviet Union makes a success of liberal reform efforts. A worst-case analysis envisages instability in Eastern Europe precipitating rivalry and mutual anxiety between a declining but much more assertive Soviet Union and a disunited Western Europe characterised by renationalised defence policies. Even if the worst case is avoided, it is possible that the European security system will have to contend with either a revival of nationalist conflicts in an Eastern Europe where ethnic passions have been freed from bloc discipline, and/or a resurgent German nationalism, against a background of political disturbance in a disintegrating Soviet Union.

In these circumstances of continued and profound uncertainty, the best course of action for the United States is a hedging strategy – one which ensures that it continues to participate in an alliance-based security structure in Europe that serves both as an insurance against a reversal of positive trends in the Soviet Union and as a way of dealing with more diffuse challenges that could result from political and economic instability in Central and Eastern Europe. Such a strategy is seen as having the further virtue of preserving the solidarity of the Western partners.

THE UNITED STATES AND EUROPEAN SECURITY IN THE 1990s

If one of the reference points for United States policy towards Europe has to be a vision of future problems, the other is the existing structures of cooperation – NATO, the EC and the Western European Union, and the set of pan-continental security institutions formed under the aegis of the Conference on Security and Cooperation in Europe (CSCE) as outlined in the Paris Charter of November 1990. Combining these structures into a viable security system that adequately addresses the set of interlocking problems facing Europe requires a middle course between, on the one hand, merely extrapolating those institutions that have worked well in the past into the future or, on the other, subjecting everything now in place to a relentless test of self-justification.

The US preference is still very clearly for NATO. The Atlantic Alliance provided the protection, the capacity for united action, and the resolve that enabled the West to prevail in the Cold War. Yet, alliances are contingent and qualified. They are specific as to time, membership and circumstances. NATO itself was a creature of the Cold War. It was the outcome of a concerted effort to secure the West against military attack, action dictated by instincts for political survival. With the dissolution of the Soviet threat, a dissolution of the alliance built to oppose it cannot be excluded.

Indeed, there are several grounds for scepticism about NATO's future. First, by its very nature, NATO has a selective membership. It is built on the principle of differentiation between those states who belong to the organisation (and thereby have exchanged a commitment of support for pledges of mutual help when in need) and those who threaten it (with an implied third category for neutrals or states marginal to its concerns). Second, this strong communality of security interest has been reified in formal structures that integrate command and control arrangements, contingency plans and forces. This institutionalisation, a sign of strength in a polarised international system, none the less limits NATO's flexibility in accepting new members and in adjusting its internal methods of consultation and coordination. Third, as an alliance, NATO is designed to perform military functions. It has limited capacity for mediation of disputes, or conducting negotiations, or directing diplomatic campaigns. Fourth, NATO reflected a particular constellation of power in which the United States provided protection through its nuclear guarantee and its military presence, and the Europeans essentially did enough to legitimise their position as allies who were worthy of protection. The Atlantic relationship was a relationship of inequality. Although this is likely to remain the case throughout the 1990s, the inequalities are likely to diminish as the United States loses economic competitiveness and the Europeans move towards a single economy. The question, therefore, is whether or not NATO can actually transform itself into the equal partnership that was envisaged at the conception of the Alliance and crystallised most coherently in the Kennedy Administration's notion of a twin-pillar alliance.

At first glance, NATO's alliance identity appears poorly suited for addressing the type of security issues that might appear in a new Europe of continental reconciliation amid political flux. Logically, a collective security body, as some have visualised the CSCE, seems a more appropriate conception. A system organised on the principle of universal membership does not differentiate among states by identifying some as threats and others as guardians of the peace, and does not depend on standing forces and a permanent command, simply creating them as necessary. Yet a CSCE-centred collective security system would have drawbacks as well as advantages for handling future security challenges. Most important, its capacity to act could be hostage to consensus politics. In the face of serious threats to the peace, actual consensus becomes far more difficult to achieve than the consensus in principle embodied in the organisation. In other words, it works best when least needed and is likely to be least effective when most needed. The sense of common political identity and collective purpose which is the hallmark of NATO, could all too easily disintegrate under pressure.

For all its weaknesses, however, NATO has been a very untypical alliance. Although the quintessential Cold War security structure, NATO was only the expression in the military field of a wider collective effort at arranging the common affairs of North America and Europe. The Alliance was part of a strategy to build an international network of collaborative enterprises that embraced the integration of commercial markets, the elaboration of monetary and financial structures, and the enhancement of a shared political culture. Hence, over the past forty years, the members of NATO have achieved a bonding, and a shared vision of how international affairs should be ordered, that go far beyond expedient security cooperation. Those assets still have value in post-Cold War Europe.

 The Bush Administration's keen awareness of NATO's attributes underlies its contention that NATO should be the primary instrument for concerting a common Atlantic approach to the reshaping of a European security system. As the one political body that links the United States to Western Europe it is seen as uniquely suited for continent-wide undertakings that, in Washington's eyes, are more likely to succeed if there is a presumption of common interest and shared outlook among the Atlantic partners. From Washington's standpoint, the distinctiveness of the industrial democracies is still the outstanding feature of the international landscape – despite the epochal events of 1989–90. For the Bush Administration, whose leading figures rank as prominent Atlanticists, how the West organises itself, and the unity it shows in addressing a fresh agenda, is the crucial element that will determine the shape of the post-Cold War world (Bush, 1990). The notion of collective political management that is central to President Bush's conception of a 'new world order' is predicated on the continuation of those internationalist attitudes among the Atlantic nations that proved so successful in the programme of postwar construction (Bush, 1990, 1991).

The challenge for President Bush and for his successor is to shape an influential world role for the United States that takes due account of the limits on American power. To do so, the specification of that modified role must conform both to the diffusion of power among friends and allies, and to the inhibitions of the American people about assuming open-ended international obligations. It follows that achieving a more equitable sharing of rights, burdens and accountability with partners is the essential precondition for realising the Bush Administration's vision of a stable world order. This basic truth makes a reconsituted, yet still vigorous, Atlantic partnership the over-riding objective of US foreign policy in the 1990s.

Yet reinvigorating the Atlantic partnership will not be easy. The retreat of Soviet power has removed much of the binding force that gave cause to NATO. Without a compelling threat, divergences have opened over appropriate structures for new conditions. During 1990 the discourse on European security structures often seemed dominated by national tastes and preferences, and characterised by claims for exclusivity and allegations of redundancy.

By mid-1991, the intra-Alliance debate over the relationship between NATO and other, emergent security bodies had regained focus as a result of the resurgence of orthodox forces in Moscow. The Soviet Union now looks an uncertain partner in the building of a 'common European home' free of military threat and ideological conflict. This reinforces Washington's con-servatism on security matters. The Bush Administration has consistently placed premiums on formal structures already in place, with a strong pref-erence for NATO to remain the keystone of Western security planning. While ready to apply a utilitarian standard in assessing proposals for revision of the organisation's forms and modalities, it has sought to preserve NATO as the one political body that links North America and Western Europe. It has looked upon innovative plans for the development of a European defence entity and the construction of a continent-wide security system based on the CSCE, as complements to NATO rather than as alternatives. Accordingly, Washington's primary benchmark for assessing those embryonic institutions has been their meaning for transatlantic solidarity.

At the same time, the Bush Administration has recognised that NATO in its traditional form would maintain neither relevance nor legitimacy in the post-Cold War era. Consequently, the Administration, in conjunction with its allies, has initiated the reform process in NATO to bring it more in line with new political and military realities in Europe. This process starts from the presumption that NATO is not only still relevant but has to contend with a wider and more diverse range of challenges during the 1990s than ever before. This was one of the main conclusions of a NATO study group dubbed the 'Legge Committee' which was set up in early 1991 to review the

Alliance's areas of strategic interest. The Committee's assessment was organised in reference to four classes of threat. The first was the residual Soviet challenge, a challenge that was related both to the continued military strength of the Soviet Union and the intensifying uncertainty about the possible consequences of either disintegration or reversion to dictatorship. In addition, the Legge Committee acknowledged the possibility of, and dangers attendant upon, instability in Eastern Europe. A third area of concern has been identified as threats on the periphery (Turkey during the Gulf War), while a fourth has been the range of contingencies that can arise outside the NATO area of responsibility and where there is no direct threat to the territory of a NATO member. If NATO is to remain effective in providing insurance against this range of contingencies then the Alliance has to change in a variety of ways. The process of adaptation, however, is already well under way.

The reform process has four main thrusts: changes in force posture, changes in strategy (especially the nuclear dimension), changes in the relationship with the nations of Central and Eastern Europe and changes in the balance of roles and responsibilities between the United States and Western Europe.

The changes in force posture were announced at the NATO defence ministers meeting in the spring of 1991 (New York Times, 1991a,b). They signified a shift from high levels of preparedness for deterrence and defence to a more relaxed posture with greater emphasis on flexibility and crisis management. Among the changes were substantial cuts in ready forces, accompanied by greater reliance on reserves, a greater emphasis on multinational forces and a new emphasis on rapid reaction forces. The existing structure of national corps is to be replaced by a structure of multinational corps, two under German command, one under US, one under Dutch, one under Belgian and a combined German–Danish command. In addition, there is to be a single German corps deployed in the Eastern part of Germany and a rapid reaction corps – a 70,000 strong force that will be under British command. The forces themselves have been divided into three categories: Main Defence Forces, Reaction Forces and Augmentation Forces. Although some of the details which still have to be worked out may involve delicate issues relating to command structures in the Alliance, force structure is perhaps the easiest area in which to make reforms.

STRATEGIC PERSPECTIVES

More difficult is the question of strategy, not least because of the difficulty of reconciling German nuclear neuralgia with the French and British conception of nuclear weapons as a key element in guaranteeing security and stability in the new Europe. This split, which was evident at the London

Summit of July 1990, has been one of the reasons why the review of strategy took rather longer than expected. The issue goes well beyond divergent national preferences. The nuclear issue cannot be seen apart from the broader questions about a reunified Germany and its place in the post-Cold War security system. With the reunification of Germany in an atmosphere of East–West reconciliation, Germany's place in the Alliance – its relationship to existing doctrines, force deployments and command structure – can no longer be taken for granted. It is not simply that the country's strategic position has changed from one of predestination to one of free–will – although, in the abstract, that is true. Rather, different circumstances cast old arrangements in a new light. The cardinal feature of the pre-existing situation was Germany's front line status in the Cold War; it was both the central stake in the struggle for power in the postwar Europe, and the prospective battlefield in the event of war. Its vulnerability and geostrategic importance made it dependent on the collective military power of its allies, above all on the nuclear guarantee given tangible expression in the thousands of United States nuclear weapons deployed in Europe and in Germany in particular.

Its apprentice status in the community of liberal democracies reinforced geostrategic inhibitions on efforts to define an alternative security position. Now there is opportunity, as well as reason, to question those elements of the previous system that singularise Germany, especially the nuclear deployments on German soil. The new conditions that alleviate the risk of Germany becoming the battlefield for World War III also open for reexamination the terms of its participation in the Alliance. That process, in turn, forces the Alliance as a whole to think through what arrangements satisfy residual security needs and to contemplate how the interest in fashioning a relationship of positive engagement with the new regimes of East Central Europe (and with the former USSR) gets factored into the equation.

Perhaps the greatest concern of the United States and at least some of the European allies is that Germany will not only be more independent and assertive but will combine this with a pacifism composed of several disturbing elements. The first is a strong reversion of Germany's dual Cold War status as the garrison for resistance to Soviet power and as prospective battlefield. The second is an optimistic reading of developments in Eastern Europe and the Soviet Union. While a third element is a striving to find an influential place in the world that conforms to economic success and new found unity without raising the ghosts of Germany's tragic past.

Such a Germany could be a security liability to the West. It would create a strong political and psychological stake in a benign vision of Europe's future that could make it psychologically difficult to read and respond to signs of a Soviet Union reverting to its antagonistic past. This could undermine Western unity at a time when it would be most needed. The problems run deeper than conjectural differences in assessing future dangers. They could have a detrimental effect on the basics of NATO strategy. A political climate suffused with Euro-optimism, and oriented by a radical break from the postwar past, is likely to generate pressures for the demilitarisation of German territory. Nuclear weapons located in Germany would be the most obvious, and probably immediate, focus of the new iconoclasm.

The challenge of maintaining NATO's nuclear component – and thereby its strategic credibility – in this atmosphere has been starkly drawn by Karl Kaiser (Kaiser, 1990). His point of departure is that nuclear deterrence cannot function effectively without political legitimacy – something that is not always present in democracies. Traditionally, legitimacy was provided by the combination of the presence of a constant threat that kept the always latent nuclear allergy at sub-clinical levels; Soviet conventional superiority; and the practical recognition that nothing degrades deterrent credibility more than worrying about it out loud. The devaluation of nuclear weapons in the present, more reassuring setting opens for public scrutiny the nuclear question. Under those circumstances, the burden of proof shifts to policies and judgements that presume the value of maintaining nuclear arms.

The crucial dilemma for NATO arises from the tension between the residual strategic value of its nuclear weapons and the growing popular aversion to those weapons in an era of apparent peace. The value of nuclear arms is both practical and symbolic. The predominant view sees them as having continuing utility as a counter to large Soviet nuclear forces that could be used for nuclear blackmail and as a residual deterrent to limited conventional aggression. Their intangible value is more difficult to specify, but of greater consequence. First, they are a facilitating element in maintaining domestic support in the United States for the military presence in Europe, albeit at lower levels. Second, they are tangible expressions of the mutual obligations and risks assumed by the United States and the European members of the Alliance. As Karl Kaiser has pointed out, the security guarantee supported by nuclear weapons is a particular expression of Alliance risk-sharing (Kaiser, 1990: 487). Indeed, it is one of the main elements around which the multinational character of the Alliance has been woven.

Kaiser, and other commentators, have become increasingly anxious because of signs that the locus of German strategic thinking is shifting in an anti-nuclear direction. Peacetime deployment of nuclear weapons on German soil is seen as undercutting key elements in the Bonn government's approach to post-Cold War security. The reason is the emphasis placed on a postulated link between the democratisation process in East Central Europe and the presence of nuclear weapons in theatre. The underlying premise is that Germany has a mission to perform in promoting liberal reform and economic development in East Central Europe that would be compromised by a continuing nuclear connection.

There are two ways in which a connection can be made between Germany's status vis-à-vis nuclear weapons and the democratisation process in Eastern Europe. The first points to the uncomfortable fact that many of the tactical systems in the NATO arsenal were intended to hit targets in Eastern Europe. Nuclear artillery and short-range missiles were key elements in NATO's flexible response strategy, serving the dual purpose of providing the means to offset Pact superiority in conventional forces while linking American troop deployments in Europe to the United States' strategic nuclear arsenal. Concrete steps are planned to downplay the importance of these theatre weapons in conformity with revised NATO doctrine, as expressed in the London Declaration of July 1990.

Nevertheless, significant numbers of short-range nuclear forces remain in Europe. They have not yet been the subject of multiple arms control negotiations between NATO and the (former) USSR. It has been an intentional policy to reserve decisions – whether on negotiated arms control or unilateral initiatives – until the conventional threat from the Soviet Union has dissipated with completion of the CFE accords and Soviet forces are completely withdrawn from Eastern Europe. Yet the outlook is for an inexorable move towards reduction of these systems. The retention of ground-based tactical nuclear arms in Germany is seen as losing its strategic rationale and political acceptance.

Anticipating both mounting pressures inside Germany for denuclearisation and a successful outcome from the CFE talks, defence planners in Washington concentrated on the new TASM as the operational link between US conventional forces in Europe and American strategic forces. Viewed as the key to keeping the doctrine of extended deterrence credible, TASM will require a secure basing mode. Washington's preference is that the deployment of TASM will prove acceptable to the Germans. If not, attention will shift elsewhere – to Italy, to Britain, *and* to France (the alternative location that makes most geographic sense). The idea of acquiring access to French air bases, even though they would remain under French control, is much discussed in the Pentagon and would be welcomed by the White House as a contingent alternative to German facilities. The idea has not generated wild enthusiasm in Paris, however.

Such a 'reconstitutional strategy' for NATO's nuclear component, though, creates a new line of discrimination among the European members of the Atlantic Alliance. Instead of being singularised as the front-line state in any future war, Germany would become privileged as a nuclear-free state where weapons-carriers and bases but no warheads would be located. Karl Kaiser argues that this is a necessary price to pay for enabling Germany to serve as a bridge to Eastern Europe. In essence his argument is that a nuclear-free Germany would be a more appealing, and stronger magnet for neighbours to the East who are anxious to avoid great power entanglements (Kaiser, 1990). It is not clear, however, that these countries want to avoid such entanglements. On the contrary, some of them have actively sought a much closer relationship with NATO without raising the question of its nuclear status – in country-specific or general terms. Indeed, this is the third area where the Alliance is taking steps to develop a new set of policies more appropriate to the post-Cold War era.

The range of options for NATO in dealing with Central and Eastern Europe is not particularly extensive. At one extreme, the Alliance could extend the security guarantees that upheld West European security throughout the Cold War to Hungary, Czechoslovakia and Poland. The advantage of this approach is that it would draw the red lines clearly on the map, thereby minimising the possibility of miscalculation, and making it less likely that the former Soviet Union would, at some point in the future, attempt to reintroduce forces into the region. The disadvantage is that it could intensify Soviet paranoia, especially that of the military, thereby encouraging the very thing it is designed to avoid. There is also a disconnect between the idea of extended security guarantees and the fact that defence spending in most NATO members is declining sharply and will continue to do so during much of the 1990s.

At the other extreme, of course, is a stance of indifference towards the Central Europeans. The difficulty with this is that the NATO members are not indifferent to the fledgling democracies of the area, especially now that they are being transformed from a Soviet forward base to a potential buffer zone, and form an economic wasteland to potential customers and trading partners. In between the two extremes of formal guarantees and indifference is the possibility of informal but closer association between the Central European states and NATO. In effect, this appears to be the option that is emerging, albeit by default rather than design (NATO, 1991). Although it has not been fully thought through it is perhaps the least unsatisfactory option for the Alliance, especially if it leads to Central Europe becoming a mutual no-go zone for both the Soviet Union and NATO.

The implication, however, is that there will remain a division of Europe; not the imposed division of the Cold War era, but differences that reflect two cardinal features of continental reality: settled conditions to the West juxta-posed with unsettled conditions in the East, and a heavy burden of geography and history that predestines the states of East Central Europe to the status of a *glacis* between Russia and the West.

While the Bush Administration appears willing to accept such a solution, it is less happy with the notion that extending the 'zone of security and peace' eastward should be accompanied by the development of an independent, West European defence identity. The idea of West European defence cooperation is something on which the United States is extremely ambivalent. There are reasons for supporting it. Washington, like its European allies, has to reconcile plans for a major scaling back of defence budgets and force levels with a more sombre assessment of Soviet capabilities. This has strengthened the Bush Administration's conviction that there has to be a shift in roles and responsibilities within the Alliance, while casting a favourable light on proposals to promote defence cooperation among the European Allies. Washington knows that a Western Europe that can act as a viable security partner offers the soundest basis for ensuring a continued American security presence on the continent that meets a standard of both public acceptability and Alliance unity. Furthermore, Washington has an interest in hearing a more coherent European view rather than what WEU Secretary-General Willem van Eekelen described as the usual cacophony of attitudes (van Eekelen, 1990a,b). This interest is underscored by the divisiveness that characterised European diplomacy during the Gulf crisis.

Yet there are also drawbacks for the United States in greater European defence cooperation. A single European voice on security matters, along with an organisational vehicle for expressing it, would challenge the United States' traditional dominance over Alliance policy. While this is a price the Bush Administration, in principle, is prepared to pay, in practice it is reluctant to accept it. In essence, the Administration wants European defence cooperation on United States terms. The prevailing conception of the WEU in Washington is one that visualises it serving primarily as an institutionalised caucus within a NATO framework and only secondarily as capable of taking concerted action on its own. While it is accepted that a European perspective has a legitimate right to assert itself, US support for such an assertion of European interests and perspectives is highly qualified. It is acceptable only if it is not done at the expense of the United States or the Atlantic link.

Indeed, by mid-1991 the debate over European defence cooperation had echoes of the debates of the early 1970s even though they lacked the acrimony of the exchanges between Henry Kissinger and French Foreign Minister, Monsieur Jobert. As in the 1970s, the debate was essentially one between the proponents of Atlantic Europe and those of European Europe. The United States was supported by Britain, the Netherlands and Portugal in arguing that the WEU should, in effect, become the European pillar of NATO. The French, however, argued very strongly in favour of a proposal which originated with Italian Foreign Minister Gianni de Michelis, and which envisaged the WEU becoming the European Community's defence wing.

The Bush Administration strenuously opposed the idea that the WEU should take instruction from the European Council or become subject to supervision by the European Community's foreign affairs commissioner. Such a design was seen as undesirable on two grounds. One was that it would open the WEU to guidance by European Community governments who are not NATO members and who do not share its outlook on security issues – today, Ireland; tomorrow, perhaps Austria, Sweden and Finland. The second and perhaps more fundamental objection was that such an arrangement would transform the flexible intra-Alliance process of consultation and deliberation into formal exchanges between the United States and the EC.[2] Not only would such a development undermine the cohesion of the Alliance, and encourage a transatlantic fault line, it would also mean that American influence in Europe – and its ability to moderate competitive economic policies by the Europeans – would diminish. Accordingly, Washington discouraged the drafting of blueprints for a modified treaty relationship between the US and its European allies.

The command status of European troops earmarked for both NATO and WEU/EC deployment raised another set of irksome issues. Security planners in Washington became concerned about several possible arrangements along these lines. They were particularly unenthusiastic about the possibility that an autonomous European capacity would exist to engage European forces in areas sensitive to the United States such as the Middle East. For different reasons Eastern Europe is also a sensitive area. There too, security planners in the Bush Administration are looking askance at the idea of the Western Europeans having an independent capability to take action on the sensitive periphery of the former USSR. The European supporters of a WEU/EC link offer the counterview that were disturbed conditions in Eastern Europe (e.g., a Hungary–Romania border conflict) to require outside intervention, it would appear less threatening to Moscow to have any Western action undertaken without US participation. As for a major threat from a resurgent Soviet Union, they believe it unimaginable that they and the US would not act jointly whatever the exact form of continental security architecture.

While such American concerns are the reverse side of the longstanding grievance about the reluctance of allies to participate on a proportionate basis in crises like that in the Gulf, they reflect a deep seated anxiety that at least some Europeans are gradually but inexorably moving away from NATO as the security institution of first resort. This is evident too in American concerns not so much over the creation of multinational European units as over the possibility that, at some time in the future, the preponderant European forces earmarked for NATO will fall under separate European commands.

For some Europeans, of course, these signs of discomfort are interpreted as evidence that what the United States really wants is not increased burden-sharing or a new division of labour but pliable allies who will continue to accept United States leadership, and who will accept both Washington's demands for support and its veto on independent European actions. Indeed, the concluding section identifies some of the tensions in United States policy towards Europe and highlights changes in attitude that must take place on both sides of the Atlantic if the Alliance is to survive, let alone prosper, through the 1990s.

CONCLUSIONS

It is arguable that the Atlantic relationship is elastic enough to permit the crystallisation of a European defence personality without jeopardising the overall pattern of cooperation. A WEU that serves simultaneously as a European caucus within NATO and a vehicle for concerting action among its self-selected membership is capable of bridging NATO and the EC. It is true, of course, that in the process of accommodating this new security reality, the Alliance would change and would lose some of the past cohesion provided by American leadership and a common interest in the perpetuation of NATO. Yet some loss of cohesion is inevitable – in the light of changes in the Soviet Union, shifting power relations between the United States and its European allies, and differentiated responses to the challege of fostering stable conditions in Eastern Europe, and to out-of-area issues. It is unrealistic to expect the West Europeans to shelter contentedly under the US security umbrella, for the allies to march in complete unison on the multifaceted campaign to extend their zone of cooperation and security eastward, or for them readily to compose their differences in how they perceive situations in other regions. Indeed, the Gulf crisis illustrated once again the problems and constraints faced by NATO when it attempts to act beyond the area of its formal responsibility. NATO was created for a specific purpose and proposals to extend its role and responsibilities to the Third World have not only been controversial but ultimately unsuccessful.

In the final analysis the problems lie on both sides of the Atlantic. The traditional divisions about the nature of a European defence identity are as alive today in Western Europe as they were in the 1960s, the 1970s and the 1980s. Moreover, the familiar US ambivalence towards European defence cooperation tends to exacerbate the internal divisions in Europe between Atlanticists and Europeanists. The irony is that the Bush Administration is very anxious that the Atlantic partners act together. In its view the break-up of the communist bloc should not be the prelude to the loosening of the bonds of solidarity in the West. Such a loosening would undermine the delicate enterprise of maintaining a constructive, yet wary engagement with the former USSR and would risk frustration and unpleasant surprises in the campaign to foster stable democracies in Eastern Europe.

At the same time, the Bush Administration has a powerful interest in the emergence of a Europe able and willing to act in concert on security matters. This would compensate for the draw down of American troops to somewhere between 100,000 and 150,000 over the next few years and would also help to transform the Atlantic relationship into a true partnership. The danger is that the centrifugal force of national instincts and habits will prevent the Europeans from taking the steps to create the capability, and to generate the will, to assume a fuller measure of responsibility for protecting their common interests.

This would be extremely unfortunate. Indeed, the costs, present and prospective, of maintaining the status quo in the Atlantic Alliance are approaching intolerable levels. Making the necessary adjustments, however, requires overcoming a formidable inertia, an inertia rooted in nearly half a century of postwar history and strengthened by success. In the final analysis, the issue is not one of organisation. However reconstituted, the long-term viability of the Alliance – and the entire network of interwoven relations associated with it – depends more on attitude than on structure. Certain features of the future situation are indisputable: above all, a larger, and more distinct European voice on all matters of concern to the Atlantic nations. The open questions are the interrelated ones of what presumptions will prevail about how to deal with the outside world they inhabit, and how collective business will be handled internally.

Achieving a more equitable sharing of responsibilities is only possible if there is a broad consensus on interests, purposes, and methods for realising them. Acceptance in principle and practice that all parties must be prepared to shoulder burdens, in turn, is the condition for facing squarely differences in interpreting the realities they are bound to deal with collectively. In the pithy words of EC President Jacques Delors: a unity of action demands a unity of analysis. Otherwise, the Alliance will be capable only of 'disparate, ill-prepared and insufficiently reasoned action' – or, fall back on the tradition of directive American leadership (Delors, 1991).

Some of these differences will survive any adjustment of Alliance responsibilities and will complicate the task of forging common policies and coordinating action. But at that point, the allies will be compelled to distinguish between genuine differences and those that reflect a desire to affirm separateness for its own sake.

European acceptance of larger responsibilities, of course, needs to be matched by an American readiness to let go of the exceptional powers it has enjoyed as leader of the Alliance. Vanity, as well as concern for practical effectiveness, lead some to claim the indispensability of US direction, albeit trimmed to reflect current economic realities. A sober appraisal suggests otherwise. The era of American supremacy is coming to a close and if the Atlantic relationship is to survive through the 1990s and beyond it must move towards the genuine partnership that was envisaged by the founders of the Alliance in 1949.

NOTES

1 This attitude was evident from statements made by senior Administration officials on the occasion of the promulgation of NATO's plan for revised force structures in May 1991 and was particularly so with Secretary of Defense Cheney's press conference at the conclusion of the Defence Planning Committee (DPC) and Nuclear Planning Group (NPG) Ministerial-level meetings on 29 May 1991. See also informal remarks reported in Washington Post 27 and 28 May 1991.

2 A precedent of sorts was set at the EC summit on 8 April 1991 when France (the then President of the WEU) convened a meeting of WEU foreign ministers to consider implementation of a collective EC-sponsored airlift to aid the Kurdish refugees. The participation of the EC's foreign affairs commissioner was also a noteworthy innovation.

REFERENCES

Bush, G. (1990) Remarks at the CSCE Conference, Paris, 19 November 1990, Washington: United States Information Service.

Bush, G. (1991) Talk on US Aims in the Gulf War, 28 January 1991, Washington: United States Information Service.

Delors, J. (1991) 'European integration and security', *Survival*, **33**, 2: 99–109.

Kaiser, K. (1990) 'From nuclear deterrence to graduated conflict control', *Survival*, **32**, 6: 483–96

Lieber, R. (1973) 'Britain joins Europe', in A. Jones (ed.) *United States Foreign Policy in a Changing World*, New York: McKay.

Mearsheimer, J. (1990) 'Back to the future: instability in Europe after the Cold War', *International Security*, **15**, 1: 5–56.

NATO (1991) *Final Communiqué of the Ministerial Meeting of the North Atlantic Council in Copenhagen, 6–7 June 1991*, Brussels: NATO Information Service.

New York Times (1991a) 31 May 1991.

New York Times (1991b) 2 June 1991.

van Eekelen, W. (1990a) 'WEU and the Gulf crisis', *Survival*, **32**, 6: 519–33.

van Eekelen, W. (1990b) 'Building a new European security order', *NATO Review*, **38**, 4: 18–23.

Waltz, K. (1964) 'The stability of a bipolar world', *Daedalus*, **93**, 3: 881–909.

9 The development of Soviet strategies in Europe

Caroline Kennedy

On coming to power in March 1985, Gorbachev almost immediately signalled his intention to develop closer relations with the West European States. This chapter examines and assesses the evolution of Soviet foreign policy in the period 1985–91. It looks at the new key concept in Moscow's strategies – the idea of a 'Common European Home'. In the period 1985–7, Moscow urged that this idea represented the basis on which a new security structure could be forged. This new vision called for the removal of nuclear weapons, and the reduction of conventional forces. At first, the strategy of denuclearisation appeared to succeed with the signing in 1987 of the INF treaty. Furthermore, Gorbachev managed to reanimate conventional arms talks by means of a series of radical concessions.

The rapid erosion of communist power throughout Eastern Europe in 1989 overtook Moscow's initiatives. The Gorbachev leadership had to deal with the collapse of the Warsaw Pact, the unification of Germany and the emergance of sovereign states on its borders. The result of these changes was that Moscow was no longer dictating the pace of change in European security affairs but rather was struggling to maintain some semblance of control.

SOVIET-RUSSIAN STRATEGIES IN EUROPE

In a speech to the Supreme Soviet in February 1985, Gorbachev announced that the USSR considered a normalisation of relations with the US to be important but 'we are not forgetting for a single moment that the world is not limited to that country alone.' (*Pravda*, 20 February 1985). Some Western analysts believed that Gorbachev would downgrade the connection with Washington in favour of strengthening links with the Western Europeans. In particular they pointed to the manner in which the Soviet leader enunciated the idea of a Common European Home, which appeared to exclude an American troop presence. During Gorbachev's visit to London in December 1984, he referred to Europe as 'our common house' (*nash obshchii dom*), and

Pravda subsequently commented that 'Washington is a stranger to that house.' (*Pravda*, 13 November 1985). Inherent in this idea was the belief that the European countries shared common interests; Soviet analysts claimed that not only was Europe bound together by geography, but also by 'historical ties' including a common political culture. (Bovin, 1985). Soviet spokesmen even asserted that European political standards were superior to those in the US. It was in Europe that the 'norms of peaceful coexistence were worked out' and the 'cowboy attitude to the problems of war and peace currently prevalent in the US is not typical of present day Europe' (Bovin, 1985).

This apparent anti-Americanism led some Western analysts to conclude that Moscow intended to force US troops out of Europe, and weaken the cohesion of the Western Alliance. Soviet strategies were not, however, as crude as this; what Moscow's policies were designed to do was primarily to strengthen economic and political ties with the Western Europeans, but also to put pressure on Washington. In the early 1980s, Soviet commentators had hoped that Western Europeans would oppose what Moscow perceived as the destabilising trends of the first Reagan Administration. In particular, Moscow attempted to inflate opposition to the SDI programme and to the presence of US medium-range missiles in Europe. West European anxieties over the SDI programme were eagerly reported in the Soviet press and there were evidently hopes of using them to exert a restraining effect on the US administration (Bovin, 1985). By the mid-1980s, however, Moscow's experience was that it was impossible to separate the US from Western Europe and that the forces which bound the centres of imperialism together were stronger than those which drew them apart (*Izvestiya*, 20 July 1986). Any hopes that the Moscow leadership had had that the West would splinter over security issues had been refuted by Western cohesion over the deployment of Cruise and Pershing II missiles in Europe. In the Gorbachev period, Soviet leaders denied any intention of attempting to break up the North Atlantic Alliance. Gorbachev commented that 'disrupting the existing political and territorial set up in Europe would result only in chaos and the worsening of the situation', and, in his book *Perestroika*, denied any such intent: 'we are far from minimizing the historical bonds which exist between Western Europe and the United States. It is absurd to treat the European policies of the Soviet Union as an expression of some anti-Americanism.' (Gorbachev, 1987)

Despite the emphasis upon West European affairs, relations with Washington remained central to Gorbachev's Westpolitik. This was apparent at the Soviet domestic level, where there was a pre-eminence of the Amerikansky in the central decision-making apparatus. At the international level it was manifested in the almost complete reversal of anti-American positions and rhetoric to which Brezhnev, Andropov and Chernenko had so tenaciously clung. The fact that Gorbachev had to place arms control at the top of his political agenda meant that any efforts to lessen the arms competition had to be directed towards the US rather than to Western Europe. It was with the former, not the latter, that Moscow had to negotiate.

THE INF AGREEMENT

One characteristic of Soviet new thinking on security was a marked accentuation of the anti-nuclear theme which had emerged during Brezhnev's last years. Nuclear war began to be redefined as nuclear catastrophe. Nuclear winter research only reinforced this assessment. In January 1986, Gorbachev set out his three-stage agenda for global nuclear disarmament. It became apparent, despite the Utopian tenor of this programme, that the denuclearisation of Europe had become a high Soviet priority on both political and military grounds. Soviet officials emphasised the inevitability of nuclear release at any level escalating into a full scale nuclear exchange. Although Soviet forces remained equipped with a whole range of nuclear weapons, and military texts continued to describe the integrated use of nuclear and non-nuclear firepower in theatre warfare, it had become apparent that the Soviet leadership had decided that the new juxtaposition of land-based shorter and medium-range nuclear missiles in Europe had enhanced the potential for crisis instability. The Gorbachev leadership, in all probability, realised that the 'war-fighting' capability of their theatre nuclear 'deterrent' forces had created ambiguity about Moscow's intentions for the West European states. This was particularly dangerous now that Soviet territory was directly threatened by the new 'Euro' missiles. This specific concern fed into a broader Soviet reappraisal of the military basis of security. Soviet leaders now emphasised that additional increments of military power did not necessarily yield greater security. In particular it was recognised that the initial deployment of SS-20 missiles had led to NATO counter deployments, and thus to an overall reduction in Soviet security.

The new Soviet foreign policy acknowledged that Soviet military capabilities had generated a perception of threat in Western states. In 1988 Razmerov, the deputy head of the department of international relations at IMEMO, declared that the USSR was perceived as a profoundly hostile concentration of political and military power, inclined to expansion and to the manipulation of military force as the main instrument for attaining its ends. This was recognised as a factor in European reluctance to conclude arms control agreements. Correspondingly, an improvement in the strategic climate would depend on a mitigation of the Soviet threat. This required not an abandonment of the European element, but rather closer attention to the region's security policy. Soviet spokesmen were careful to emphasise the 'European' aspect of the INF agreement, despite the fact that it was a superpower bilateral agreement. Indeed, Soviet concessions during the negotiations towards the INF treaty can be interpreted as part of a broader diplomatic effort to reshape West European security thinking.

The concessions made by Moscow during the INF negotiations are worthy of some consideration. First, Moscow agreed to the long standing Western assertion that French and British nuclear arsenals were separate and independent, and that they should not be included in the agreement but should be discussed in a future round of strategic cuts. Hitherto, the USSR had demonstrated considerable concern over the projected modernisation of the British and French forces. This Soviet concession signalled recognition that Western nuclear decision making was not monolithic and that states had the right to negotiate separately. It also signalled rejection of the traditional notion that the USSR had to be as strong militarily as any potential coalition of antagonistic powers. In order to achieve an agreement, Gorbachev was compelled to exercise pragmatism and compromise. As Shevardnadze explained in February 1988: 'the maintenance of deadlock at the talks on the English and French systems would have meant the absence of any accord at all'.

Moscow recognised that the West Europeans perceived a massive Soviet threat, and that as a result London and Paris would not readily dismantle their nuclear systems. By agreeing to postpone their inclusion, Moscow could secure an immediate agreement on Western theatre systems and could use this experience to allay European fears and undercut any future rationale for independent forces. An agreement on INF also meant that the French and British forces would no longer be tied to US forces so that European nuclear arms could be negotiated separately in the future.

A second major concession made by Moscow was their agreement to dismantle a great many more missiles than the Western states. This suggests a fundamental reassessment of the value of the SS-20 missiles. Bessmertnykh, who was at this time a deputy foreign minister, criticised the original deployment for over-emphasising military considerations and underrating political criteria. The decision to withdraw the missiles conformed to the new thinking on nuclear weapons and in particular to the aim of denuclearisation in Europe. Soviet leaders stressed the benefits for European security when they stated that an important feature of the INF treaty was that Europe would no longer be safe for limited nuclear war.

In more general terms, following on from this new assessment of security, the Soviet political leadership understood that their military 'assets' could be traded for increments in the political basis of security. Some Soviet evaluations of the SS-20 deployment pointed out the disastrous effects it had had, specifically on relations with the West Europeans. An article in 1988 commented that:

> The long experience of elaborating the treaty on intermediate-range and shorter-range missiles is a progeny of difficult mistakes in our policy in Europe... the decision to replace SS–4 and SS–5 missiles with more sophisticated SS-20 missiles was motivated by technological advances rather than by political analysis.
>
> (Vybornov *et al.*, 1988)

It is the politically successful nature of the INF treaty which Soviet leaders stress. Vorontsov, the first deputy minister of foreign affairs stated that:

> Arithmetical calculations of the correlation of weapons in terms of each type were not the only things to be taken into account, but that it was necessary to give the whole cause of nuclear disarmament a decisive push forward to make the first step – which is always the most difficult – towards this end.
>
> (SWB, 1988b)

The Soviet political leadership hoped that this agreement on nuclear systems would open the way for more arms control agreements. Leading Politburo member Ligachev for example stated that:

> [This] treaty can and must open the way towards a 50 per cent reduction in strategic offensive weapons of the USA and Soviet Union, stopping nuclear tests, eradication of tactical, nuclear and conventional weapons and armed forces and a ban on chemical weapons.
>
> (SWB, 1988a)

It was believed that Europe was fertile ground for such an approach.

Gorbachev was the first Soviet leader to understand the link between nuclear and conventional arms control. His view was made clear at the December 1987 Washington superpower summit (the occasion for the formal signing of the INF Treaty) when the Soviet leader acknowledged a need to address the issue of conventional force asymmetry: Soviet political leaders accepted that conventional cuts were a necessary step before further nuclear arms cuts. One Soviet commentator stated that:

> Nuclear disarmament is not possible without conventional disarmament because nuclear weapons are regarded as an insurance against conventional weapons being used and for as long as the concentration of forces on one side or the other appears threatening or dangerous to the other side.
>
> (Moscow Home Service, 15 January 1989)

This approach demonstrated a much greater awareness than hitherto of the linkage in official Western circles between Soviet conventional forces and Western nuclear requirements.

MILITARY DOCTRINE AND CONVENTIONAL ARMS CONTROL

In the pre-Gorbachev period, two premises underpinned the Warsaw Pact approach to conventional arms cuts in Europe. The first was that the territorial status quo had to be maintained, while the second was the refusal to countenance suggestions that the Warsaw Pact possessed a numerical superiority over NATO. However, by 1987, the Soviet political élite had formulated a new approach to military doctrine which profoundly affected the 'old' assumptions in Europe. The 'new' military doctrine contained the following five key ideas: first, that the prevention of war is the most fundamental objective of Soviet military doctrine; second, that war cannot in any circumstances be considered the continuation of politics; third, that security is interdependent; fourth, that security cannot depend upon military technical means alone; and fifth, that Soviet security requirements must be based upon new ideas of 'defensive defence' and 'reasonable security' (Bluth, 1990: 237). It was this latter concept that was most crucial to the new approach to arms control in Europe. In essence it signified that the East merely required forces that were adequate for defence. This meant that the East could abandon its traditional emphasis upon offensive operations with its corresponding requirements for large forces.

The first indication of the new Soviet approach came in April 1986. During a visit to East Germany, Gorbachev proposed the reduction of conventional forces in Europe, 'from the Atlantic to the Urals'. This call was elaborated in the 'Budapest' appeal of the Political Consultative Committee of the Warsaw Pact on 11 July 1986 and again in May 1987. At its meeting in Berlin, the Warsaw Pact officially adopted 'reasonable sufficiency' and 'defensive defence' as its new military doctrine. At the meeting, it was stated that the Warsaw Pact would 'strictly comply with the limits of sufficiency for defence, for repelling possible aggression'. The Pact aimed to rectify numerical imbalances and aimed at the 'reduction of the armed forces (such that) neither side while ensuring its defence, would have the means for making a surprise attack on the other side or for starting offensive operations in general'. It also pointed to the need to prevent the threat of surprise attack and to withdraw the most 'offensive' types of weapons from zones of contact. However, despite this public commitment, a central issue was the extent to which these declarations of principles and proposals elaborated at Berlin would actually be adopted by the Soviet leadership, as these issues had generated an intense debate among the Soviet political and military élites.

As early as 1986, it was apparent that some senior Soviet military officers did not wholly share Gorbachev's vision of a new 'politicised' military doctrine or indeed his benign vision of the West. Army General Valentin Varennikov, for example, the then deputy chief of the General Staff, stated that:

> The Soviet Union cannot fail to take into account that in practice imperialism still leans on military aspects... the USA and the other NATO countries are not heading for agreement. To the contrary, they are striving in every way possible to break out into the lead in the military technical aspect.
>
> (Varennikov, 1987)

Even in the wake of the Berlin declaration, Kulikov stated that the Western threat to the USSR was real. Marshal Akhromeev expressed reservations about Western ambitions and accused the West of still trying to attain 'world supremacy' (*Krasnaia Zvezda*, 9 May 1987).

The debate over the meaning and implementation of a doctrine of 'reasonable sufficiency' became more intense during 1987–8. In March 1986 in a report to the Party Congress, Gorbachev had put forward his view of what reasonable suffficiency should mean. In particular he spoke of it as 'purely defensive in nature' (*Pravda*, 7 March 1986). In a speech to the Trade Union Congress in February 1987, Gorbachev stated that in line with reasonable sufficiency 'we will not take a single step over and above the demands and requirements of reasonable, sufficient defence' (*Pravda*, 26 February 1987). Gorbachev was trying to achieve two goals through this endorsement of a new military doctrine. First, he wanted to place a lower priority upon defence needs and make corresponding cuts in the defence budget, but second, he wanted to assert the control of civilian members of the party over military affairs.

It would seem to have been Gorbachev's insistence upon making unilateral cuts which particularly incurred military opposition. The Soviet military were determined that any arms reductions had to be reciprocal. General Moiseev stated that reasonable sufficiency had to 'depend upon the position and the actions of the USA and NATO as a whole' (Skorodenko, 1989). In January 1989 Marshal Akhromeev stated that although he supported the need for military reforms there were limits:

> Defence sufficiency cannot be interpreted one sidedly, without regard to the developing correlation of forces. It would be even more of a mistake to understand it as unilateral disarmament or unilateral lessening of our defence.
>
> (FBIS-SOV, 1988)

Despite military reservations, in December 1988 Gorbachev announced unilateral force reductions in line with his interpretation of the new Soviet military doctrine based on principles of reasonable sufficiency and defensive defence. This involved a total reduction of 500,000 troops, including 50,000 from Eastern Europe. Six tank divisions were to be withdrawn from Eastern Germany, Czechoslovakia and Hungary and disbanded. Assault landing troops and bridging equipment were also to be withdrawn. In total, 10,000 tanks, 8,500 artillery units and 800 aircraft were to be withdrawn from Eastern Europe and the European part of the USSR. In protest at this, Marshal Akhromeev announced his resignation.

THE CFE TALKS

Mainly because of the unilateral cuts in conventional Soviet forces in Europe, by January 1989 a mandate for negotiation on conventional armed forces in Europe had been agreed and the CFE negotiations began in Vienna on 8 March 1989. NATO put forward its proposals which emphasised the desirability of reducing equipment. NATO proposed overall ceilings on equipment within the Atlantic to the Urals (ATTU) region (specifically tanks, artillery and armoured personnel carriers) and a 'sufficiency rule' according to which no country would be permitted to have more than 30 per cent of its overall total of equipment in the ATTU area. NATO also wanted four inner zones in the region, each with its own sub-limits, the purpose of which would be to restrict the possibilities for a surprise attack. The Warsaw Pact, on the other hand, proposed a three-stage scheme for disarmament in the region. It was envisaged that the stages take place from 1991–4, 1994–7 and from 1997–2000. The Warsaw Pact sought the restructuring of both alliances onto strictly non-offensive principles. In particular, the Warsaw Pact wanted to include shorter range nuclear systems which conformed to their desire for the denuclearisation of Europe. They also wanted to include naval forces in the CFE talks as a way of limiting an area of Western superiority (an initiative resisted by NATO). Finally the Warsaw Pact attempted to negotiate limits on NATO aircraft which could be used for the new strategy of follow-on forces attack (FOFA).

The CFE talks were interrupted by what became known as the Bush Plan, announced during the NATO summit in Brussels on the 19 May 1990. The American President declared that the United States was prepared to accept a limit of 275,000 American and Soviet ground and air personnel stationed outside national boundaries in the ATTU area. He also announced the expansion of the NATO proposal to include reductions to equal ceilings in numbers of helicopters and all land based aircraft in the ATTU area at a level of 15 per cent below current NATO levels. In January 1990, Bush amended these proposals to a limit of 195,000 American and Soviet troops in Central Europe, but with the United States permitted to keep another 30,000 troops in an 'outer zone' comprising Italy, Spain, Turkey and the UK. This proposal required a reduction of some 60,000 American and 370,000 Soviet troops inside the Central Front, but the 20,000 American troops in Europe outside the zone meant that the USSR was accepting a position of near conventional inferiority in the Central Front. Despite this, the plan was accepted by Soviet Foreign Minister Shevardnadze at the foreign ministers' meeting in Ottawa in February 1990 (Bluth, 1990).

The interesting question is why Moscow accepted such a proposal. By early 1990, Moscow had very little choice but to try and maintain a holding operation of its position in Eastern Europe and particularly in Eastern Germany. Even as the CFE talks proceeded, the Soviet position was profoundly influenced by the events in Eastern Europe. The collapse of communist power throughout the Eastern bloc and the movement towards German unification undermined the very premise upon which the CFE talks had been founded, namely the existence of a two-bloc structure in Europe. In 1990, Moscow was left trying to salvage something of its former position in the Eastern bloc.

MOSCOW AND THE GERMAN QUESTION

For many years before 1990, the USSR and the Federal Republic of Germany had shared a common interest in détente and in particular in economic cooperation, but on the West German side this was always placed against loyalties and attachments to the West and on the Soviet side by a fear of German influence in the East. Initially Kohl compared Gorbachev to Goebbels, and the Soviet press continued to complain about 'German revanchism' and 'militarism'. From 1987 onwards, however, as it became obvious that Moscow was prepared to accept radical reforms in Eastern Europe, Moscow and Bonn began to move closer together. The central question for the USSR's European diplomacy was the problem of the security status of the soon-to-be-unified German state. After the opening of the Berlin Wall, the Soviet leadership was cautious in its comments on the possibility of German unification, but in February 1990 Gorbachev said that this was a question for the Germans themselves to decide but that the settlement could not be dealt with in isolation from an overall European security context and the building of new structures in Europe. At this stage, Soviet commentators were still hopeful that the process would be protracted, one that would take years not months to complete (*Pravda*, 11 February 1990). It was stated repeatedly that NATO membership for the united Germany was totally unacceptable. In April, Gorbachev declared that NATO membership for a unified Germany would not be tolerated by the Soviet people, while Soviet spokesmen began to put forward the idea once more of a Common European Home, with new security structures in which the division of Germany could not be overcome without overcoming the separation of Europe. Valentin Falin, the head of the Central Committee's International Department, proposed that German neutrality, guaranteed by the other thirty-three Helsinki signatories would be the best solution (Holden, 1989). In talks with the Chairman of the EC Council of Ministers in April 1990, Gorbachev stated that unification must be simultaneous with the process of creating a new European security system. Foreign Minister Shevardnadze suggested that Germany might be a member of both military alliances, and in his speech to the '2 plus 4' foreign ministers in May, emphasised the dangers of unification. As an alternative he offered the idea of a 'greater Europe' security mechanism, which would act in conjunction with the '2 plus 4.' By May, the Soviet position had softened and Gorbachev was suggesting that Germany might participate in NATO, but on the same basis as France – that is that the country remain outside the integrated military command structures, an option rejected by West German Defence Minister Stoltenberg.

The underlying thread of the Soviet position on Germany was an attempt to solve the problem through a neutrality guaranteed by all-European security structures. At the opening of the CSCE human rights meeting in Copenhagen, for example, Shevardnadze and Baker discussed plans for drawing up a political agreement between NATO and the Warsaw Pact. The Soviet Foreign Minister put forward proposals for the strengthening of the CSCE process. He suggested a council of heads of state which would meet every two years; a committee of foreign ministers, which would meet more frequently and a permanent secretariat with a centre for ensuring stability (*Izvestiya*, 6 June 1990). However, the major flaw in this Soviet scheme was that it did not take account of the speed with which the two Germanys were moving towards unification. Indeed, although the Soviet side continued to put forward suggestions for the resolution of the German problem within new pan-European structures, it was premised upon the continued existence of two political blocs. On 11 June 1990, in Brest-Litovsk, Shevardnadze held a meeting with Genscher concerning Germany's membership of NATO. They discussed prospects for a new type of relationship between NATO and the Warsaw Pact, while on 22 June at the second ministerial meeting in the '2 plus 4' series, Shevardnadze suggested that for a five-year period after unification, East Germany should continue to be a member of the Warsaw Pact. Any progress towards full unification would, the Soviet Foreign Minister suggested, be dependent upon agreement on all-European security structures to eventually replace the existing arrangements. However, despite Moscow's professed desire for a new pan-European security structure, given its economic and political weakness it had little to bargain with, against a Western Alliance determined to maintain the cohesion of NATO.

On 15 July 1990, talks began in Moscow between Gorbachev and Kohl, and an agreement was reached on the conditions for German unification. Moscow succumbed to the Western demand that Germany should be free to choose which alliance it wished to belong to; that Soviet troops would be withdrawn from the Eastern part of the country over a maximum period of four years; that in this interim period, only German territorial defence troops would be present on that territory; and that German forces would be reduced to an overall total of 370,000 in a four-year period. Germany would also renounce the manufacture or possession of nuclear, chemical and biological weapons, and Bonn agreed to sign treaties with Moscow on political, security and economic relations which would provide German financial support for the relocation of Soviet forces which had been stationed on East German soil (Malcolm, 1990: 46). When this treaty for German unity was signed at the final '2 plus 4' session, Moscow pressed to extract economic concessions in return for its acquiescence. In particular the Soviet political leadership wanted Bonn to take on the formidable responsibilities of supplying industrial and consumer goods to Eastern Europe and the USSR. The Federal Republic agreed to a twenty-year agreement on economic, industrial and technical cooperation and agreed to contribute DM12 billion towards the cost of rehousing Soviet troops removed from Eastern Germany (Malcolm, 1990: 46).

This agreement on German unity was not officially tied to the conventional arms talks taking place in Vienna, but the resolution of the German issue opened the way for a resolution of differences in the CFE talks. Moscow still pressed for some form of compensation for their withdrawal from Eastern Europe and for the fact that the Warsaw Pact was no longer a functioning military alliance. In particular they argued that the sufficiency rule should be amended to allow them to retain 40 per cent of each category of equipment. In the autumn of 1990, a compromise was struck between the two sides which went some way towards this, while Moscow in return did not insist on limits on manpower (Bluth, 1990: 240).

On 19 November 1990, the CFE treaty was signed by leaders of NATO and the Warsaw Pact. It is difficult to see the treaty as anything but a defeat for Moscow's military leadership. It codified the retreat of Soviet military forces from Central and Eastern Europe. During the second half of 1990, military resistance to Gorbachev's leadership on security and arms control issues had become increasingly apparent. The Soviet military had openly voiced its concern about the deteriorating situation in the USSR as a whole and their loss of prestige abroad. The Soviet military even circumvented the CFE treaty by moving approximately 60,000 pieces of Soviet military equipment (including approximately 20,000 tanks) east of the Urals and therefore outside the terms of the treaty. While the actual military value of the equipment moved was questionable, of more significance is the fact that the Soviet military élite were obviously opposed to Gorbachev's 'concesions' in the European theatre.

The collapse of the Warsaw Pact and the unification of Germany inspired a fundamental reassessment of security requirements in Moscow. From 1986 until 1989 Moscow had advocated the value of a nuclear-free Europe, and pushed for the eradication of both intermediate and shorter-range nuclear systems. However, by late 1989, Moscow was proclaiming the value of a continued nuclear deterrent. Moscow's preferred option was to maintain some nuclear forces, albeit at lower levels, and Soviet analysts began to discuss the benefits of a 'minimum nuclear deterrent'. Moscow believed it necessary in the light of its conventional arms cuts to rely on nuclear forces. Ironically then, by late 1989 Moscow found itself no longer pushing the arms control agenda in Europe but maintaining the position that nuclear forces were a safeguard against the uncertainties of the future.

THE SOVIET MILITARY COUP AND ITS IMPLICATIONS FOR BOTH SOVIET AND EUROPEAN SECURITY

Sergei Karaganov, the deputy director of the Soviet Institute dealing with European issues, stated that the Soviet Union was a regional power, not a superpower (*Guardian*, 22 November 1989). He suggested that the USSR actively sought a continued US military presence in Europe and that it was through NATO and the Warsaw Pact that a 'new' European Security structure should be built. However, by late 1990, this 'vision' was not possible. The Warsaw Pact had collapsed, Soviet troops were in retreat, Germany was unified in NATO and even more problematically for Moscow, several Soviet republics were actively claiming their right to secede. It is this latter issue which appears to have prompted the attempted removal of Gorbachev from power during 19–21 August by the more conservatively-minded members of the Soviet élite. A treaty was due to be signed which would have permitted union republics autonomy within a loose confederation. The attempted coup was a last-ditch stand to prevent the final collapse of the USSR. Its failure hinged upon both the inability and unwillingness of the Soviet security forces (the KGB, the interior police and the army) to act in a coherent manner, and subdue the demonstrations against the coup. In particular the Soviet army proved to be internally divided and at the lower levels more reform-minded than its leaders had assumed.

The aftermath of the coup raised many issues for Soviet security and indeed for Europe which now has an unstable, fragmenting ex-empire to its east. Gorbachev's vision of a Common European Home, in which both military alliances would gradually be dissolved, and all security issues dealt with through the CSCE is outmoded. The West has made it clear that NATO will remain intact and that the CSCE process will not usurp NATO. The integration of 'Eastern' states into Western organisations such as NATO and the EC will be based upon criteria dictated by the West. This will include the adoption of free market principles, and democratic political models. There will also be a requirement for states to be 'stable'.

It is this latter requirement which will effectively exclude the majority of the states of the former USSR. With the break-up of the Soviet Union many issues are thrown into doubt. The first is, in crude terms, that if Moscow relinquishes its central military control whose finger will be on the nuclear button? Will nuclear weapons systems be controlled by the individual republics such as Uzbekistan? Who would the West negotiate with in any future arms control talks? And what does this mean for nuclear proliferation? It is not at all clear what the attitude of the republics will be to such questions of nuclear control. Some like the Ukraine have disavowed any intention to hold nuclear systems, but most of the republics have made it clear that they intend to assert control of their own armed forces. Some have chosen to maintain 'national' conventional forces, with compulsory military service, and defence doctrines modelled along 'defensive territorial defence'. Some analysts in the new republics have actually proposed that an arrangement, such as in NATO, might be possible whereby there might be some form of 'central' body through which all due republics might coordinate their defence decision making. However, this raises the issue of whether the new republics will share a common vision of security. There are many outstanding territorial and ethnic tensions between the various republics and a pessimistic assessment might point to due danger of some of the new individual and independent armies embroiled over issues such as Nagorno Karabakh.

Given this state of flux, it is difficult to predict the future of the Soviet republics and indeed what the current instability means for European security. However, it must be questionable whether the current Western policy of 'excluding' the states in the East from institutions such as NATO and the EC is wise. A stable future lies in tying the East into pan-European security structures not locking it out.

REFERENCES

Bluth, C. (1990) 'Military strategy and security issues', in A. Pravda (ed.) *Yearbook of Soviet Foreign Relations*, London: I.B. Tauris.
Bovin, A. (1985), in *Izvestia*, 25 September 1985.
FBIS-SOV (1988) 4 January 1988: 1.

Gorbachev, M. S. (1987) *Perestroika: New Thinking for our Country and the World*, London: Harper Collins.

Holden, G. (1989) *Soviet Military Reform*, London: Pluto Press.

Malcolm, N. (1990) 'Western Europe', in A. Pravda (ed.) *Yearbook of Soviet Foreign Relations*, London: I.B. Tauris.

Pravda, A. (1990) *Yearbook of Soviet Foreign Relations*, London: I. B. Tauris.

Skodorenko, P. (1989) 'O voennykh doktrinakh i mezhdnnavodnoi bezopasnosti', *Vestnik Pro* May 1989.

SWB (1988a) Soviet TV broadcast 0700 GMT, 9 February 1988, *Summary of World Broadcasts: Soviet Union*, 0072 c/2.

SWB (1988b) Soviet TV broadcast 2105 GMT, 15 February 1988, *Summary of World Broadcasts: Soviet Union*, 0084 A1/5.

Varrenikov, V. (1987) 'Na strazhe i bezopasnosti narodov', *Partiinaia Zhizv*, 5 March 1987: 9–10.

Vybornov, S., Gusenkov, A. and Leontiev, V. (1988) 'Nothing is simple in Europe', *International Affairs* (Moscow), 1988, 3: 34–41.

10 British perspectives on the future of European security

Len Scott

In the 1980s defence and disarmament became subjects of intense political debate and popular concern in Britain. Defence was a central issue in the general elections of 1983 and 1987. Opposition to nuclear weapons and to British, NATO and American defence policies gave rise to an anti-nuclear mass movement larger, more heterogeneous and arguably more successful than its predecessor in the 1950s. The result was that in the early 1980s the British political and intellectual consensus on defence and security in Europe fractured.

The challenge of heterodox thinking on defence and security has grown in cogency and, with the end of the Cold War, in relevance. The advent of Mikhail Gorbachev, the collapse of Marxism-Leninism in Eastern Europe and the unification of Germany have wrought a transformation in the military equations and political geometry of European security. Orthodox thinking and policy making has now responded to these changing circumstances. At the same time the high tide of anti-nuclear opposition has receded and there are grounds to believe that a new political consensus has begun to emerge.

The reaction of the British government to the end of the Cold War and future challenges for European security was summed up by the Defence Secretary, Tom King, in 1990 when he argued, that despite changing circumstances:

> The basic elements remain firm – the vital role of the Atlantic Alliance, and of the presence of United States forces in Europe as its military keystone; the need for nuclear weapons to help prevent war; and the continuing value of a British contribution in Germany; and the importance of flexibility and versatility in our forces, for roles beyond as well as within NATO.
>
> (Ministry of Defence, 1990: 5)

This chapter will focus on two of these principal tenets of British policy, which have been, and are likely to be, central to British political and academic debates about European security in the 1990s: the role of nuclear weapons and the role of NATO. The context of those debates will be very different from the past but their form and content will nevertheless reflect the arguments and analyses of the last decade.

WHITHER THE BOMB?

In the 1980s nuclear weapons were at the centre of the British debate about European security. In particular the issue of Cruise and Pershing precipitated the disintegration of the British political consensus in the early 1980s. Later the INF negotiations became one of the main vehicles of rapprochement between the superpowers. The emergence of Mikhail Gorbachev, the departure of Ronald Reagan, and the end of the Cold War have had significant implications for the politics of nuclear weapons in Britain and indeed in Europe. In particular the Labour Party under Neil Kinnock changed its policy on nuclear disarmament. But the end of the Cold War has not meant the end of the arms race or the removal of nuclear weapons from European territory, nor did the British government's 1990 review of defence policy signal any fundamental reappraisal of British nuclear weapons policy.

Whenever there has been debate about British defence policy it has mainly focused on nuclear weapons and nuclear disarmament. In the 1980s this centred on both British nuclear weapons (mainly Trident) and American nuclear weapons (mainly Cruise). The latter was of greatest political importance because it was the deployment of ground launched Cruise missiles and Pershing IIs in Western Europe that led to the rise of the anti-nuclear movements, and the ensuing collapse of the British political consensus on defence. Cruise caused great public concern because the missiles were seen to herald an American willingness to use Europe as a nuclear battlefield. Opposition to Trident and the maintenance of a British deterrent reflected different concerns, part of a general campaign in support of nuclear disarmament and against the nuclear arms race. The policy of the Major government remains to build four Trident submarines each equipped with sixteen missiles which in turn can carry up to eight nuclear warheads. While the Ministry of Defence continues to argue that Trident will be a minimum deterrent critics have opposed the escalation involved in Britain's acquisition of a new generation of strategic nuclear weapons.

The relevance of British strategic nuclear weapons to European security has long been in doubt. Most advocates of Polaris and Trident have seen them as an independent or national deterrent. Critics, including the Labour Party, have poured scorn on the idea of independence. Some have ascribed the desire for a national deterrent to post-imperial sentiment. Others, including two former Chiefs of the Defence Staff, Field-Marshal Lord Carver and Lord Mountbatten, questioned the credibility of a policy that envisaged Britain using nuclear weapons against the Soviet Union when the United States was not prepared to do so. The formal position of successive British governments (since Denis Healey first introduced the idea in the 1960s) is that British strategic nuclear weapons contribute to European security by providing a second centre of decision-making within the Alliance. However this rationale has not featured much in recent British debates which have focused on the question of an independent deterrent, by which is meant a nuclear force capable of withstanding a massive Soviet nuclear attack on the United Kingdom and able to engage in nuclear retaliation against centres of Soviet state power.

One idea that gained some ground (but not much) in the 1980s was that of a joint British–French nuclear force. The SDP-Liberal alliance argued for greater British–French nuclear collaboration and former Prime Minister Edward Heath advocated a Franco-British deterrent (Heath, 1988: 207). Pressure for France and Britain to participate in follow-on negotiations to the Strategic Arms Reductions Talks (START) is likely to grow. According to a 1989 United States Congressional Research Service report, on present plans, and after START, by 2005 the British and French arsenals could be equal to one-fifth of US forces (compared with just 2 per cent in 1985) and to nearly a quarter of Soviet strategic forces (Preece and Freeman, 1989: 19–22).[1] George Bush's proposals to eliminate multiple warheads on land-based missiles and Mikhail Gorbachev's counter proposal to negotiate a further 50 per cent reduction in strategic forces would increase the military significance and political saliency of the European arsenals. Already the French government no longer intends to develop a mobile land-based missile to replace its eighteen intermediate range ballistic missiles, but remains intent on modernising its strategic forces. So too is the Conservative government in Britain, and this policy is shared by its Labour and Liberal-Democratic opponents.

There is certainly no reason to believe that a Major government or indeed any Conservative or Conservative-led administration will abandon the idea of a national deterrent in general or the Trident system in particular. For many Conservative MPs this may well reflect visceral notions of national prestige which nuclear weapons are believed to endow. For others the end of the Cold War has been met with a measure of caution. They feel that change can be confounded or reversed and that the Gulf war showed that Britain could become involved in confrontations with ruthless dictators armed with weapons of mass destruction. This cautionary instinct has been articulated by Sir Michael Quinlan, Permanent Under-Secretary at the Ministry of Defence, who told the Soviet General Staff in November 1990:

> It would be foolish for us in the West to expect you, or for you to expect us, to act today as though that ideal condition of permanent trust and confidence had been completely established in the East–West context... I

believe that on both sides we must still recognise honestly that we are not yet at, or even perhaps very near, the point at which the military insurance element becomes entirely irrelevant between us.

(Quinlan, 1991: 295)

Moreover, he argued:

Except perhaps in a future too remote and uncertain for the prospect of it to shape policy today – the retention of nuclear weapons in smaller but still significant numbers on each side, at both the strategic and non-strategic levels, will remain a prudent and positive element in the construction of a dependable international system for preserving peace among the countries of East and West.

(Quinlan, 1991: 293)

This statement of government thinking by its senior defence mandarin no doubt resonates with sentiment inside the Conservative Party. It was nevertheless at variance with the sentiment, if not the stated policy, of the official Opposition at the time.

The Labour Party has an eclectic history on nuclear issues. Labour governments took many of the key decisions in British nuclear policy. In opposition, anti-nuclear feeling had a decisive influence on party policy in the late 1950s/early 1960s and in the 1980s. Since 1980 the Labour Party has been led by two members of the Campaign for Nuclear Disarmament – Michael Foot and Neil Kinnock.[2] In 1983 and 1987 Labour campaigned on a 'non-nuclear' defence policy. In both elections the issue cost the party votes and in 1983 exposed internal divisions. In 1989 after a lengthy and comprehensive review of policy as a whole significant changes on defence were agreed (Labour Party, 1990). This was widely portrayed as the abandonment of 'unilateralism' in favour of 'multilateralism'. In particular Trident was no longer to be unconditionally scrapped but dismantled as part of a negotiating process with the Soviet Union. In April 1991 Neil Kinnock went further and made it clear that a Labour government would not 'get rid of all nuclear weapons for as long as others have them' (*Guardian*, 1991b). This was later amplified by the Shadow Foreign Secretary, Gerald Kaufman, who explained:

We believe that Britain ought to remain as a participant in those negotiations [follow-on START talks] until they are successfully and finally concluded with an agreement by all thermo-nuclear powers to eliminate those weapons.

(Kaufman, 1991)

This might seem to offer a plausible disarmament strategy, in so far as the signing of START is being followed by further talks on strategic arms,

Mikhail Gorbachev has outlined a plan for global nuclear disarmament and President Mitterrand has indicated that France could participate in future nuclear arms negotiations. However there have been no indications that the United States government is even contemplating nuclear disarmament. A strong national consensus remains on the need to modernise all three elements of the strategic triad of intercontinental ballistic missiles (ICBMs), nuclear armed submarines (SSBNs) and long-range bombers. Likewise the former Soviet Union continues to introduce new strategic nuclear systems, including SS–24 and SS–25 mobile ICBMs and Delta IV and Typhoon class SSBNs (IISS, 1990: 210). British participation in START 2 may assist the arms control process, but these negotiations will only be designed to reduce rather than abolish strategic weapons. The prospect of global nuclear disarmament may not be an illusion, but it is certainly a mirage in so far as it is inconceivable that global nuclear disarmament can be achieved by the year 2000. While the START treaty is an important arms control agreement it will only cut the levels of strategic nuclear warheads back to where they were in the early 1980s. One estimate has suggested that under the treaty the United States will still have over 10,000 strategic warheads while the former Soviet Union will keep over 8,000 (*Jane's Defence Weekly*, 1991). Progress on further START negotiations on the Bush and Gorbachev proposals of September/October 1991 would yield significant reductions, but this will continue to fall well short of the goal of a non-nuclear world by the year 2000.

Nevertheless Labour is right in saying that there will be growing pressure to include the British and French forces in START 2. Hitherto, successive American Presidents have fended off Soviet demands to include the British Polaris and Trident weapons in the arms control process. However Trident will represent a significant increase in the number of targets Britain can destroy. It will, moreover, be able to destroy hardened Soviet targets, including ICBM silos, which Polaris cannot. The qualitative change is as important as the quantitative. These developments will increase Soviet pressure to include the British Trident in arms negotiations.

The Labour Party proposes to build only three Trident submarines on grounds of cost (Labour Party, 1990: 1987), although this policy would have been reviewed by an incoming Labour government if the contract for the fourth submarine had already been signed (O'Neill, 1991). Hitherto successive governments have accepted the argument of the service chiefs that four SSBNs is the minimum required to maintain at least one submarine on station, invulnerable to a surprise 'bolt out of the blue' attack. This has been the basis on which Britain has operated an independent deterrent, although successive governments have not made clear why this requirement is essential for a second centre of decision making. It is not known when the entire Polaris fleet will be phased out. A mixed Polaris–Trident fleet will operate beyond the lifetime of this Parliament, on present plans. Nevertheless

Labour's policy would mean eventually discarding the traditional conception of an independent deterrent or revising the criteria for deterring a 'bolt from the blue' attack so that a three-submarine fleet will suffice.

A strategic capability of this kind is only needed if the former Soviet Union is the potential enemy. Trident is not necessary to deter putative nuclear threats from the developing world. Even if such threats exist Britain has other nuclear capabilities able to deter them. Without a Soviet threat there is no credible rationale for an intercontinental range ballistic missile system of this kind.[3] In Britain the demise of the Soviet threat may well encourage proponents of an independent strategic capability to search for potential enemies.

THE BOMB AND EUROPE

British strategic nuclear weapons have a dual identity. On one hand they serve as an independent national deterrent. On the other, since 1963, they have been committed to NATO, where they are part of an arsenal which reached its peak in the 1960/1970s when over 7,000 nuclear warheads were at the disposal of military commanders. To examine the role of these weapons it is necessary to look at NATO strategy. For the last forty years the existence of some sort of Soviet threat was taken for granted. In the 1980s this was challenged by those who argued that the scale of the threat was exaggerated and by those who pointed to the inherent implausibility of the Soviet desire to conquer Western Europe. New thinking about common security in Europe challenged traditional ways of analysing the threat. In the 1960s proponents of strategic arms control had emphasised the objective of strategic stability with the aim of managing both the arms race and political crises that might precipitate war. European advocates of alternative security went much further. They saw military reform as a vehicle of political change, and began to broaden the debate about the nature of security beyond the realm of the purely military. Yet disarmament and denuclearisation were, and remain, at the heart of their thinking.

Proponents of alternative defence argue that their ideas set the agenda for the 1980s. Yet debate remains over the respective paternity claims of the Reagan Administration, NATO, Gorbachev and the Campaign for Nuclear Disarmament, for the Zero Option and the Intermediate Nuclear Forces (INF) treaty. Whoever set the agenda for whatever debates in the 1980s, the Thatcher government continued to press the case for a strategy of flexible response for NATO and an independent British strategic deterrent into the twenty-first century. However reform in the Soviet Union and the changes in Soviet foreign policy brought about by Mikhail Gorbachev have transformed European security. The renunciation of the Brezhnev doctrine in

Eastern Europe precipitated the collapse of the Warsaw Pact and the beginning of the withdrawal of Soviet forces from Eastern Europe. The Soviet Union has accepted the unification of Germany with relative, indeed remarkable, equanimity. The military consequences of these developments have been enormous. So too are the implications of the conventional arms control process achieved in the Conference on Security and Cooperation which resulted in the treaty on Conventional Forces in Europe (CFE) signed in November 1990.

For NATO the outstanding achievement of CFE was to establish the principle of parity which required massive and disproportionate cuts in Soviet conventional forces. However two things are clear. The first is that a substantial part of the military infrastructure of the Cold War still exists in Europe, as it does in Soviet-American relations. Second, despite unilateral withdrawals of tactical nuclear weapons and while NATO is reviewing its strategy, there is no immediate prospect of the denuclearisation of Europe or even Germany, or the abandonment of strategies based on nuclear weapons. It is also clear that the British government has played, and may well continue to play, a central role in ensuring that this continues, although the political composition of future British governments would affect some important decisions, notably in the field of nuclear modernisation.

One pillar of the Cold War has disappeared, the Warsaw Pact. So too has Soviet conventional superiority. Yet despite enormous reductions the level of forces in Europe remains very high by historical standards. When the Germans invaded the Soviet Union in 1941, for example, they possessed at most 3,300 tanks (Cooper and Lucas, 1976: 42).[4] By 1994 NATO will possess some 20,000. More significantly with the disintegration of the Warsaw Pact the military balance will no longer be seen in terms of WTO versus NATO but the former USSR versus NATO. The West, for example will have 20,000 tanks as against no more than 13,300 for the former Soviet Union. The criticisms of NATO strategy which emphasised the qualitative aspects of the military balance are likely to acquire a new relevance in this environment. One debate has been how far Western qualitative advantages have offset Soviet numbers. If NATO's qualitative advantages continue to hold good then the changes in the numerical balance could provide NATO with a meaningful degree of conventional superiority. The performance of Allied forces in the Gulf war against Soviet equipped and trained Iraqi forces provides a graphic illustration of the relevance of these questions. These arguments will reinforce the claim that NATO no longer needs its panoply of tactical and theatre nuclear weapons and that it can discard a strategy based on threatening to initiate nuclear war. The fact that the former Soviet Union can no longer be perceived to enjoy conventional superiority has profound implications for NATO strategy, which has traditionally been based on a preparedness to initiate nuclear war to avoid losing a conventional one. Post-Cold War Western strategy remains wedded to the employment of tactical, theatre and strategic nuclear forces in the event of war in Europe. The incredibility of such a strategy has long provoked criticism from across the political spectrum in Western Europe and across the Atlantic, but in these new circumstances this will be increased by claims of conceptual obsolescence.

NATO's nuclear strategy has long reflected national and conceptual disagreements and compromises. The end of the Cold War is unlikely to change this fact. Quinlan makes clear the British government's view that the role of nuclear weapons is neither a consequence of NATO's need to compensate for conventional inferiority nor to deter Soviet nuclear weapons (Quinlan, 1991: 299–301). They are there to make the costs of war out of all proportion to the gains, and to do so in perpetuity. However the increasing demands in Germany for the abandonment of nuclear weapons which can only reach German territory will be a potent factor in the politics of the Western alliance. Allied to long-standing US disquiet about the burdens of a first-use strategy this could prove a decisive axis for reform within NATO. Given the problems of negotiating limits on dual-key systems (artillery and aircraft) the optimal strategy was for NATO to withdraw the weapons unilaterally, as it had done before. (Since 1979 some 3,000 of 7,000 nuclear warheads had been withdrawn from Western Europe in this manner, prior to Bush's initiative.)

The debate about first use and the issue of the deployment of non-strategic nuclear weapons are separate though related. In theory NATO could retain a strategy of flexible response even if it did not have any nuclear weapons based in Europe. Yet the indications are that even if NATO is embarked upon the reform of its nuclear strategy, a Conservative government will wish to retain a level of nuclear forces on German territory for political reasons as well as traditional military ones. This is to prevent German political isolation in the face of Soviet pressure for the denuclearisation of Europe, which was the logic behind NATO's decision to deploy INF forces in five NATO countries, but which may be of diminishing importance in the future if the former Soviet Union continues to accept the presence of some American nuclear forces as the price of a continuing American military presence in Europe. Indeed it appears that the Soviet government now recognises some advantages in an American presence in Western Europe as a bulwark against future German revanchism. It is also clear that the British government will seek to link agreement to changes in NATO strategy to a programme of modernisation, even though the political difficulties of this were illustrated over the saga of the follow-on to the Lance missile.

The Labour Party's embrace of multilateral disarmament and the further change in policy in 1991 suggest that while it has crossed the Rubicon, it has not yet stopped travelling. A degree of ambiguity surrounds Labour's future plans and the 1989 policy statement's position on NATO strategy may be superseded after the general election. On the other hand the effective abandonment of disarmament on strategic nuclear weapons may reinforce the intra-party need for a more radical stance on non-strategic weapons. Equally tactical weapons in Europe do not raise the same kind of electoral issues and electoral liabilities that Polaris and Trident are seen to do for the party. Labour had long been committed to the elimination of short-range nuclear missiles (the 'third-zero option') and battlefield nuclear weapons and naturally applauded Bush's action. At the same time a radical review of NATO strategy is unlikely to amount to the denuclearisation of Germany. Furthermore the implications of reducing NATO nuclear weapons in Western Europe may be to increase dependence on those weapons based in Britain. There may well be pressure to increase the numbers or capabilities of nuclear capable aircraft based in Britain. Greater attention may also focus on the possible 'theatre support role' of the British Trident force which, with its greater accuracy, will be capable of targeting Soviet military assets previously assigned to NATO's nuclear bombers.

NATO: A SOLUTION IN SEARCH OF A PROBLEM?

NATO has existed to safeguard Western Europe by deterring the Soviet Union from attacking or seeking to coerce its members. The Alliance's supporters argue that it has triumphed. In 1990 Mrs Thatcher described it as 'the most successful alliance in history' (*Guardian*, 1990a). Its detractors have questioned the existence of an imminent (or immanent) Soviet threat. Either way, there is now general agreement that Western Europe is not threatened by the Soviet Union. As a result NATO has begun to search for a new role, if not a new *raison d'être*. It is clear that some of the new thinking about this may well reflect rather old ideas.

The original aim of NATO was famously described by its first Secretary-General, Lord Ismay, to be 'to keep the Russians out, the Americans in and the Germans down'. The position of Germany in this equation changed quickly as the military imperative of strong collective defence necessitated West German rearmament. One result was the decision by Churchill and Eden in 1954 to make the unprecedented commitment of British forces to the continent in peacetime. The political rationale was to reassure French and other opinion about the possible revival of German militarism. Political considerations have subsequently played a decisive role in sustaining the British Army on the Rhine (BAOR) in the face of arguments by the Navy and others for a rationalisation of Britain's strategic roles. While BAOR could not expect to survive CFE without radical cuts, its continued existence in the wake of the 'Options for Change' exercise in 1990 probably owes as much to political than military considerations.

The burden of Germany's history is still a potent factor in European affairs but the relative ease with which unification took place is an indication of the successful integration of West Germany into the fabric of the Western Alliance and the European Community. Unification does present political and economic challenges. In military terms the anomaly of NATO territory which cannot be defended by NATO armies could present problems in the future. On the other hand unification provides an opportunity for Germany to become fully integrated into the new Europe. British foreign policy could play a crucial supportive role in ensuring that it does (Treverton, 1990). Yet British suspicions of German revanchism have been articulated by the former Trade Secretary, Nicholas Ridley and some of the academic advisers who had Mrs Thatcher's ear in 1990.

Prime Minister Major was quick to distance his government from the impressions created by his predecessor. Nevertheless one of the arguments advanced in support of an Atlantic Alliance is that it provides reassurance to Germany's neighbours (and the Soviet Union), and a necessary framework for integrating a united Germany into the new Europe. As Professor Sir Michael Howard has argued, one reason for keeping NATO:

is generally admitted but seldom mentioned in polite society. There *is* a German problem. It may only be a problem of perception, but it exists none the less. An alliance without the United States would be an alliance dominated by Germany. The peoples both of Central Europe and the Soviet Union, rightly or wrongly, would see this as a threat. Even the Western European allies would be uneasy; not so much because of the record of Wilhemine and Nazi Germany as because of more deep-rooted instincts about the need for a Balance of Power in Europe.

(Howard, 1990: 105)

For Howard the 'sacrosanct' element of Lord Ismay's equation remains the American commitment to Europe. Since the start of the Cold War there has been an enduring bipartisan consensus on the importance of the 'special relationship' between Britain and United States, despite much criticism (particularly from the Left) during the Vietnam War and over the policies of the Reagan Administration. Ironically the lowest point of British-American relations came under Conservative administrations: most dramatically with Eden's Suez policy, but also under Edward Heath. It was Heath who took Britain into the European Community in 1973 and who has since strongly argued that Britain's future lay in Europe rather than in any special transatlantic relationship (Heath, 1988: 207). Many others have shared the view that it was necessary to choose between the US relationship and Europe, though not all (most notably Margaret Thatcher) have shared Heath's enthusiasm for Europe. On the other hand is the argument that the special relationship and enthusiasm for European integration are entirely compatible. Indeed the most consistent proponents of this have been the Americans themselves. From the Marshall Plan to Macmillan's attempts at membership of the EC to Britain's eventual entry in 1973, the Americans have been enthusiastic supporters of a greater British economic, political and military role in Europe. Successive American governments (urged on by Congress) have wanted Europeans to do more (and pay more) for their own defence. Nevertheless opponents of a new defence role for the EC have cited American disquiet at the possible diminution of the role of NATO.[5]

For over forty years British governments have been deeply concerned with the American military commitment to Europe's security. In part this reflected fears about American isolationism and the possible withdrawal of American ground forces from Europe. More importantly British and West European policy-makers became concerned about the credibility of the American commitment to initiate nuclear war with the Soviet Union in the event of a Warsaw Pact attack on Western Europe. The American nuclear guarantee has been regarded as central to the NATO enterprise. The development of Soviet intercontinental capabilities created great problems for this guarantee. The strategy of flexible response adopted in 1967 and the 1979 NATO decision on Cruise and Pershing were each rooted in the perception that reform was necessary to bolster extended deterrence. British governments played a major part within the Alliance in developing these policies and it is clear that the current government attaches great importance to preserving an American nuclear role (and associated deployments) in Europe. The trends in Labour Party thinking suggest that a future Labour government will not fundamentally challenge this, even though it may take a different position on specific decisions (e.g. the TASM) within NATO.

OLD WINE, NEW BOTTLES? OLD WHINES, NEW BATTLES?

In the British defence debate in the 1980s the issue of nuclear weapons and the role of the United States in Europe were enmeshed. Principally this was because the deployment of Cruise and Pershing II missiles together with ill-considered statements by American leaders gave the impression that Europe was becoming a prospective battlefield for nuclear exchanges that would not extend to the Soviet Union or the United States. In the 1980s, opposition to Cruise and other aspects of NATO strategy and American foreign policy led to arguments for Britain to leave NATO. In 1983 the Alternative Defence Commission argued that if NATO was not willing to renounce nuclear strategies Britain should withdraw from the alliance (Alternative Defence Commission, 1983: 9). A second report in 1985 reiterated this view and spelt out the conditions (including the idea of a timetable) on which Britain might remain a member. The authors stated that 'whether or not to remain in NATO is the most important question for Britain without the Bomb'. (Alternative Defence Commission, 1985: 22–3) However they argued:

> Ultimately, peace in Europe requires the dissolution of the two blocs, yet an immediate British withdrawal from NATO, far from being a step in this direction, might be dangerously destabilising, even precipitating a more hazardous realignment than at present.
>
> (Alternative Defence Commission, 1985: 27)

This thinking resonated with that of the Labour Party which made its commitment to membership of NATO clear but supported the establishment of:

> a European nuclear weapons-free zone and a new European-wide security system, leading to the ultimate replacement of the present division of Europe into NATO and the Warsaw Pact by the dissolution of the two blocs.
>
> (Labour Party, 1984: 18)

Despite its embrace of nuclear disarmament Labour remained committed to membership of NATO. However elsewhere antipathy to NATO's nuclear policies led to antipathy to NATO itself. Groups like the campaign for European Nuclear Disarmament (END) and the Campaign for Nuclear Disarmament (CND), advocated an end to the bloc system. Influential figures in the peace movement, such as Professor E.P. Thompson saw one of the primary purposes of nuclear disarmament in Europe to be to free Europe from the hegemonic hold of the superpowers (Thompson, 1980). Successive CND annual conferences voted for British withdrawal from NATO, though the national leadership did not regard the issue as a campaigning priority. Illustrative of the arguments against membership of NATO were those of Jonathon Porritt, one of the leading figures of the Ecology Party, who in advocating British non-alignment in 1984 stated that:

> NATO is more likely to be the cause of war than the agent of peace... Our withdrawal from NATO might well bring about its break-up, but that will assuredly happen anyway as other countries come to reject dependence on nuclear weapons.
>
> (Porritt, 1985: 353)

News of NATO's death was much exaggerated. The obituaries came at the high tide of anti-nuclear opposition. Even before the end of the Cold War the Labour Party had signalled a firmer commitment to the Alliance even though it still urged radical reform of NATO strategy. The 1987 Labour manifesto declared: 'Labour's defence policy is based squarely and firmly on Britain's membership of NATO. We are determined to make the most useful possible contribution to the alliance' (Labour Party, 1987: 15). It might have been expected that the end of the Cold War would have raised fundamental questions about the need for the NATO alliance or Britain's membership. Yet so far there have been remarkably few voices in Britain in favour of abolition. Some have questioned the continuing need for NATO. The outgoing Director of the Royal Institute of International Affairs, Admiral Sir James Eberle, has argued that NATO has accomplished its aim of bringing the division of Europe to a peaceful end and that the only remaining task is the dissolution of the organisation (*Guardian*, 1990c). But a firm political consensus now exists between the three main parties on the need to maintain the Alliance for the foreseeable future, even if debates on the relevance of other institutions and frameworks, in particular the EC and CSCE, are emerging.

The British government has taken the view that NATO is the best vehicle for the preservation of the American commitment to Europe and that the American commitment to Europe remains essential to European security. During the negotiation of the CFE treaty the Thatcher Administration was anxious to fix a level below which American troops in Europe would not be reduced. It is also clear that the British government is strongly against the elimination of all non-strategic nuclear forces, and will wish to ensure an American nuclear presence on mainland Europe as well as in Britain. The preference for NATO over the EC is primarily based on the perceived need for an American commitment.[6] The debate about the EC's role has gathered pace since the 1980s when the Community first began to develop its own foreign policy, notably on the Middle East, Central America and Southern Africa. The treaty on political and economic union has provided an opportunity for taking the debate and indeed the EC's role further. This raises the question of the future of the Western European Union (WEU). The British government favours the idea of using it as a bridge between NATO and the EC. Advocates of an EC defence role have suggested the organisation could be brought within the Community's structure (*Guardian*, 1990c).[7] This would not only strengthen the European as against the Atlantic pillar of Western security but would provide a vehicle for greater French participation in security issues. In particular it provides a possible framework for British and French nuclear collaboration or indeed some form of 'Euro-deterrent', based on strategic and/or non-strategic nuclear weapons. The alternative would be for the French to reintegrate themselves into the military structure of NATO which would require a quite fundamental change of attitude by the French government (although according to one account, collaboration in nuclear policy and nuclear strategy has been going on in great secrecy since the 1970s between the French government and both the United States and NATO (Ullman, 1989)).

The British view has been to support moves to strengthen the European pillar provided this was not at the expense of the American commitment. In the field of arms procurement, and particularly when Michael Heseltine was Defence Secretary, the British government was an advocate of a European as opposed to an American approach. The idea of future collaboration with the French on an air-launched nuclear missile may well be an option for a British government determined to press on with non-strategic nuclear modernisation.

The Labour Party has been if anything more forthright than the Conservatives in rejecting a defence role for the EC. In the past it expressed opposition to the idea of a third bloc and what it described as 'Euro-Gaullism' (Labour Party, 1984: 16) and this attitude appears to have hardened with the Gulf War (*Guardian*, 1991a). Jacques Delors has claimed that the divergence of views apparent before and during the War provides another argument for moving towards a form of political union embracing a common foreign and security policy (Delors, 1991: 99). The more likely conclusion to be drawn in Whitehall and Westminster is that an EC security policy is at best inappropriate, at worst unworkable. Yet just as with doubts about European economic integration eventual British involvement may well reflect calculations about the national costs of being excluded rather than the international benefits of the enterprise itself.

The arguments about the respective merits of NATO and the EC as the institutional basis of European security are political as much as military. However, in one area an EC defence organisation might proffer a framework for an 'out-of-area' military capability which would not be possible for NATO without amending the articles of the NATO treaty which govern the basis on which NATO can resort to force and the geographical area in which it can do so. An 'out-of-area' capability has been a long-simmering issue within the Alliance and in June 1990 Mrs Thatcher strongly endorsed the idea (*Guardian*, 1990b). The Gulf War demonstrated the considerable problems in getting the necessary European political will to intervene outside Europe. In Britain there would be equally considerable problems in maintaining a political consensus on an 'out-of-area' capability be it under the auspices of NATO or the EC. Edward Heath has described the idea of a NATO worldwide peacekeeping force as a 'new imperialism to replace that banished after the Second World War' (Hyde-Price, 1991a). It is difficult to see how a political consensus could be maintained on this. Despite changes on its policies on nuclear weapons and defence spending Labour is highly unlikely to embrace the idea. At the same time the Gulf War showed both the opportunities for *ad hoc* military cooperation and the emerging possibility of a revitalised United Nations.

HOW MANY TRENDS MAKE A PARADIGM SHIFT?

The bipolar world of NATO and the Warsaw Pact is no more. For some the resulting uncertainties of the multipolar system make for a more dangerous environment (Mearsheimer, 1990). There clearly are problems with nationalism, revanchism and ethnic antagonism in Eastern Europe and indeed within the boundaries of the former Soviet Union. There will be costs to pay for the end of the Cold War, and these will be paid for by those least able to afford them – mainly Eastern Europeans. In the West the ghost of Sarajevo still lurks in the shadows. There is nervousness that the 'Balkanisation' of Eastern Europe could lead us back to 1914. Yet however unpredictable the future (and however ingenious the strategists' scenarios) it is still extremely difficult to see how the political problems affecting the new democracies of Eastern Europe could take us back to the divisions and antagonisms of the two blocs. Ethnic violence and revanchism do pose threats to Europeans, but they are not the same kind of threats to European security that have existed for forty years. Moreover efforts to deal with these sorts of problems can promote better political relations between the countries (or peoples) involved. The conflict in Northern Ireland for example has led to a framework of cooperation between Britain and Ireland and a new relationship between London and Dublin which may well play an important role in any future political settlement.

Much of the debate about the new Europe has been about appropriate frameworks and the relevant 'security architecture' for the 1990s. There is of course nothing inevitable about the primacy of institutions, as Adrian Hyde-Price has argued (Hyde-Price, 1991a). None the less the trend toward supranational integration is a potent factor in European affairs. Western Europe is advancing towards some form of political and economic union. Eastern European countries, noticeably Hungary and Poland are keen to follow, and also to explore the possibility of joining NATO as their former Warsaw Pact colleagues in East Germany did. The Soviet Union's request to do likewise has not been treated with the same degree of seriousness that its applications to join the International Monetary Fund and the World Bank have done. Yet while President Gorbachev may have fallen short of some Western expectations his embrace of the market portended a revolution in Soviet society as profound as his original embrace of glasnost and perestroika.

NATO believes that it preserved European security by deterrence. It is clear that the British government believes that nuclear weapons cannot be discarded, a view increasingly shared by the leadership of the Labour Party. The relevance of policies and institutions that were designed to deter a threat which no longer exists can, and will, be called into question. Similar criticisms will be made of the idea of an EC defence policy, although the role of the community in the Yugoslavian crisis may enhance the EC's credibility in the field of European security, at least *vis-à-vis* the CSCE.

The principal political objective of the European Economic Community was to ensure that Western Europeans, and in particular the French and Germans, would never again go to war with each other. This objective has now been achieved. War between the democracies in Western Europe is quite inconceivable. This is not due to the military balance between these countries or because of some notion of nuclear deterrence (even if France does target tactical nuclear missiles on Germany). It is because Britain and France and Germany together with the other countries of Western Europe have developed political, economic and cultural institutions which have rendered war unthinkable as an act of policy between them. This represents a paradigmatic shift in relations between countries whose conflicts twice this century brought war on a global scale. The long-term implications for European security of the possible liberalisation and democratisation of the Soviet Union is potentially more profound than the shifts in the military balance or in nuclear weapons policies (Hyde-Price, 1991b).

The real challenge, and one which the debates about the future of European security are already addressing, is how the success of the West Europeans can be created on a pan-European scale. One response has been to focus on new institutions. Mike Gapes, the Senior International Officer of the Labour Party has argued that:

> Co-operation between the more political NATO and the new political/military remnants of the Warsaw Pact should be developed as the basis for a European Security Organisation. It could develop, in time into the European Regional Security body of the United Nations which many envisaged when the UN organisation was established in San Francisco in 1945.
>
> (Gapes, 1990: 18)

This proposal is of interest not least because of the underlying scepticism about CSCE as a possible replacement for NATO.[8] The idea of CSCE as the future European Security structure has gained ground in some of the former members of the Soviet bloc (Hyde-Price, 1991a). In Britain the view that NATO has served its purpose and can now be replaced by CSCE can be expected to gain ground, not just on the left. General Sir Hugh Beach has argued:

It is time now for NATO, giving credence to its own recognition of a European identity in the domain of security, to work toward its gradual absorption (together with that of the effectively defunct Warsaw Pact) into the wider all-European grouping provided by the CSCE.

(Beach, 1990)

CSCE of course includes the United States which is important for those, like the British government, who are anxious to preserve an American role in Europe (although there is no suggestion that the government sees CSCE as an alternative to NATO).

Since 1990 the CSCE has begun to acquire an institutional existence, and this is likely to grow. The development of a new role is likely to develop on an *ad hoc* basis. Support could well depend on future success, and comparisons with the EC over their roles in the Yugoslavian crisis may not augur too well for CSCE. Likewise external diplomatic pressure on the Soviet Union over its behaviour in the Baltic states is more likely to be effective at the bilateral US–USSR level or in a concerted US–EC approach than through CSCE where the Soviets can block such pressure. Advocates of common security nevertheless see CSCE as the natural post-Cold War architecture for the European home, not least because CSCE has always been concerned with a broader canvas than just military policy. CSCE's promotion of human rights and political development make it the obvious institution for developing the new democratic Europe.

A decade ago anyone able to predict the contours and outcome of the European security debate of the 1980s would have forsaken political analysis and become very rich as a fortune teller. It is possible to identify trends in international politics, for example international borders are becoming more porous to the movement of information, capital, people and above all, ideas. European-wide institutions reflect and encourage these trends. To paraphrase Mikhail Gorbachev, Europe has groped, and continues to grope, its way toward an integral and interdependent existence. Equally Europe cannot escape from its history or its geography, and it is clear that there are powerful centrifugal forces within the Soviet Union. Predicting how these trends will interact to shape the political, economic and military parameters of the future Europe poses enormous challenges for analysts and policy makers.

The future cannot mirror the past. Yet British debates on European security in the 1990s cannot but reflect the debates of the 1980s and before. The focus of the latter may no longer be appropriate. The INF treaty has removed Cruise, Pershing and the SS-20. The CFE treaty and Soviet unilateral cuts have fundamentally changed the conventional military balance. Conventional arms control talks in the 1990s may make useful if unspectacular progress in the building of further mutual confidence. Yet the strategies and institutions of the Cold War – nuclear weapons and NATO – will remain at the heart of British debates on European security for some time, even as a new political consensus develops. Increasingly that debate – and British government policy – will acquire a peculiarly schizophrenic quality. The continuing existence of military and nuclear hardware means that arguments about strategy and defence policy will continue, while the political context of these debates renders them ever more divorced from reality. There is a point where worst-case analysis becomes clinical paranoia. Nevertheless the felt need for a 'military insurance policy' is certain to obtain in Britain, whoever is in government throughout the 1990s. The debate about the political and economic foundations of European security will go forward. Military power and nuclear weapons may well wither away in political terms, rather in the manner that Engels saw the state withering away in Socialist society. There are good reasons to be optimistic about the future of European security. There are also good reasons to believe that the future will be as unpredictable as the recent past has been exhilharating.

NOTES

1 As the actual reductions will be less than 50 per cent the figures for the European proportions need to be amended accordingly.
2 Neil Kinnock allowed his membership of CND to lapse in 1991 (*Sunday Times*, 1991).
3 Strategists at the RAND Corporation nevertheless devised a scenario in which the British Trident is fired at the People's Republic of China in a limited nuclear war fought over Hong Kong (Digby et al, 1988: 103–7).
4 Over a third of these were Panzer 1s and 2s which were training models equipped only with machine guns and/or light cannons.
5 See reports of a letter from US Secretary of State Baker to EC governments seeking assurances that EC defence and foreign policy will not weaken NATO (*Guardian*, 1991c).
6 There are also problems with the neutrality of Ireland, though advocates of an EC security role regard these as manageable (Heath, 1988: 206).
7 Other British advocates of an EC defence role would prefer not to use the WEU as the vehicle of integration with the EC (*Independent*, 1991).
8 See the comments of the deputy Shadow Foreign Secretary George Robertson (Robertson, 1990: 701).

REFERENCES

Alternative Defence Commission (1983) *Defence without the Bomb*, London: Taylor & Francis.
Alternative Defence Commission (1985) *Without the Bomb – Non-Nuclear Defence Policies for Britain*, London: Paladin.
Beach, H. (1990) 'New spirit that heralds the end of NATO', *Guardian*, 23 August 1990.

Cooper, M. and Lucas, J. (1976) *Panzer – The Armoured Force of the Third Reich*, London: Macdonald & Jane's.

Delors, J. (1991) 'European integration and security', *Survival*, **33**, 2: 99–109.

Digby, J., Eliot, M. and Schabe, W. (1988) *How Nuclear War Might Start: Scenarios from the Early 21st Century*, Santa Monica: RAND.

Gapes, M. (1990) *After the Cold War – Building on Alliances*, Fabian Pamphlet 540, London: Fabian Society.

Guardian (1990a) 'No alternative to NATO for united Germany, says Hurd', 8 June 1990.

Guardian (1990b) 'Thatcher calls on NATO to move into new areas', 8 June 1990.

Guardian (1990c) 'Admiral calls for dissolution of NATO', 13 December 1990.

Guardian (1991a) 'Kinnock upset by war shy EC', 24 January 1991.

Guardian (1991b)'Kinnock blocks Tory thrust on defence', 17 April 1991.

Guardian (1991c) 'EC defence moves worry Washington', 29 April 1991.

Heath, E. (1988) 'European unity over the next ten years: from Community to Union', *International Affairs*, **64**, 2: 199–207.

Howard, M. (1990) 'The remaking of Europe', *Survival*, **32**, 2: 99–106.

Hyde-Price, A. (1991a) *European Security Beyond the Cold War*, London: Sage.

Hyde-Price, A. (1991b) *The USSR and the West: A Medium Term Strategy*, Fabian Pamphlet 548, London: Fabian Society.

IISS (1990) *The Military Balance 1990–91*, London: Brassey's.

Independent (1991) 'EC best for defence', 16 March 1991.

Jane's Defence Weekly (1991) 'USA and Soviets agree to START cuts', 27 July 1991, 131.

Kaufman, G. (1991) 'Leading the way to peace', *Guardian* 10 July 1991.

Labour Party (1984) *Defence and Security for Britain*, London: Labour Party.

Labour Party (1987) *Britain Can Make It*, London: Labour Party.

Labour Party (1990) *Meet the Challenge – Make the Change: The Final Report of Labour's Policy Review for the 1990s*, London: Labour Party.

Mearsheimer, J. (1990) 'Back to the future: instability in Europe after the Cold War', *International Security*, **15**, 1: 5–56.

Ministry of Defence (1990) *Statement on the Defence Estimates 1990, vol. 1*, Cm 1022-I, London: HMSO.

O'Neill, M. (1991) *Hansard*, 27 June 1991, cols 1187–8.

Porritt, J. (1985) 'Green peace', in F. Holroyd (ed.) *Thinking about Nuclear Weapons*, London: Croom Helm, 344–61.

Preece, C. and Freeman, J. (1989) *British and French Strategic Force Modernisation*, Washington D. C.: Library of Congress, Congressional Research Paper.

Quinlan, M. (1991) 'Nuclear weapons and the abolition of war', *International Affairs*, **67**, 2: 293–301.

Robertson, G. (1990) 'Britain in the new Europe', *International Affairs*, **66**, 4: 697–702.

Sunday Times (1991) 'How I learned to stop worrying... and love the bomb', 14 July 1991.

Thompson, E. (1980) 'Protest and survive', in E. P. Thompson and D. Smith (eds) *Protest and Survive*, London: Penguin.

Treverton, G. (1990) 'Britain's role in the 1990s: an American view', *International Affairs*, **66**, 4: 703–10.

Ullman, R. (1989) 'The covert French connection', *Foreign Policy*, 75: 3–33.

11 French security policy and the new European order

Frederic Bozo

From the French perspective, 1989–91 not only brought about profound changes in the structure of the European system, but provided a litmus test for the validity of a set of assumptions and attitudes towards European security which have constituted the French security model and its specificity for almost three decades (Bozo, forthcoming). Because the key rationale behind France's East–West, West–West and national security policies since the time of de Gaulle in the 1960s has been that of French diplomacy's stated ambition to overcome the bloc system, the fall of the Berlin Wall was in many ways a moment of truth. In fact, the initial French reaction to the surprisingly quick demise of the 'Yalta' order after November 1989 gave the impression that the country was not as ready to face the consequences of these historic changes as its international rhetoric suggested, thus leading to apparently ill-advised policies and inconsistent attitudes in the initial 'post-Wall' period. Yet the immediate concerns of the year 1989–90, even though they may have not yet been completely overcome, are nevertheless likely to progressively yield to the realisation of the country's mid- to long-term interests and constraints. Thus, if upcoming opportunities are not missed, France will be able to play her part in the new European order.

CONCERNS: FRANCE'S POLICIES IN THE IMMEDIATE POST-WALL PERIOD

An analysis of France's initial concerns and reactions *vis-à-vis* the changing European security system must begin with an assessment of French attitudes towards the prospect of German unification in the year or so after the fall of the Berlin Wall (Kolboom, 1991; Trean, 1991). This may not, however, be the best yardstick of the country's readiness at that time to face the consequences of the demise of the 'Yalta' order. Initial French attitudes have, not surprisingly, been characterised by some degree of subjectivity. Nor have they stemmed primarily from an objective anticipation of the role and status of a united Germany in a post-Cold War Europe, but rather from experiences of the past: negative reactions have mostly been influenced by reminiscences of the pre–1945 era, and positive ones by the tradition of post-Second World War Franco-German reconciliation.

Yet positive attitudes have clearly prevailed, and the French have, by and large, welcomed German unity. In comparison with Germany's other partners (particularly Britain), public opinion has proved warmly supportive (*Economist*, 1990a). Official France was arguably less enthusiastic, and unsurprisingly talk of 'the return of Bismarck' and the like was heard in the media and some limited sections of the political and intellectual élites. But the majority of political leaders have also shown support for unification (albeit with various levels of emotion and with the predictable exception of the Communists). As to President Mitterrand, he unambiguously recognised the right of the Germans to unity as soon as July 1989. Many in France and in Germany however have criticised his lack of demonstrative enthusiasm and apparent failure to grasp the historic dimension of the event. His unemotional approach was illustrated by his answer to the question: 'Are you afraid of the reunification of Germany?' asked a few days before the fall of the Wall. 'I am not afraid of reunification' he said. 'I think the Germans' aspiration to unification is legitimate, if they have the will and the ability to achieve it. France will adapt her policies in order to act in conformity with Europe's interests and her own' (Mitterrand–Kohl, 1989). Beyond this rather cold rhetoric, Mitterrand's main miscalculation seems, with hindsight, to have been his underestimation of the pace of unification, which made him appear as willing to slow down or even postpone the process.[1] While it is doubtful that such was his intention, it certainly fostered German misreadings of the French attitude. All this led to a temporary chill in the Franco-German relationship which, as Karl Kaiser and Thierry de Montbrial wrote, 'survived dangerous moments' in 1990 (Kaiser and de Montbrial, 1990). But to a large extent this may have been unavoidable. After all, the pace of the unification process caught most Germans by surprise and was bound to create misunderstandings within the Franco-German context.

Attitudes towards German unity per se have arguably been less revealing about French concerns in 1989–90 than have the debates as to the East–West and West–West institutional frameworks in which it ought to be accomplished. As de Gaulle frequently insisted, 'the German problem is essentially the European problem'. Indeed, France's European policies in the context of German unification tell a lot about her initial perceptions, reactions and concerns. The most striking feature of these policies is that they have favoured the West–West framework as the best suited to manage changes in European security. In the immediate aftermath of the fall of the Wall, Mitterrand made it clear that he considered the deepening and speeding up of West European integration among the Twelve as the best response to this new challenge. He asked, and obtained Germany's commitment to the process of strengthening the Community economically and politically in parallel with achieving unification. In April 1990, a Kohl–Mitterrand joint proposal to convene an intergovernmental conference to prepare for political union again confirmed Germany's support for this approach. Even more significantly, Mitterrand's approach to European unification throughout most of 1990 was marked by an unusually strong insistence on his federalist conception of the EC build-up. By stressing the 'federal finality' of the Community, he moved France's approach to European integration further away from the traditional Gaullist conception of the EC than at any time in the previous three decades, at least rhetorically (*Le Monde*, 1990a). The implicit motive was of course that economic and political unification within the EC would alleviate the risk of a hegemonic Germany by inserting it in the fabric of supranational European integration.

In parallel with this, in the immediate post-Wall period France logically recognised NATO as another institution fit to play a major role. No essential difference of approach was shown with Washington or London on the issue of the military status of a united Germany and, notably, its full membership in the Alliance. Paris seemed to believe at that time that NATO integration was an effective instrument to contain the future politico-military might of its neighbour. As a consequence, the possibility of normalising France–NATO relations was discreetly envisaged and discussed with allies, particularly with the US at the April 1990 Key Largo meeting between Presidents Mitterrand and Bush.

The limits and pitfalls of France's initial strongly West–West response to the new security challenges were quickly revealed however. At the EC level, the logic of deepening the integration process along federalist lines as a safeguard against German hegemony was beginning to be questioned. Could it not lead to the very opposite result and facilitate German domination, as well as require France's surrendering parts of her independence? (*Economist*, 1990b).[2] Mitterrand himself may have been troubled by such concerns, for he imperceptibly moved to a far less integrationist approach as 1990 drew to a close. This change of approach was formalised in the Kohl–Mitterrand letter on political union of 6 December 1990, with its strong emphasis on intergovernmental rather than supranational decision-making processes. At the NATO level, the limits of France's initial approach were even more clear. It was progressively realised that the initial pro-Alliance reaction and policy of normalisation of NATO ties could push France back into the Atlantic fold and jeopardise her strategic autonomy and independent status, particularly if a US-German 'partnership', as offered by Bush in Mainz in 1989, were to dominate the Alliance in the future. The NATO London summit in July 1990 thus led to a sudden interruption of the rapprochement between France and NATO. Mitterrand refused to endorse the transformation of flexible response into a 'last resort' strategy and, above all, to have France participate in the effort to set up new multinational forces. As if to distance himself even more clearly from the process of NATO reform, he announced his unilateral intention to withdraw all 50,000 French forces from Germany in the next four years, a gesture which was met with disillusionment in the Federal Republic and interpreted as a signal of France's return to the 'sanctuary'. At any rate this episode seemed to illustrate Mitterrand's perception of the risks of relying too much on the consolidation and deepening of Western institutions as the best response to the challenges of the new European agenda.

Yet, in spite of the shortcomings of this West–West approach, the more traditional East–West security framework did not appear to be a real priority on the French agenda in that period. To be sure, Mitterrand's diplomacy in late 1989 and throughout most of 1990 seemed to attach much importance to the emerging pan-European dimension. During his meeting with Gorbachev on 6 December 1989 in Kiev (which was widely interpreted in the FRG as an attempt to check unification with an old-fashioned 'alliance de revers', a reflection of both the German paranoia and French awkwardness which prevailed then), he joined with him in calling for a CSCE summit by the end of 1990 and later offered to host such a meeting in Paris. Then he went on to launch the idea of a European 'Confederation' designed to offer the new Eastern and Central European democracies a chance to tie themselves to the 'hard core' of European construction (i.e. the EC) long before they became eligible for full membership of the Community. Finally, he promoted the idea of a Bank for European Reconstruction and Development (BERD).

However emphatic or spectacular these initiatives were, they seem to have stemmed mainly from a desire to preserve a classical Gaullist façade rather than a true willingness to promote a new security architecture for the 'Grande Europe'. In practice, they proved of limited impact. France did host the November 1990 CSCE summit meeting in Paris, but in the preparation phase the French diplomacy seemed more in agreement with the cautious American and British stance than with the German and Soviet insistence on institutionalising the CSCE and giving it a stronger security role. For instance, France was far more reluctant than Germany to give the new Conflict Prevention Centre (CPC) more than a technical role and opposed the idea of making it the embryo for a future European Security Council, i.e. an instrument of collective security. As for the Confederation, it has remained, for quite some time, at best an empty shell, if not a slogan, and Mitterrand has been astonishingly sparing of explanations and details on his concept (Vedrine and Musitelli, 1991).

France's lack of enthusiasm for initiatives designed to strengthen the pan-European dimension of security proved particularly strong in the defence and security issues. Not only did the French diplomacy favour full NATO membership for a united Germany but, for a while at least, it showed suspicion *vis-à-vis* German intentions in that realm. In what appeared as a typical reminiscence of the 'Rapallo' mythology, Paris voiced unofficial but harsh criticism of the German-Soviet cooperation treaty of 9 November 1990, article 3 of which was interpreted by some in Paris as a 'reinsurance' clause reminiscent of the German-Russian treaty of 1887. This was, it was argued in the Quai d'Orsay, essentially incompatible with the spirit of West European solidarity and showed that the new Germany would prove a less reliable security partner in the future. Needless to say, the Franco-Soviet treaty signed on 29 October 1990 was devoid of such a clause. This diplomatic skirmish was highly illustrative of French concerns *vis-à-vis* Germany's perceived propensity to promote pan-European arrangements in which the West European (and to a lesser extent Atlantic) dimension would be diluted.

To sum up, France's response to the German and European challenges in the year or so after the fall of the Berlin Wall has been characterised by three main features. First, in spite of apparently significant initiatives such as the Confederation, French policies have been predominantly reactive. Of course, most key players of the European game were taken by surprise in the immediate post-Wall era, and France was no exception. Even the US has, arguably, done no more than closely follow Germany's heels. But in the case of France this relative passivity must be contrasted to a long Gaullist tradition of vision and activism in European security affairs. Moreover, French initiatives have often had to react not only to the rapidly evolving European context, but also to the negative impact of previous initiatives. This has created the impression of frequent adjustments, if not about turns. In spite (or maybe as a result) of Mitterrand's legendary tactical aptitude, this conveyed the impression of a lack of strategic direction, if not reluctance to accept those changes.

Second, as a consequence of this, French policies have been characterised by a deliberate tendency to multiply the institutional responses to the new German and European challenges, and to avoid giving a clearcut exclusivity to one particular framework. To be sure, the European Community was clearly identified as France's privileged forum for post-Cold War Europe. But Mitterrand did not push this West European bias to the point where other institutions would be excluded. In fact, it may be argued that the French initiatives have systematically searched for an institutional plurality, even redundancy, in which Western forums such as the EC, NATO or the WEU would not exclude pan-European ones such as the CSCE or the European Confederation. Such policies were of course typical of Mitterrand's habit of always keeping as many options open as possible. They may indeed have been well suited to a period of rapid change and uncertainty. But as a result of this approach his initiatives have sometimes seemed hesitant, if not contradictory. In fact, one of the most frequent criticisms of his approach has been his alleged inability to make clear choices (or, perhaps even more relevantly, to express his choices clearly).

Last but not least, the Gaullist model which has made up the French diplomatic and defence framework for three decades, although not altogether abandoned was handled roughly as a result of these initiatives. Not only were these reactive, often half-way policies, contrasting sharply with the General's visionary style, but, in substance, they departed from the Gaullist paradigm and its emphasis on the necessity to promote strong pan-European arrangements, its rejection of a federalist West European construction and of an integrated, American-led Atlantic Alliance. And yet, somewhat inconsistently, in the final analysis the key Gaullist assumption of French defence policy – the necessity to preserve the country's national sovereignty and strategic autonomy – was not called into question, in spite of Mitterrand's initial integrationist reaction (Hoffmann, 1990). This blend of Gaullist, Europeanist and Atlanticist policies was not only seemingly inconsistent, but it also fostered a somewhat paradoxical and above all damaging perception of French *repli sur soi* among allies.

Thus, France arguably fluffed her entry into the 'post-Yalta' world, the prospect of which she had been cherishing for decades. Some have commented that it was paradoxical that France should have put aside de Gaulle's heritage at a time when his prophecies on the future of Europe were at long last coming true, while others have argued that Mitterrand was only adapting the Gaullist framework to the realities of 1989–90. But at any rate, France gave an impression of reluctance to accept Germany's reunification and Europe's new order, a muddled record which can be explained by several interrelated factors. First, after two decades of immobility in European security following the Gaullist era, France had in many ways reached an accommodation with the status quo. A revisionist power in the 1960s, the country had progressively become more satisfied with the 'Yalta' order during the 1970s and 1980s. After all, France's position in the bipolar system had been reasonably enjoyable. On the one hand she had managed to remain aloof from the stifling Western structures such as NATO, thus preserving her autonomy and independence while enjoying a fair degree of security, and on the other she had managed to get political credit from her continuously denouncing the bloc system and having developed a specific, long-term concept of Europe's security architecture. Thus, when the revolution of 1989 finally brought about the changes France had advocated for so long, its initial reaction was one of limited enthusiasm. Moreover, France's real influence and leverage were quite limited in this period of rapid transition. At a time when the superpowers themselves had little impact over the ongoing changes in European security and, most of all, over the German unification process, France's role was, much like Britain's, bound to be at best secondary. This was the case during the 2 plus 4 conference in which the only substantial French input was to state the necessity to settle the issue of the Oder–Neisse line prior to concluding a treaty (a wholly justified concern, but one which, again, in the short term, did not help alleviate Franco-German misunderstandings). This was also the case within the Atlantic Alliance, where France's influence was small as a result of her specific status. This limited French ability to play a significant role in the overhaul of NATO.

Perhaps the most fundamental feature of French policy, however, was a major dilemma which France faced (or rather perceived herself as facing in the immediate post-Wall period) over integration and independence. On the one hand France could play the card of Western integration as the best way to absorb German might in the EC and to maintain a balance of power within the Alliance thanks to a continued strong US presence. But she might then eventually have to pay the price of this policy in terms of her own independence and status. On the other hand, France could promote European policies of a more genuinely Gaullist vein, with a view to establishing a collective security system from the Atlantic to the Urals, in which France would not be constrained in entangling Western structures. But this would create the risk of leaving Germany at the centre of Europe, with no institutional checks and balances, and without the possibility of France providing the balance by itself. Torn between two opposing, and perhaps equally irrelevant or obsolete approaches, France tried to combine the two of them, hoping to reap the benefits of both while escaping the pitfalls of both. Needless to say, it has not been a successful attempt, as it led to apparently ill-advised attitudes and inconsistent initiatives.

CONSTRAINTS: THE NECESSITY FOR CHOICES

In the initial post-Wall period, French attitudes and initiatives were therefore mostly influenced by immediate perceptions and concerns, particularly those dealing with the unification of Germany and its consequences. They were mostly shaped not by efforts to anticipate the future European system, but by applying old conceptual frameworks. This has been perhaps an unavoidable phase. But now that the initial post-Wall period is over, the question becomes will France be able to elaborate and implement long term policies in which important choices will have to be made? And what will be be the terms of those choices? To answer this question, one must first look at the constraints within which these policies will have to be conceived in the years ahead.

It is important to bear in mind the actual timeframe in which these constraints will emerge. When Mitterrand said in Bonn, on 3 November 1989 that 'given the pace of events, I would be surprised if the next ten years should pass without our having to face a new structure in Europe', he may have made an underestimation if by 'structure in Europe' he meant 'status of Germany', for the unification process took less than a year (Mitterrand–Kohl, 1990). But if he was pointing to the overall European security system, this time-frame is not irrelevant. To be sure, a series of major events took place in the very short term, including: a NATO summit in the fall of 1991 to define the new tasks of the Alliance; the signing by the end of 1991 of a treaty on EC political union; and the gathering in 1992 of a new CSCE summit in Helsinki with a likely substantial arms control agenda. Yet these events will need to be confirmed by subsequent evolutions. The concrete strategic consequences of the 1989 revolutions in the security field will make themselves felt progressively. Indeed, it will take the first half of the decade for the 1990 CFE treaty to be fully implemented and for the Soviet forces to withdraw completely from the territory of the former GDR, not to mention the negotiation and implementation of a CFE2 treaty or the strengthening of CSCE's current embryonic collective security mechanisms. It will also take some years for the Western forces now stationed in Germany and elsewhere in Europe to reach a stable, much lower level and to undergo the profound restructuring prompted by the political and strategic upheaval of the past two years or so. Finally, the emergence of a tangible West European defence and security structure will almost certainly not happen before the second half of the decade at best, even if political union is formally established in 1991. Thus, it is within this mid- to long-term time frame that France's major security choices will have to be made. They will result from a combination of mid- to long-term objectives and constraints which must now be reviewed.

The West-West dimension of security, both at the Atlantic and West European levels, could well prove the most challenging in the years ahead. At the Alliance level, the old France–NATO equation will be likely to come under pressure (Bozo, 1991a). After all, France's specific position within the Alliance so far (beside motivations dealing with Gaullist ideas of *grandeur*) stemmed mainly from the stated objective of overcoming the bloc system, which justified her non-integrated status and zealous preservation of an autonomous defence and deterrent posture. But this rationale is now being challenged precisely because 'Europe has entered a new, promising era' as 'the division of Europe is... being overcome', as France and her allies have recognised in the London Declaration (NATO, 1990). As the Alliance itself adapts to this new situation, both in words ('we solemnly state that we are no longer adversaries') (NATO, 1990) and deeds ('we must profoundly alter the way we think about defence') France's reluctance to change the nature of its overall relationship with NATO could ironically lead to her being perceived as the last defender of the status quo. Moreover, France's aloofness from Allied military structures is likely in the long run to have far less military relevance as the actual degree of NATO peacetime integration recedes. For, unlike forward defence, most national NATO forces are likely in the future to remain stationed on their home territories in peacetime, coming under NATO command only in a crisis or in a conflict, a modular, flexible formula far more compatible with France's concept of allied military operations.[3] Ironically enough, present trends within NATO's military organisation may well have the effect of generalising the French pattern of participation, thus making the issue of integration far less divisive.

The same *de facto* convergence is likely to appear as far as strategic doctrines are concerned (Bozo, 1991b). The opposition between flexible response and France's deterrent concept stemmed from profound divergences, most of all over the issue of the nuclear threshold. For the past three decades, France rejected the NATO strategy because of its alleged objective of postponing nuclear first use in a major conflict in Europe, and criticised flexible response as a war-fighting doctrine as opposed to her own war prevention nuclear concept. But as the Soviet threat recedes, and particularly after the reduction in capabilities after 1994–5, most predictable scenarios of conflict in Europe will not require the threat (let alone the use) of nuclear weapons since they will not involve the 'vital interests' of nuclear countries. Both France and her nuclear allies in NATO will *de facto* have to adapt their thinking to a situation of minimal deterrence in which nuclear weapons will be truly 'last resort' weapons, as the London Declaration put it – even though Mitterrand vigorously opposed this wording with the traditional French arguments. The nuclear element, although still essential, should become politically and strategically less preponderant for Western security, thus making the antagonism between France and NATO over nuclear doctrines increasingly irrelevant.

In sum, the military and strategic changes likely to take place in the next few years may well remove the constraints which have fostered the controversies between France and NATO for three decades. But this is only one side of the coin. France's NATO policies in the foreseeable future should be increasingly intertwined with her initiatives in the field of West European defence and security cooperation. France will naturally continue to favour the emergence of a politically and strategically more autonomous Western Europe, probably the most permanent feature of her international policy since the Second World War. But this ambitious objective will have to adapt to the realities and constraints which have become progressively clearer and have been confirmed by the lessons of the Gulf War and the role Europe has – or has not – played (Bozo and Paolini, 1991). Indeed, the advent of a concrete

European political and strategic entity is a far-reaching objective, unlikely to happen in the short or mid-term. Even if a treaty on political union is signed by the end of 1991, it most certainly will not establish in the near future an organisation capable of defending Europe. Moreover, a European political and strategic entity cannot be thought of as an integrated, supranational institution on the model, say, of the European Defence Community. The Kohl-Mitterrand letter on political union mentioned above has bluntly recentred the exercise to an intergovernmental approach. Today's reality of European national perspectives – again amply demonstrated during the Gulf crisis – simply does not allow the establishment of a centralised decision-making process with a common military instrument. As the French Foreign Minister Roland Dumas pointed out:

> Let us be realistic: it [a common defence policy] is not feasible point-blank... The objective is not to replace today's national responsibilities by a collective approach: security is the concern of all, and defence that of each and everyone.
>
> *(Le Monde*, 1990b)

Because the emergence of a European defence organisation is not a short-term possibility for political, military and financial reasons, NATO will remain, for some time at least, the key organisation for the defence of Europe – a fact France has had to recognise. As Mitterrand himself put it, 'the defence of Western Europe, today and for many years to come, cannot be conceived of but within the bounds of the Atlantic Alliance' (*Le Monde*, 1991a).

These constraints, which French policies will have to take into account in pursuing the objective of European unification, will, in the short term, cause a dilemma which is not entirely new. On the one hand, France cannot hope to enhance European political and strategic unity without accepting NATO as a point of departure and, therefore, without accepting some kind of a rapprochement with NATO so as to increase France's leverage within the Alliance and accelerate its Europeanisation. But on the other hand, such a rapprochement is risky (even though it has become possible at the military and strategic levels) until Europe has achieved a concrete degree of political existence, for it could simply lead to France's return into the Atlantic fold with no real European progress. As a result, France's margin of manoeuvre will be limited. This does not mean that an active French policy will be impossible, but that changes will be progressive and initiatives will have to be pragmatic.

The necessity for choices in the next few years will also be felt at the level of France's national defence policy. In a Europe in which a certain degree of 'renationalisation' of defence policies seems inevitable given the vanishing Soviet threat, individual defence choices will be critical. France's programmatic, structural and doctrinal options will have a substantial impact on the country's ability to pursue its overall European security objectives and, needless to say, to defend itself. Until recently, fundamental defence choices have been postponed as a result of the uncertainties of the post-Wall period (Howorth, 1990). But under the combined pressure of financial constraints and the end of the Cold War, it is being acknowledged that real choices with long-term implications will have to be made in the next few years. Moreover the Gulf War, which demonstrated the relative deficiencies of the French defence posture in the new world security context, has had a catalytic effect. Indeed, departing from this traditional wait-and-see policy and willingess to avoid jeopardising the sacrosanct defence 'consensus', the President himself declared in the immediate aftermath of the Gulf War that 'a debate on the internal equilibrium of our forces, on their composition and their nature, is necessary. It should begin this year in Parliament' (*Liberation*, 1991).

Both nuclear and conventional forces will have to come under scrutiny. With regard to the former, a reform of nuclear doctrine and, most of all, its political presentation will be needed if French politico-strategic isolation in Europe is to be avoided. France's traditional insistence on the absolute primacy of nuclear deterrence ('*le tout-nucleaire*') will, as hinted above, become increasingly irrelevant in the new context. Paris will have to accept that nuclear arms are last-resort weapons, something which is not a doctrine but a fact of life. Maintaining a declaratory, let alone an operational policy of early nuclear use would also be politically damaging: the threat of rapid escalation in a Europe now rid of overwhelming Soviet military superiority would antagonise other nations in Europe, particularly those now weary of nuclear weapons. Finally, France will have to make efforts to overcome the contradiction between her primarily national, indeed hexagonal, conception of nuclear deterrence and her advocation of European Union. Whereas it has been possible to live with this up to now, it is likely to become less sustainable in the new context. The fact that the nuclear element will be less central in France's and Europe's security should facilitate this adaptation (Paolini, 1991).

Such a reform of nuclear policy is bound to have an impact on the nuclear force structure. With almost one-third of defence procurement going into nuclear weapons, genuine technological independence, and a complete panoply of strategic weapons for each leg of the triad, France today is often described as a mini-nuclear superpower. Although France's nuclear posture was supposed to be minimal, in the new strategic environment the question 'how much is enough?' will have to be asked seriously. As a result of both the politico-strategic trends described above and of budgetary constraints, nuclear priority will likely be abandoned and the nuclear arsenal will, for the first time, stop expanding. For a number of reasons the ground leg may be gradually phased out: the growing vulnerability of the silo-based missiles on the Plateau d'Albion; the difficulty in developing a mobile follow-on missile; and their association with the concept of national sanctuary. The strategic triad could therefore, at least in the long run, become a dyad. Moreover, cuts in the other two legs will likely be considered. Even though the SLBMs will remain the cornerstone of France's deterrent posture, defence planners will probably face a choice between quantity and quality as intensive efforts will be needed to preserve their invulnerability (*Le Monde*, 1991b).

Conventional forces will also have to undergo profound changes. So far, their concept, format and structures have been shaped almost exclusively by the strategic realities of the Cold War. Because of the nuclear priority conventional forces have been treated as the poor relations of French defence, despite a continuous qualitative build-up since the late 1960s. Even more importantly, they have only marginally been thought of in terms of employment and mostly in terms of deterrence. Apart from their near permanent commitment in a post colonial context (involving small forces mostly in low intensity warfare) French conventional forces have been tailor-made for the European theatre in which they were facing a massive threat to France's vital interests. As a result, they have not been well designed for grey-area contingencies of a less than all-out confrontation at the border of the national territory. To be sure, efforts were made throughout the 1980s to make them ready for such situations, including the creation of an army rapid action force (Force d'Action Rapide – FAR) in 1984. In 1989 an ambitious plan was announced shortly before the sweeping changes in Central and Eastern Europe, to adapt the army, air and naval forces to a strategic environment in which multiple risks inside or outside Europe, rather than a unidirectional threat, will need to be addressed. But France's relatively limited military commitment in the Gulf War has illustrated the necessity to maintain this effort if France is to remain, strategically, a medium power with global ambitions and capabilities. This will require further modernisation of the conventional forces in order to upgrade their mobility, projection capabilities and, last but not least, C3I capabilities. Indeed, the most important military lesson drawn from the Gulf War by the French military – a lesson which also applies to the Central and Eastern European context – is about the strategic role of reconnaissance and intelligence capabilities (above all those provided by satellites) in crisis management and actual operations. Yet the most challenging item on the list of necessary reforms may well be the conscription system. The limited number of French troops sent to the Gulf as compared with Britain was not so much the consequence of more limited operational capabilities than a reflection of the fact that conscripts may not be used in military contingencies in which the country's vital interests are not at stake. A higher degree of professionalisation of the French forces will thus be needed in order to increase intervention capabilities, but for obvious political, social and economic reasons this will be a limited evolution, and one which, in any event, will need to be continued by an overall diminution of manpower, particularly in the army.

These changes in France's defence posture in the years ahead, and above all the necessary shift in the balance between nuclear deterrence and conventional defence, will have to be made in a difficult budgetary context. Even though France has been an exception among Western powers in maintaining a defence budget which has not declined in real terms, this will probably have to change in the future. Whatever the evolution of the defence budget in real terms, it is almost certain that it will at best stagnate as a function of the GNP, thus reflecting the nation's changing priorities. Whereas defence spending came close to a level of 4 per cent of the GNP in the mid-1980s, it is likely to remain around 3.5 per cent at most in the foreseeable future, a figure which sets quite narrow limits for the evolution of France's defence posture, and one which makes real strategic choices a necessity rather than making marginal cuts across the board (Seguin, 1991).[4]

Finally, options will have to be defined by France in the East–West dimension of the evolving European system. So far this has clearly not been a priority, even though efforts were made to conceal the French preference for existing Western forums and, to begin with, the EC. Yet some signs show that this benign neglect may, in the longer run, become harmful for France's role and status. In 1990 the Czechoslovak leadership endorsed the Confederation concept and agreed to co-host a meeting in Prague to launch it in June 1991 under the joint chairmanship of Mitterrand and Havel. Now there are reports that they and other Central and Eastern European governments are weary of this approach, which have been interpreted by some as a blow to Mitterrand's ambitious scheme (Fitchett, 1991). Not only are East and Central Europeans grieved by France's apparent inability to give substance to this concept, but they are also distressed by the notion that the Confederation might be a way to postpone their entry into the EC and other Western institutions. Indeed, Mitterrand may have underestimated the attraction the Community (and even NATO) holds for the new democracies. France has been a killjoy for their hopes of rapidly joining the West by being the most vocal critic of NATO's pretensions to play a role *vis-à-vis* these countries and by stressing the need for them to be patient as to EC membership (a political mistake that German diplomacy has carefully avoided). The fundamental issue here is whether the prospect of belonging to a Gaullist 'Grande Europe' makes any sense to the Czechs, Poles and others.

The relative failure, so far, of the Confederation is of course probably not prohibitive. Yet it comes as a warning for the years ahead: France will have to decide what role she should play with regard to the political and economic re-emergence of Central and Eastern Europe's democracies and, most of all, with regard to their security problems. (In a different way of course, the same question will apply to the former Soviet Union.) This means that a clear and consistent French perspective on the respective roles of the main organisations and forums *vis-à-vis* the ex-bloc countries should be offered. Perhaps even more importantly, this dimension of the new European system will require a more dynamic presence, both in political, economic and last but not least, cultural terms. The risks of inactivity or indecision in that realm are considerable: what is at stake in France's strategy with regard to the 'other Europe' is whether or not she will go into eclipse as a European power, particularly *vis-à-vis* Germany.

OPPORTUNITIES: LOST OR YET TO BE FOUND?

France's future in Europe in the decade ahead appears to be a choice between two evils. On the one hand, refusing to take into account the emerging trends in European security and to adapt French East–West, West–West and national security policies accordingly would lead to isolation. But on the other hand, relinquishing the specificity of the Gaullist model (or what remains of it) may be rightfully dreaded as likely to lead to a drop in France's status and international influence. Of course, this choice between isolation and normalisation is one between two different but equally unattractive forms of marginalisation in the new European system. Thus, for France, the question 'what is to be done?' in the next few years amounts to asking whether an escape from this dilemma may be found and how.

Judging from ongoing developments, in the short term the answer may at first glance seem to be negative. France's record so far is muddled compared to her ambitions. The rather poor showing of the Confederation project highlights the narrowness of the margin of manoeuvre left between the objectives and the constraints of France's policies and seems to confirm the difficulties France will have in finding a new role in the new pan-European context. But this impression is even stronger at the West–West level and particularly in the light of France's aspiration to West European political and strategic unification, the most constant goal in French security policy post-Second World War and one of France's main tools of international influence and status. Current events confirm Mitterrand's unwilling recognition of the Atlantic Alliance as the inevitable basis of West European security, and the ongoing reform of NATO does not fit well with French West European ambitions. At the military level (for France's allies have, paradoxically, agreed on a new force structure before reaching consensus on a new strategy and on the new political tasks of the Alliance) the new Rapid Reaction Force (RRF) concept launched in May 1991 by the integrated members of NATO, cannot be seen from Paris but as a successful pre-emption of French goals. If implemented, the RRF will apparently constitute a European force within NATO, capable of operating on behalf of European members in situations out of the NATO treaty area in which America's allies would want to be on their own. By refusing to associate its own forces (notably the Force d'Action Rapide) with this new force structure, and by staunchly criticising this effort as a façade transformation, Paris has once again risked creating an impression of opposing changes within the Alliance and of clinging to the dogma of strategic independence.

Some in France have criticised Mitterrand's decision not to participate actively in the reform of NATO and its tentative Europeanisation. By remaining aloof from the new structures, particularly from the Rapid Reaction Force (RRF), critics point out that France will be marginalised in what will remain the main defence forum on the continent for the years to come, in the name of her chimeric plans for West European political and strategic unification. As a result Britain, thanks to her skilful NATO policy and more flexible approach to the Community after Thatcher, is now credited with pragmatically taking the lead in the movement to give the Europeans a bigger role in the Alliance while continuing to reap the benefit of her special relationship with the United States. Not only will France be isolated in the Western alliance, the argument goes, but by the same token the effective transformation of NATO and the emergence of a truly autonomous European entity, of which France is the only possible catalyst, will be delayed. In other words, because she clung to twenty-five-year old attitudes and principles despite a completely new environment, France may have missed an historic opportunity to take the lead in the transformations which it had advocated for so long, a mistake she is likely to have to pay for in the years to come (Lellouche, 1991).

While it is true that in the short term these events may appear to be a setback for France, or at least a lost opportunity, decisions made after the July 1990 NATO London summit and in the first half of 1991 may not have been as mistaken as critics argue. It is doubtful whether other options were truly available and, most of all, whether France had enough leverage to risk trading off her specific NATO status so as to be in a position to actually promote far-reaching changes from within. In other words, the dilemma between rapprochement with NATO to accelerate its Europeanisation and retaining French independence was still insuperable and imposed a wait-and-see attitude. Granted, Paris did not even come up with its own version of a transformed Alliance, thus making it virtually impossible for other Europeans to endorse it. But it is clear that French options, had they been put on the table, would not have been accepted by France's partners. Paris was unlikely to obtain tangible results because of economic and financial constraints, because of doubts as to the strategic viability of a genuinely European defence organisation and, last but not least, because of fears that its creation would hasten the US disengagement from Europe (particularly given Washington's policy of deliberately fuelling those fears). In short because of the considerable inertia which characterises the security policies of individual West European countries and of the United States, such a success would have been highly unlikely at this time. As de Gaulle once put it, 'one must not ask for what one cannot get', a precept which seems to have influenced Mitterrand once again. Hence a feeling of *déjà vu* was apparent, reminiscent of episodes such as the 'Year of Europe' in which France appeared as stubbornly isolated in the Atlantic Community.

Yet, this may be only a short-term situation. Even though NATO today seems to sail before the wind, this may be but a volatile impression. At the political level, as far as the new tasks of the Alliance are concerned, the American-led effort to give it some relevance *vis-à-vis* the security problems of Central and East European nations or in the global North–South context is likely to reach its own natural limits as European members (and not only France) widely oppose these roles, and favour other institutions such as the CSCE or the UN to fulfil them. Events in Yugoslavia in summer 1991 have already confirmed the limited relevance of NATO in such contingencies. And at the military level, the plans which have been agreed upon within the Alliance remain to be implemented in practice. The Rapid Reaction Force in particular will require considerable efforts on the part of participating states, which, except for Britain, are far from already having the capabilities for such operations. It also remains to be seen what exactly the Force's missions will be. Some NATO members (not only France) already question the rationale behind such a force in a post-Cold War context. As a result, the Rapid Reaction Force is likely to remain a virtuality, or at least to depend to a very large extent on US support (in which case it would not be a truly European force). In sum, the reform of the Atlantic Alliance may well soon appear as a *trompe l'oeil* behind which the long-term trend of American disengagement and loosening of the Allied military structures will continue. In spite of the current talk of a 'unipolar world' in the aftermath of the sweeping US-led victory in the Gulf War, an American-led NATO is not certain to emerge, at the end of the day, as the be-all and end-all of Western security. If these predictions are confirmed (as French policy-makers obviously anticipate) then the real opportunities for France may still be ahead.

While keeping aloof from NATO for the time being, France retains valuable assets for influencing the evolution of Western structures. When it comes to capabilities and intentions, the Gulf crisis and war have demonstrated that France can deliver in spite of her specific status. The overall excellent relationship between Paris and Washington, which has been constantly built up over the past decade or so (in spite of punctual psychodramas), confirms France's key role in any new transatlantic bargain. To be sure, NATO has survived without France for almost three decades. But in a much more volatile European environment, in the absence of a massive threat, and with the likelihood of an inward-looking Germany, France's participation may well appear more vital, thus paving the way for future compromises. To sum up, Mitterrand's apparent bet on mid- to long-term trends may well prove a good one. If such is the case, he will have made the right choice in keeping assets to bargain with when the time is ripe. In spite of the present apparent setback, France may thus be likely to quickly return to its traditional ambitions and West European activism. The main question of course remains how this will be done, but it is already clear that because of the constraints discussed above, future French policies will have both to continue to provide vision so as to keep the necessary momentum, and, more importantly, tactical flexibility so as to obtain tangible, if progressive results. In other words, it will have to be a far more pragmatic approach than in the past.

A prerequisite for the initiation of such policies is the signing of a political union treaty. This is seen from Paris as signalling a clear commitment on the part of the Twelve to build up a European political and eventually military organisation. Even though the treaty will almost certainly not create such an entity in the immediate future, and is likely to remain for some time at best a statement of principle, it will represent a significant token for France's European policies. It will provide the long-term perspective and the legal framework needed to stimulate the progressive edification of a concrete strategic entity. And, equally important because it will alleviate France's fears of the Atlantisation of her European ambitions and international status, it will take some heat out of and inject flexibility into the France–NATO relationship.

Once this prerequisite is obtained, France's policy is likely to be dual-track, both at the European and NATO levels. At the European level, France will have to further 'Europeanise' her defence in order to give its West European ambitions political credibility and operational substance. Once the principle of political union is agreed upon, Paris will both have to, and be in a position to, make more concrete offers with regard to the West European strategic identity. To some extent, the patterns of European military cooperation developed in the 1980s (such as the Franco-German defence cooperation or the Italian-Spanish-French cooperation in the Mediterranean) will be useful frameworks for these initiatives. But French initiatives will need to be much more far-reaching than these efforts, the scope of which was at that time limited by the constraints of the bipolar game. Two main directions seem to be promising for these initiatives. The first is space and satellite technology. In 1994 France will be the first non-superpower nation (albeit with a measure of Italian and Spanish support) to launch a military intelligence satellite. Because such capabilities are likely to be key strategic assets in the new environment, France will certainly try to foster a strong West European partnership in that realm. French policy makers indeed rightly underline the fact that military space technology is now of the same strategic importance as nuclear capabilities were in the Cold War and they have no difficulty arguing that European autonomy, whether within NATO or not, means nothing if the proper C3I assets are not available independently. As for the second direction, it could consist of intensifying efforts aimed at increasing the interoperability of European national forces, particularly for intervention out of the NATO area. 'Europeanising' the Force d'Action Rapide by promoting common operational standards and joint manoeuvres with other similar European units, would be the key element in that effort. Such peacetime cooperation could of course be implemented in a WEU framework, with a view to being able to set up a truly autonomous force with a European command system in a crisis. The aim would be to offer France's European allies an alternative to the British-led, NATO integrated RRF. The French concept could attract nations with a specific strategic perspective (such as Italy and Spain in the Mediterranean) or interested in a more genuinely European effort than the RRF entails (such as Germany). This would have to be a pragmatic policy, aimed not at countering NATO but at developing complementary structures between the existing or transformed Alliance, and Europe. Because military cooperation will be increasingly characterised by the flexibility and plasticity of command structures, France's European allies should not perceive this policy as an attempt to undermine NATO but as an effort to extend the spectrum of allied military architectures in the direction of European autonomy.[5]

The corollary of this Europeanisation and the second track of France's approach would have to be a rapprochement with NATO. This would be needed for technical reasons, but also for political ones. At the technical level, France's more active presence in NATO structures would facilitate more flexible cooperation among Europeans, and indeed between Europeans and Americans. At the political level, it would represent a token of France's new readiness to recognise the NATO framework as still essential for West European defence and for the transatlantic link. In practical terms, this rapprochement would not have to be conceived of in terms of France's 'reintegration' into NATO, which would be both militarily irrelevant and politically incompatible with the objective of European unity and autonomy, but as a pragmatic institutional bridge building (for instance, France's return to the military committee would be then conceivable). This rapprochement should result from a carefully balanced approach aiming at both pro-gressively normalising France's participation in NATO (short of military integration) and developing a genuine European security and, in the longer run, defence identity.

To conclude this discussion of France's opportunities in European security for the years to come one must thus look beyond the present relative disappointment. True, recent events in NATO as well as the overall post Gulf War atmosphere do foster an impression of a reduced French influence and failure to push key objectives in European security. But it must be realised that behind the scenes, long-term trends are at work which could prove more favourable for French designs, if the opportunities are not missed.

NOTES

1 Typically, Mitterrand's visit to the GDR in late December 1989, a few days after his meeting with Gorbachev in Kiev (see below), was interpreted as a sign of his belief that a reformed and democratic East Germany could survive as a separate country and society.
2 The risks entailed by a federalist approach to European unification were highlighted when Kohl declared on French television 29 March 1990: 'As for me, the objective is to build the United States of Europe... but I am curious to see whether everybody is ready for that', a remark which implicitly questioned France's strong European rhetoric.
3 This will notably be the case for NATO's Rapid Reaction Force, discussed below (Hitchens, 1991).
4 The August 1991 coup in the Soviet Union, which took place as the defence budget for 1992 was being debated, probably saved a few billion francs. But this is only a respite.
5 As a result of the increased flexibility of military arrangements, forces earmarked for the Rapid Reaction Force, if it is set up, could well cooperate with the non-integrated Force d'Action Rapide in peacetime. (The FAR could well be France's future military contribution to NATO in a clearly identified East–West, NATO-related contingency.) Both the British-led RRF and a potential WEU French-led equivalent must be conceived of in terms of crisis, or wartime integration, thus allowing a building-block, modular approach (Heisbourg, 1991).

REFERENCES

Bozo, F. (1991a) 'La France et l'OTAN: vers une nouvelle Alliance', *Defense Nationale*, January 1991: 19–33.
Bozo, F. (1991b) 'La France, l'OTAN et l'avenir de la dissuasion en Europe', *Politique Etrangère*, 1991, 2: 513–25.
Bozo, F. (forthcoming) 'Paradigm lost: the French experience with détente', in R. Davy (ed.) *European Detente: A Reappraisal*, London: RIIA.
Bozo, F. and Paolini, J. (1991) 'L'Europe entre elle-meme et le Golfe', *Politique Etrangère*, 1991, 1: 179–92.
Economist (1990a) 27 January 1990.
Economist (1990b) ' France pulls away from de Gaulle', 15 December 1990.

Fitchett, J. (1991) 'Czechs cool to meeting sought by Mitterrand', *International Herald Tribune*, 10 June 1991.

Heisbourg, F. (1991) 'Europeans could have their force', *International Herald Tribune*, 29 May 1991.

Hitchens, T. (1991) 'NATO leaders mull change to flexible rapid-reaction forces', *Defense News*, 1 April 1991.

Hoffmann, S. (1990) 'The case for leadership', *Foreign Policy*, 81: 20–38.

Howorth, J. (1990) 'France since the Berlin Wall: defence and diplomacy', *The World Today*, July 1990: 125–30.

Kaiser, K. and de Montbrial, T. (1990) 'France and Germany: the tasks ahead', *International Herald Tribune*, 14 December 1990.

Kolboom, I. (1991) *Vom Geteilten zum vereinten Deutschland,* Deutschland-Bilder in Frankreich, Arbeitspapier zu Internationalen Politik, 61, Bonn, DGAP.

Le Monde (1990a) Interview with President Mitterand, 20 June 1990.

Le Monde (1990b) 12 October 1990.

Le Monde (1991a) 13 April 1991.

Le Monde (1991b) 8 June 1991.

Lellouche, P. (1991) 'OTAN: l'"atlantisation"', *Le Point*, 1 June 1991.

Liberation (1991) 4 March 1991.

Mitterrand–Kohl (1990) text of a joint press conference held in Bonn, 3 November 1990, *Politique Etrangère de la France*, November–December 1990: 4.

NATO (1990) *London Declaration on a Transformed North Atlantic Alliance*, Brussels: NATO Information Service.

Paolini, J. (1991) 'La France, L'Europe et la bombe', *Commentaire*, 54.

Seguin, P. (1991) 'La nouvelle armée francaise', *Le Monde*, 6 June 1991.

Trean, C. (1991) 'La France et le nouvel ordre européen', *Politique Etrangère*, 1991, 1: 81–98.

Vedrine, H. and Musitelli, J. (1991) 'Les changements des années 1989–1990 et l'Europe de la prochaine décennie', *Politique Etrangère*, 1991, 1: 165–77.

12 Security policy in the Federal Republic of Germany

The search for a new identity

Norbert Ropers

THE NEW CHALLENGES FACED BY GERMAN SECURITY

With the end of the East–West conflict and the unification of the two German states, 1990 brought fundamental changes to the new Federal Republic, and particularly its security. For four decades the two German states had lain at the juncture of the East–West conflict, and military plans and capabilities had been geared primarily to their territory; now the Federal Republic lies at the centre of a continent whose states profess, via the 'Paris Charter', the common principles of the market economy, pluralist democracy, and peaceful cooperation. The prospects of a lasting European peace order and a markedly reduced level of armaments and of military personnel have seldom been as good as today. However, the new situation has also brought uncertainties and risks which German security policy cannot and should not ignore.

Five specific security challenges face the Federal Republic. At the top of the list come the foreign policy aspects of German unification, which, within a short time, have given the country complete sovereignty in international law but which have also confronted it with a host of new expectations from its neighbours and partners. The clearest expression of the expectations (and fears) that exist *vis-à-vis* the new and enlarged Germany was given in the positions of the various countries at the start of the so-called 2 plus 4 negotiations, the 'negotiations to bring about German unity' (Schlotter, 1991). What the Western partners were chiefly interested in was 'binding' the new Germany into the framework of the existing Western alliances and organisations, in order to counter the threat of any erosion of transatlantic/ Western European relations and the possibility of any 'special German way'. The Soviet Union, on the other hand, started off wanting to use German unification as a lever to get rid of the old alliance structures and to incorporate the united Germany into a new, pan-European security structure.

At German instigation, it was the Western position that finally prevailed at the end of the 2 plus 4 negotiations. However, in return for allowing the new Germany to be linked into the Western security system, the Soviet Union obtained a series of Western concessions and German undertakings. One of the most important of these is that Germany will reduce its forces to 370,000 by the mid-1990s and that no nuclear weapons or non-German NATO troops may be deployed on the territory of the former GDR. Furthermore, in the 2 plus 4 treaty, the Federal Republic reiterated its renunciation of the right to produce, own, or use nuclear, biological, or chemical weapons (*Bulletin des Presses*, 1990).

The results of the 2 plus 4 negotiations mark out some important framework conditions for future German security policy. At the same time, the expectations and fears that were voiced in East and West in the course of the negotiations have made it clear that the memory of Germany's role between 1871 and 1939 has by no means faded. The relief shown by most of Germany's neighbours over the 2 plus 4 solution was probably due not least to the fact that this seemed to guarantee a more stable way of harnessing a united Germany than did the alternative schemes for a new, pan-European peace structure.

A basic dilemma faced by future German foreign policy, now that the East–West conflict is over and unification has been achieved, results from the contradictory expectations being directed at the country from outside. On the one hand there are fears that Germany might become too strong and might once again attempt to secure supremacy in Europe. On the other hand there is the expectation that, precisely because of this strength, Germany should play a more active role in Europe than it has done up to now. What consequences this dilemma has in the individual practical areas of security will be examined more closely below, but before that, it is necessary to examine a second set of security challenges, namely the internal problems posed by unification.

These challenges consist chiefly of two related processes: the integration of the remnants of the Nationale Volksarmee (NVA) into the Federal Army, and the reduction of overall Federal Army manpower to 370,000 men and of weapons levels to the ceilings set out in the CFE I treaty. The size of the NVA had already decreased rapidly immediately after the peaceful revolution which took place in the GDR in late 1989. By summer 1990 it had shrunk from 173,000 men to just under 100,000 (IAP-Dienst Sicherheitspolitik, 1990). However, the Federal government's plan to integrate the now-shrunken NVA into the Federal Army was greeted with reserve by many West German soldiers because the former hostility between the two armies had created a considerable psychological barrier. In particular, the idea of having to accept as superiors those NVA officers who had previously been responsible for inculcating an enemy image of West Germany in the GDR stirred up adverse emotions. Conversely, after unification in October 1990, many NVA soldiers felt discriminated against because of the circumstances of the takeover and because of their inferior financial position compared to their fellow soldiers from the West.

In summer 1991 the integration of the East German units was formally concluded. One of the more important ways this was achieved was through a disproportionate reduction in the number of units in eastern Germany. Thus in May 1991 there were only 56,000 German soldiers still stationed there (*Frankfurter Allgemeine Zeitung*, 1991c). None the less, the psychological-cum-social barriers between conscripts and professionals from East and West will probably make proper integration of the Federal Army as a whole difficult for some time to come.

Besides this, the political debates about the future structure of the Federal Army indicate that because of the changes in overall conditions, military aspects will play a markedly less important role. Thus in discussions about the regional distribution of the garrisons that would remain, the arguments that were advanced concerned mainly regional and structural aspects and had very little to do with military strategy.[1]

The third challenge with which German security policy is presented stems from the substantial demilitarisation in Central Europe. This involves not only the plans for reduction that have already been agreed, but also the possibility of further disarmament and conversion. The disarmament measures agreed in CFE I provide for substantially reduced weapon ceilings that would have been considered inconceivable just a few years ago (*Europa Archiv*, 1990). These will completely remove any Soviet ability to launch a surprise attack on Western Europe, a key assumption behind Western strategic planning. In addition, it is likely that there will be drastic reductions in military personnel in the wake of any follow-up negotiations. It is already certain that in addition to reductions in the Federal Army, there will be a drastic cutback in foreign troops stationed in Central Europe. The Soviet Union will withdraw its 380,000 men from the former GDR by the mid-1990s; its withdrawal from Czechoslovakia and Hungary has already been concluded; and its troops are to be withdrawn from Poland by the mid-1990s. As regards NATO forces the United States and Britain have announced a reduction in their troops by more than half their present strength, and France will limit its involvement to participation in the Franco-German brigade. This means that in a few years there will be one million fewer soldiers in Central Europe than at the end of the 1980s.

The financial savings made possible by these reductions in personnel will be modest in the short term however: compensation and pensions must be paid and money spent on removals, (accumulated) ecological burdens must be cleared away, and there is a general trend towards more cost-intensive arms equipment. In the case of the Western troops stationed in the former Federal Republic, there is the added consideration that they represent an important factor in regional economies, not least from the point of view of the German civilians they employ. The effect of conventional disarmament on employment is therefore negative for the Federal Republic (Wellman, 1989: 415ff). Of course this is not the only determining factor; the alternative uses to which the military budget may be put, and the conversion strategies implemented by the arms industry are also important considerations (Kiy and Lobbe, 1990).

In sum then, this third challenge is ambivalent. On the one hand, in view of the actual and potential demilitarisation in Central Europe, it would seem obvious that security policy should be radically revised, and not simply 'carried on' as before but at a lower level. On the other hand, precisely because of the extent of demilitarisation, there have begun to be stirrings among a number of vested interests and interest groups who would like to preserve as much of the former structures as is possible.

The fourth challenge lies in the radical shift in security problems in Europe (Enders, 1990). In addition to the disappearance of any Soviet ability to launch a surprise attack on Western Europe, the dissolution of the Warsaw Pact and the strong Western orientation of the Eastern states of Central Europe has provided NATO with a new 'security glacis'. The former Soviet Union will no doubt remain the most important power on the Continent in military terms, but the problems in regard to security stem not so much from this fact as from the diverse difficulties associated with the transformation of the former socialist societies. Chief among these are the tendencies to fragmentation of the multinational states of Yugoslavia and the Soviet Union, as well as the ethno-nationalist conflicts in Eastern and Southern Europe (Giessman, 1991). The risks of violent confrontation to which these give rise cannot be resolved by the traditional Western policies of alliance and deterrence.

A further problem arises from the economic gulf between Western and Eastern Europe. Apart from the fact that such an imbalance is not compatible in the long term with a 'pan-European peace order', this gulf prejudices the prospects of success of the reforms being implemented in the former socialist countries. One expression of this is the steep rise in migration from the East to the West which has occurred since 1989. Estimates differ as to the extent of future emigration that may be expected from the former Soviet Union and the Eastern European countries. According to surveys conducted in spring 1991, four to five million people have concrete plans to emigrate during the next three years (Stolting, 1991). The chief motives here are undoubtedly economic. Additional migratory movements of unknown size may be prompted by the current ethno-nationalist conflicts and by the uncertain situation in the former Soviet Union. The option that is sometimes alluded to of deflecting the expected migratory floods with military barriers however seems highly problematic.

The Federal Republic is particularly affected by this development. In the first place, within the framework of détente it strongly supported measures to make freedom of movement between East and West a reality, and it would therefore not appear very credible if it now spoke up in favour of the imposition of new barriers. In the second place, its geographical position means that it is less able than other Western European states to abstract itself from the developments in Eastern Europe. In addition, there are historical relations and economic and cultural links with these countries, all of which means that Germany must pay particular attention to the new security risks and interests of its Eastern European neighbours.

The fifth challenge is that of security threats from outside Europe. This was widely discussed in the wake of the 1991 Gulf War, particularly after Germany's cautious approach was subjected to massive criticism by some Western allies. What should the nature of Germany's participation in military activities outside the NATO area be? What political role should Germany play in the world, now that the 'special role' forced on it by division has come to an end? Of course, these questions can only be answered against the background of an appraisal of the principal dangers for the future. Do these risks take the form primarily of military confrontations, to be settled by the despatch of troops from Europe? Probably not: current world security problems consist at root of a fatal interweaving and reinforcement of political, economic, and ecological trends which inhibit the development of the majority of countries of the developing world; which intensify the ecological risks to the planet; and which aggravate ethno-nationalist and religious conflicts, and conflicts between states (SEF, 1991). Together with the spread of technologies of mass destruction and the transfer of arms, these form the background to the diverse threats of war outside Europe. A security policy that sees itself as a prophylactic policy of war prevention must therefore begin to tackle the structures of conflict in good time. In this connection, the discussion about 'out-of-area' operations by the Federal Army seems totally inadequate. It does not do justice to the far-reaching challenges of global survival.

THE EVOLUTION OF GERMAN SECURITY POLICY, AND ITS IMPLICATIONS

How German security policy will respond to the new challenges depends not least on the self-image which it has had up to now, and on the security structures and capabilities which have been built up over several decades.

After the catastrophe of National Socialism and of Germany's unconditional capitulation in the Second World War, all things military in Germany seemed to have been discredited for the foreseeable future. In addition, as late as 1949 the occupation forces, through the 'Petersburg Agreement', obligated the Federal government to 'maintain the demilitarisation of the Federal territory and to strive, by all means in its power, to prevent armed forces of whatever kind being raised again' (Siegler, 1979: 93).

With the advent of the Cold War, however, the situation in Europe changed radically. West German rearmament began to be discussed, at first in expert circles and then publicly. The driving force here was the United States, who, in view of the strong military presence of the Soviet Union in Central Europe, could see no alternative to German rearmament if a sufficient conventional balance were to be established on the European continent. In addition, remilitarisation offered the Federal government under Adenauer the opportunity of extending its room for manoeuvre in foreign policy (Jopp, 1981). In order to overcome opposition and reservations not only within the Federal Republic but above all in France and Britain, the Federal Army was from the outset closely integrated into NATO. The justification for the existence of NATO and for the existence of the Federal Army – in terms of the threat from the East – were almost identical. This legitimisation of West German rearmament has continued to shape the security policy debate in the Federal Republic to this day. Defence within the NATO framework (together with the gradual Western integration of the 1950s and the Ostpolitik of the 1970s), forms one of the three core ideas underlying the Federal Republic's foreign policy. Unification with the GDR has tended to reinforce this self-image, since the countervailing foreign policy of the other Germany was so manifestly unsuccessful (von Bredow and Jager, 1991: 35–6).

One expression of how Germany has seen its security up to now is provided by the restrictive conditions imposed by the Basic Law – or the restrictive interpretation of them (Deiseroth, 1991). Article 87a of the Basic Law states that:

1 The Federation raises forces for the purposes of defence.
2 Excepting for the purposes of defence, these forces may be used only as expressly allowed by this Basic Law.

What Article 87a means by 'defence' is not expressly stated in the German constitution. Even the Constitutional Court has not, to date, passed any judgements on this question. Until the debate on German participation in the 1991 Gulf War, however, all the parties represented in the Bundestag were agreed that to send the Federal Army into action was permissible only in the case of a direct attack on German territory or within the framework of the reciprocal defence obligations enshrined in the North Atlantic Treaty. Any other military intervention, whether outside the NATO area or within the framework of UN peacekeeping forces, was classified as constitutionally inadmissible.

The ending of the East–West conflict has called into question the image the Federal Republic has had of itself up to now in security terms. The legitimisation of German military power by reference to a threat of attack from the East no longer holds water. What legitimisation can take its place? Or does the very fact of a changed situation offer the opportunity of creating a 'Federal Republic Without an Army' (FRWA)? Or is it perhaps time to recognise the existence of armies as 'normal expressions' of nation-state sovereignty that do not need any concrete 'threat' to justify them?

THE RESPONSE OF THE POLITICAL PARTIES

All political parties in the Federal Republic agree that, following the end of the East–West conflict and the unification of Germany, foreign policy and security policy are subject to substantial pressure for change. The most popular metaphor used is that of Germany's enhanced 'role on the world stage' or of its increased 'responsibility'. Given the size of unified Germany, given its newly-won sovereignty, its geopolitical position, and its diverse international links and transnational interconnections, the country must now at long last 'come to political maturity' (Woyke, 1991). The country's position as an 'economic giant' and a 'political dwarf', so long bemoaned by certain German politicians, has, it is claimed, finally been superseded. However, ideas about what direction this 'maturing process' should take, and about the extent of desired changes, differ considerably.

Because of its governmental responsibility and the way it could manipulate its divided roles, the coalition comprising the CDU, CSU, and FDP had the most flexibility in shaping the process of change in security. All the parties were and are agreed that NATO should continue to form the backbone of German security policy, but there were and are differences on three counts:

1 The necessity of developing the Western Alliance into a more 'political alliance';
2 the enlargement of NATO by the creation of new Western European and pan-European security structures;
3 the extension of the geographic field of operations of the Federal Army.

As might be expected, the most conservative reactions to the new international situation came from the CSU. However, the party had obvious difficulty in putting its foreign policy ideas into some sort of programme and getting the same kind of support for them as they had managed to do before the death of Franz Josef Strauss. Its critical comments on the course adopted by Foreign Minister Genscher seemed often to be fuelled by a resentful reluctance to entrust to him alone what, in the period of radical change in 1989/90, was a highly popular area of political creativity. It was only in relation to the controversy over the German role in the Gulf War that the party developed the beginnings of an independent foreign policy programme (*Frankfurter Allgemeine Zeitung*, 1991d). The central idea in the CSU's programme for the 1990 Federal elections was that of 'watchfulness as the price of freedom'; stress was also laid on the continuing importance of NATO and the Federal Army as a still-necessary counterweight to the Soviet military superpower (CSU, 1990, 10–12). The need for, or desirability of, new European security structures did not figure in this programme. In other statements by leading CSU politicians they were mentioned merely as 'worth examining' (Tandler, 1990).

The conservative coalition's reaction to the new security situation is clearest in its appraisal of the demilitarisation steps agreed to date. Deputy Chairman of the party, Gerold Tandler, commented on the limiting of future Federal Army strength to 370,000 men and on the definitive renunciation of the right to produce, store, or use ABC weapons that: '(They) have created a situation in which it is impossible to make more extensive demands for a weakening of defence-readiness' (Tandler, 1990).

In contrast, the CDU's position on future security policy was from the outset more nuanced, although even in their case there was a prevailing tendency to push the military aspects into the foreground. Thus Defence Minister Stoltenberg began early on to try to adjust NATO ideas to fit the new circumstances in Europe. In place of 'forward defence', he proposed a scheme of 'borderline defence' to take account of the changed situation in Central Europe. The concept of nuclear 'deterrence' was to be replaced by one of 'reinsurance', in which the presence of a 'reciprocal minimum of nuclear means in Europe' would be agreed. What was decisive, said Stoltenberg, was that 'we gear our defence-concept to a broad spectrum of potential future military risks' (Stoltenberg, 1990: 9). Up to now, though, the question of how these proposals might be translated into practical terms has remained vague, not least because within NATO opinions differ as to the nature of future military risks and what may be done to counter them (Kamp, 1990).

A more broadly formulated understanding of security policy informed the 'CDU Points of Reference on Foreign Policy', unveiled by the party's General Secretary, Volker Ruhe, in February 1991 (CDU-Bundestages-chaftsstelle, 1991). Here too, NATO appears as the indispensable guarantor of Western Europe's Atlantic security ties. However, stress is laid on the dynamic character of these ties: they are to help create a 'new security structure' in Europe which both takes account of the interests of the Central and South-East European states and fosters peaceful change in the Soviet Union. In response to the part played by Germany in the Gulf War, there is a demand that the member states of the European Community should 'share a common destiny'. One way to achieve this, it is claimed, is to create multinational European units. These kinds of proposals had already been discussed several times during the debates about the security aspects of German unification. However, at that time they were geared rather to finding a new formula for coping with the presence of foreign troops on German territory, one that would fit in with the new status of Germany and the changed East–West situation. Here, said Volker Ruhe, the 'mixed task-forces' would have the function of building a 'psychological' bridge leading to world wide military commitment (Ruhe, 1991). But within which organisation these units were to be established remained an open question. In subsequent statements, it was the WEU that was most often mentioned in this connection. On the different question of whether troops may be sent into action at the behest only of the United Nations or also at that of other multinational institutions, the majority of CDU politicians now tend towards the latter position. The Federal Republic should not, said Volker Ruhe, be any different in this respect from its neighbours France and Britain (*Frankfurter Allgemeine Zeitung*, 1991a). Meanwhile Chancellor Kohl declared that the decision about whether it was permissible to send the Federal Army into action outside the NATO area would be a central issue during the current legislative period. If it did not prove possible to come to a new constitutional arrangement about this, he said, the problem would inevitably become a bone of contention in the next Federal election campaign (*Frankfurter Allgemeine Zeitung*, 1991b).

One explanation for the CDU and CSU efforts to develop an individual foreign policy profile is undoubtedly the dominant position of Foreign Minister Genscher and his ideas within the Federal government. His attempts – sometimes labelled 'Genscherism' – to establish a pan-European partnership of stability involving the United States and the Soviet Union had begun to win broad support by the end of the 1980s if not before. However, the identification of this policy with Genscher, or with the FDP, led to considerable resentment in the CDU and CSU. Genscher and the FDP lay much greater stress than does the CDU on the importance of new, pan-European security structures (FDP, 1991; Genscher, 1990). In this regard, the CSCE is to be developed into the main 'pillar of, and forum for, a new cooperative system of stability in Europe that fully involves the Soviet Union as a partner with equal rights' (Genscher, 1990: 476). From the liberal point of view, the CSCE conflict-prevention centre that has now been established in Vienna forms the nucleus of a European security council. NATO and the EC should also assume a more strongly pan-European function – NATO through a change to a more political alliance and also via its linking function *vis-à-vis* Eastern European countries; and the EC through a gradual opening up of membership to Central European states and through economic support for other neighbours in the East.

Overall, the FDP sees the security of united Germany as consisting not so much in the creation of military structures and strategies as in a comprehensive Europeanisation of political, economic, and technological structures. The ultimate goal is a:

> United States of Europe in the shape of a federative republic with: a parliament directly elected by proportional representation and upholding all the rights and duties of a democratic community; a government elected by parliament; a president; and a strong chamber to represent member-states.
>
> (FDP, 1991: 2)

The emphasis on civilian priorities does not, of course, exclude the possibility that the FDP, like the CDU, will support a change in the Basic Law in order to enable the use of the Federal Army outside the NATO area. However, this use would remain strictly confined to missions carried out at the behest of the United Nations.

The SPD had greater difficulty agreeing on a new, post-Cold War security concept. The speed with which Chancellor Kohl and Foreign Minister Genscher pushed through German unification, with the proviso that all-Germany would be a member of NATO, had put the party sharply on the defensive. Its intention to bring about the dissolution of the blocs in East and West – a goal that still figured in its Berlin programme of 1989 – suddenly had at least half the ground cut from under it. In the federal elections of December 1990 the party received dramatic confirmation that its ideas for policy on Germany could not command majority support.

Finally, views within the SPD about military engagements outside the NATO area became polarised as a result of the debate about the German role in the Gulf War. The wing of the party that is critical of the military stressed that in future the safeguarding of peace should depend primarily on a prophylactic policy of war prevention using civilian means (Muller, 1991). The prime necessity, so the argument went, was therefore to strengthen these structures. What is meant here is, *inter alia*, the reform of the United Nations (its democratisation and improved supranational effectiveness), and the expansion of the CSCE into a comprehensive, pan-European security system. From this perspective, a change in the Basic Law to allow military engagements by the Federal Army outside the NATO area seems a case of mistaken priorities. Precisely because of Germany's historical responsibility, the country should pursue a foreign policy of strictly civilian orientation. Against this background, even UN peacekeeping missions were, and continue to be, rejected on the grounds that there is too great a danger that they will serve as a 'lead-in' to further military engagements.

In contrast, the 'pragmatic' wing of the SPD emphasises the international pressure the Federal Republic is facing (Hofmann, 1991). A prophylactic policy of war prevention is held to be just as important by this group. In the transitional period, however, Germany would miss out on some important opportunities to exert influence if it went in for complete 'out of area' abstinence; and conversely it could more easily be drawn into unwanted constellations by other powers.

The SPD's party conference in Bremen in May 1991 ended with a compromise between these two positions. Having first expressed the desire to see the United Nations developed into a worldwide collective security system, the decisive passage reads as follows:

> We reject any extension of the functions of NATO and the WEU aimed at a possible engagement of their troops outside the area covered by the North Atlantic Treaty and we reject the raising of taskforces for this purpose. A change in the Basic Law which aims to make it possible for the Federal Army to engage in this or any other kind of out-of-area operation is incompatible with our policies in regard to peace and security. We reject any German participation in military engagements carried out under UN command or with UN authority. The Federal Republic must, however, be in a position to participate in peacekeeping measures (UN peacekeeping missions) within the framework of the United Nations.
>
> *(Suddeutsche Zeitung, 1991)*

In addition, the SPD, like the FDP, proposes the creation of a civilian peace corps, which would be used within the framework of the United Nations to combat environmental damage, provide humanitarian aid, and help out in catastrophes.

Within the SPD there is no dispute about the fact that a new, pan-European security structure should be developed under the aegis of the CSCE. The ideas of the party in this regard largely coincide with those of the FDP. There is, however, one important difference and that is in relation to whether increased West European cooperation on security within the EC and the WEU advances this objective or not. A large section of the SPD sees a danger here that the neutral and non-aligned states and the states of Eastern Europe will be excluded (Bahr, 1991a). There is also a considerable degree of consensus over the desirability of a radical change in military strategy and doctrine in Europe. As early as the second half of the 1980s, the concept of 'structural incapacity for attack', and of a concomitant drastic reduction in forces, had won acceptance within the party (SPD, 1989). Following the radical changes in Europe, and following the success of the CSCE negotiations in Vienna, the possibility that this idea might actually be realised became a tangible one. In a proposal entitled 'The Federal Army in Transition', the SPD attempted to set out in concrete terms the consequences in terms of military planning (SPD, 1990). Because of the developments that were taking place, this plan was soon superseded; in it, however, the SPD gave early support to the idea of further reductions in the 370,000-man Federal Army to 200,000–250,000 (though this plan did not prevent the party opposing Defence Minister Stoltenberg's plans for cuts on grounds related to regional policy) (*Frankfurter Allgemeine Zeitung*, 1991e).

The small parties on the left or Green edge of the political spectrum had even greater problems than the SPD in adjusting to the new situation in regard to foreign and security policy. The SED's successor, the PDS (represented in the Bundestag by the PDS/Left List) had rejected NATO membership from the outset, and had demanded a comprehensive policy of disarmament. Its proposals for alternative security structures were, however, meagre and divorced from reality. Nevertheless, the party did succeed in evoking some response within the context of the peace movement's campaign against German participation in the Gulf War (mainly because it was the party which made the most radical stand in the Bundestag against an extension of the Federal Army's area of operations) (PDS, 1991).

For the Greens, peace, together with ecology, had been a central policy interest from the outset (Meyer and Zadra, 1991). However, their core demands – the dissolution of the blocs and radical disarmament – were so far removed from practical politics of the 1980s that it was often difficult to make out any concrete 'Green' positions on particular security issues. When, at the end of the 1980s, it began to look as if there would be a chance to take the first steps towards disarmament and towards putting the blocs into some kind of perspective, the Greens missed the opportunity of introducing further small steps into the political debate. Even further removed from reality was the Greens' rejection of German unification, which persisted until mid-1990. This was one of the factors which led to the defeat of the (West German) Greens in the federal elections of 1990. Since then, although there have been signs of a pragmatic turn-around in the party, there is still a considerable potential for conflict – something that is demonstrated *inter alia* by the split among German intellectuals over the Gulf War (Tuckfeld and Muller, 1991).

SECURITY POLICY IN UNITED GERMANY: FUTURE TRAITS

At first glance, the various parties' policies seem to differ considerably from one another. A closer look, however, reveals that the differences relate to a small, albeit highly important, set of issues. There is a broad consensus on a large number of other points, reflecting the continuity of thinking on security in the Federal Republic. The lively debate about the security identity of united Germany therefore also turns on the question of how the traditional lines pursued in the 'old' Federal Republic can be continued in the enlarged Germany. One indication of this was the many statements made and interviews given about the German role in the Gulf War (Brandt, 1991; Weizsacker, 1991). In what follows, six aspects of this debate will be outlined, ranging from broad consensus to clear disagreement. From this there will emerge a picture not only of the new security identity which each of the various political groupings in the Federal Republic is aiming at, but also the German view of German national interests.

The first point concerns the basic consensus over the fact that the new Federal Republic should be tied to the West. This consensus had existed in the old Federal Republic since at least the start of the 1960s, following the SPD's acceptance of the course set by Adenauer of integration into the West. Involvement in the Atlantic Alliance and in Western European integration were also part of this process. During the radical upheavals of 1989/90, endorsement of Western integration actually increased among the West Germans. The proportion of those who thought that 'NATO was the sole safeguard... of peace in Europe' increased from 53 per cent to 64 per cent by September 1990, while the proportion of supporters of a 'neutral Europe' had dropped from 26 per cent to 21 per cent. On the less discriminating question of whether united Germany should be a member of NATO, more than two-thirds of West Germans were in favour in June 1990 (Veen, 1991: 32 and 40). As might be expected, this proportion was much smaller among East Germans, whereas the latter were much more open-minded from the outset on the issue of integration into the EC.[2]

This spectrum of opinion reflects both the political course taken by German unification, under the banner of NATO membership, and the differing political socialization in western and eastern Germany. In time, East German attitudes will probably fall in line with West German. However, the difficult process of unification also harbours the risk of anti-Western feeling among certain groups in eastern Germany for whom that process will bring at least temporary disadvantages.

The overwhelming endorsement of the idea of keeping united Germany integrated in the West does not, of course, mean automatic endorsement of all security measures taken by the Western Alliance. The best example of this is the crisis over nuclear policy in the first half of the 1980s. In just the same way, attachment to the West should not be thought of as an expression of permanent support for the present structures of the Western Alliance. In a period of transition this attachment undoubtedly had an important stabilising function; but it is ill-prepared to meet the new security challenges. A long-term attachment of the Germans to the West therefore necessitates a reinforcement of Western European integration and a reform of Atlanticism (Czempiel, 1990).

The second basic consensus in (West) German foreign policy was achieved when, at the start of the 1980s, the CDU/CSU took up the main aspects of Ostpolitik instituted by the social-democratic-cum-liberal coalition. The basic idea behind Ostpolitik was that, because of its special relations with the GDR and the other countries of Eastern Europe, and because of its precarious situation at the heart of the East-West conflict, the only chance the Federal Republic had of gradually overcoming the confrontation was through acknowledgement of the status quo, a comprehensive renunciation of force, and the settlement by treaty of the arguments it had with its Eastern neighbours. Egon Bahr's long-reviled formula 'change through rapprochement' summarised this policy.[3]

What role this strategy played in eroding communism and in prompting the revolutions in Eastern Europe remains a matter of dispute between the supporters and critics of détente. What is indisputable, however, is that the rapid realisation of German unity could not have been achieved had it not been for the comprehensive understanding with the Soviet Union. This understanding was reflected in the 2 plus 4 agreement, and in four further bilateral agreements:

1 the 'agreement on the conditions regulating the temporary presence of Soviet troops on the territory of the Federal Republic of Germany and on the arrangements for their planned withdrawal';
2 a 'transition agreement', in which the FRG undertakes to make available a sum of 12,000 million DM and an interest-free credit of over 3,000 million DM to cover the continued presence and withdrawal of the Soviet troops, the major part of this being earmarked for the construction of housing;
3 the 'agreement on neighbourliness, partnership, and cooperation', which is intended to go beyond renunciation of force and the promise of non-aggression and provide active spurs to cooperation and understanding;
4 the 'agreements on the development of comprehensive cooperation in the fields of technology, economics, and science' (*Europa Archiv*, 1991a).

Together with the promises of financial aid and credit and credit-guarantees amounting to more than 60,000 million DM, these agreements constituted a special link between the Soviet Union and the Federal Republic of Germany. To describe them as 'buying off' the Soviets' entitlements as victors in the Second World War and the presence of its troops in eastern Germany does not do justice to the intentions of the political leadership in the two countries. These measures cannot be understood without reference to the tragic history of Soviet-German relations in the twentieth century, and to the desire that these relations should in future take the shape of a pan-European partnership of stability. On the Soviet side, in addition to direct economic support, the expectation that Germany will act as a bridge to the Western community of nations as a whole, and thus also to a further opening-up and modernisation of the country, also undoubtedly plays a role (Portugalov, 1990).

In the Federal Republic, this policy *vis-à-vis* the Soviet Union enjoys wide support among both the political parties and the people at large. The same is true of the policy of agreements with the newly emerged democracies in Central Europe (Poland, Czechoslovakia, and Hungary). There is, however, one reservation here, in regard to Poland. This is because a small but politically very well-organised minority of exiles has up to now made the settling of the situation with this country problematic. The (electorally-motivated) regard which Chancellor Kohl showed this group also led to a long delay in the unambiguous acceptance of the German-Polish border. As a result of internal and external pressure, however, this question was event-ually settled – initially by identical resolutions in both German parliaments, and, following unification, by a German-Polish border treaty. As with the Soviet Union, a comprehensive agreement on neighbourly relations was also concluded with Poland (*Europa Archiv*, 1991b).

The third point of consensus in the debate on security policy concerns disarmament of short-range and battlefield nuclear weapons. However, this unanimity is only as recent as 1989, when the CDU/CSU adopted the FDP's critical stance in the debate about the modernisation of short-range missiles. The decisive factor in their change of attitude was the fact that these weapons, which could only be intended for use on German (or Czech) soil, were rejected by the West German population. The Federal government clearly wished to prevent a revival of the peace movement along the lines of the early 1980s. At the 1990 London summit, the Alliance, at German insistence, declared itself willing to negotiate on the question of complete abolition of short-range land-based nuclear weapons. But at the same time, NATO decided that (airborne) nuclear forces were to continue to be based in Europe. Furthermore, the latest developments show that the nuclear powers' interest in negotiating away these weapons is very slight, despite the radical changes in the military/strategic situation in Europe. From the German point of view, the situation is aggravated both by France's plans to deploy forty new 'Hades' short-range missiles, with a range of 480 km, near the German border, and by Britain's intention to develop a new nuclear stand-off weapon (TASM) and use it to equip the squadrons of Tornados it has deployed in the Federal Republic (*Der Spiegel*, 1991).

The SPD has shown the firmest commitment on this issue, arguing that short-range and battlefield nuclear weapons should not only not be modernised but should 'be withdrawn from all countries that have no power to use these systems. This includes airborne nuclear stand-off weapons.' (Horn, 1990). The FDP's position, in a nutshell, is that: 'land-based nuclear weapons no longer have any place on German territory' (FDP, 1991: 7). The position of the CDU/CSU is less clear: the hope is expressed that it will be possible to achieve the complete abolition of nuclear artillery and short-range land-based nuclear weapons in the course of further negotiations between the nuclear powers; a 'denuclearised Europe' is, however, rejected (Stoltenberg, 1990: 9–10). It remains unclear how the presence of the remaining nuclear aircraft is to be reconciled with the idea that nuclear weapons are to be used only as a 'last resort' (Kamp, 1990: 69). Regardless of how the CDU/CSU politicians who deal with security matters judge this question, it is probable that the leadership of these parties reject the notion of having nuclear weapons deployed on German soil.

With the fourth aspect of the security debate, the question of a new European security architecture, there is a wide range of opinion. The positions of the different parties were outlined in the previous section. With the exception of the Greens and the PDS, they all argue in favour of a gradual transformation of existing alliances and institutions. This involves: the development of NATO as a political alliance; the extension of Western European cooperation on security within the framework of the WEU, EC, and EPC; and the institutionalisation of the CSCE. There is no doubt that the individual parties emphasise different aspects, but one thing they have in common is a cautious attitude to any global schemes for new peace and security structures. The more lively and more radical debate about the architecture of the future 'European house' is taking place in the 'approaches' to the political parties, in journalism, and in academic circles (Krell, 1991; Senghaas, 1990; Weidenfeld, 1990). There is a clearer articulation here of the hitches and contradictions that will result from the parallel development of new Atlantic, West European, and pan-European security structures. One point worth noting in connection with the German quest for a new identity in security is that the majority of the writers are looking for a form of institutionalisation of security policy which will accommodate the interests of Western and Eastern neighbours alike and do so as soon as possible. A decisive factor here is the fear that if this is not done, Europe will collapse into three very heterogeneous parts, with highly problematic consequences in terms of security:

An institutionally petrified western Europe, a crisis-ridden Soviet Union which would still have the largest military potential in Europe at its disposal, and, caught between the two, an eastern Europe whose chance to win a hearing through the medium of pan-European institutions would have been squandered.

(Senghaas, 1991: 15)

The most widely propagated concept is that of a regional system of collective security, but one that includes various models of preventive conflict-resolution (IFSH, 1990). The organisations envisaged as bases for this are NATO (which would be extended eastwards) and the CSCE. Under the rubric 'guideposts from peace theory', Dieter Senghaas has also summarised four criteria derived from peace research which should be observed in the reshaping of Europe:

1 The requirement that states should be founded on the rule of law (since this principle of organisation between states fosters peaceful foreign policy);
2 The requirement that response to expectations be predictable (to be achieved through institutionalised cooperation);
3 The requirement that the economic situation be equalised (since the reconstruction of Eastern Europe is in the West's own obvious interests);
4 The requirement that empathy be shown (for developmental difficulties being experienced by the peripheral areas of Europe) (Senghaas, 1991).

The fifth aspect of the security debate concerns the fundamental question of the status and nature of the military apparatus. Is the existence of the Federal Army a quasi-'natural' expression of the Federal Republic's sovereignty as a nation-state, or has its existence been generally called into question by the disappearance of the threat from the East? What tasks should the future Federal Army be assigned? What consequences does this have in regard to the size and structure of the armed forces? Does the Federal Republic still need a conscript army or can the required tasks be better executed with a professional army? Very different answers to these questions are currently under discussion. They range from the 'Federal Republic Without an Army' initiative – which is modelled on a similar citizens' initiative in Switzerland and aims to bring about the dissolution of the Federal Army without replacement – to the attempt to fix the strength of the Federal Army permanently at the new 370,000-man level. However, the politically significant debate rarely extends to the extreme of complete abolition of the Federal Army; rather, what is happening is that radical critics are trying to make their proposals socially acceptable by suggesting the transformation of the military apparatus through greater involvement in civilian tasks (natural disasters, environmental protection, development aid, or for humanitarian purposes) (Bahr, 1990; Vogt, 1990: 1–37).

The supporters of the 'normality thesis' concede that the Federal Army owes its creation to contingent factors. But now it is time, they say, not to look for some other contingent justification but to regard the military as a permanent expression of the country's status as a nation-state, and as an example of self-assertion based on loyalty to the constitution (Isensee, 1991). At the centre of the public debate about this issue one finds the metaphors of the fire-brigade, of the police, or of insurance in general, but one also finds allusions to the international importance of the Federal Republic and to the pressures to conform imposed by the international system.[4]

One not inconsequential illustration of the controversy over the future of the military in Germany is the debate about military service. Up to now it has been regarded as an important element in the democratic legitimisation of the German armed forces. To date, official policy, and the majority of SPD politicians, have categorically rejected the idea of abolishing compulsory military service (de Maiziere, 1991: 274–83). However, if there is a reduction in the size of the Federal Army to less than 370,000 men, it will probably be questionable whether compulsory military service can be maintained in its present form. Moreover, most of the arguments for retaining compulsory military service seem hardly convincing when one looks at the new challenges (Kuhlmann and Lippert, 1991).

Probably of even greater significance for the future status of the military is the sixth security issue, namely the controversy over an out-of-area role for the Federal Army. As has been intimated several times already, this question was a catalyst for most of the proposals in regard to united Germany's new international political role. The controversy was unleashed as a result of the criticism voiced by several allies in regard to the Federal Republic's inadequate involvement in the military alliance against Saddam Hussein. In fact, the Federal Republic was involved on a massive scale in this war, as the main base for the marshalling of Western troops, as the financer of allied military expenditure, and via its economic support for major Arab states; publicly, however, this role was underplayed (Gillesen, 1991). The Bonn government sought to do justice both to the expectations of its Western partners and to the cautious mood in the Federal Republic. The chief determinant of action was the consensus that existed between the parties to the effect that the Basic Law did not allow the Federal Army to be sent into action outside the NATO area. This consensus lasted until the escalation of the Gulf conflict. Since then, the parties' opinions have diverged considerably (Kamp, 1991).

If one assumes that an out-of-area role requires a change in the constitution – and all parties were agreed on this until a few months ago – the consent of the SPD is needed to achieve the necessary two-thirds majority. What the SPD parliamentary party's final decision will be on this issue is still an open question. But in view of the resolutions of the SPD party conference in

Bremen, and of the FDP's situation at the time of writing, the CDU/CSU will probably not obtain the majority for constitutional change which it needs to realise its wish to send the Federal Army on out-of-area missions without a UN mandate (within the framework of a 'European intervention-force' for example).

One can, however, conceive of another way in which these difficulties might be circumvented. Since the interpretation of the relevant articles of the Basic Law is not clear-cut, there have been attempts to gradually circumvent the current restrictions on the basis of national obligations or various 'material constraints'. However, in view of the degree to which this issue has been politicized, it is doubtful whether a consensus for such a course could be achieved within the Federal government.

CONCLUSIONS

Leading politicians, journalists, and academics are agreed that united Germany should assume 'a greater degree of responsibility in the world'. But what this new, 'more responsible' role should look like is a matter of dispute. In simplified terms, it may be said that two extreme stances are distinguishable here. Some consider that restricting West German security policy to the task of countering the dangers within East–West relations, and renouncing a militarily backed 'policy of strength' are approaches which have proved their worth. The Federal Republic's success as an economic power, they claim, is probably due in no small measure to the fact that it comes closer to the concept of a 'civilian power' than any of its Western neighbours, with the exception of Japan. However, continues the argument, if it was to have been able to counter Western accusations that its civilian-power policy was greatly lacking in credibility, the Federal Republic should have been more consistent in the past in halting the export of technologies of mass destruction. Following the drastic reduction in the threat from the East, security policy should not go off in search of new dangers to be deterred or combated by military means. Instead, it is high time to come to grips with the real challenges to peace and security in the world: abject poverty in the greater part of the Third World, but also in many parts of the East; indebtedness and extreme economic disparities within and between states; the destruction of the natural bases of life; and the rapid disappearance of resources. Of course, say this group, we cannot for the time being do without the military apparatus – as a form of 'reinsurance' and to help direct a process of peaceful change in the international system. The army could, however, undergo a further, substantial reduction in size to a level 10–20 per cent of current strength. It should be the long-term objective of German security policy to overcome the use of force between states by means of a global peace-order involving a central, or at least a collective, monopoly on force. Under such an order, the Federal Republic would also be required to participate militarily. However, one would first have to ensure – initially through a reform of the United Nations and the creation of collective regional security systems – that these institutions were actually functioning and could not be misused by particular leading powers.

The contrary position holds that these preconditions for German participation in international security systems are unrealistic. Only through active involvement – including military involvement – in actions conducted by multinational alliances for the purposes of safeguarding or establishing peace will the Federal Republic secure the chance to create, and increase the efficiency of collective security structures. Besides, the contingent legitimisation of the Federal Republic's current military apparatus was, in any case, provisional in nature. Now that full sovereignty has been secured and German unity achieved, military forces are a normal expression of national self-assertion. The size and structure of the armed forces should be decided in consultation with allies and with those with whom treaties have been concluded, and they should be calculated and designed in such a way as to meet the new military risks inside and outside Europe. One should, however, also take into account various other factors that are not determined by exclusively military considerations, such as the maintenance of compulsory military service and appropriate reflection of status. Besides this, international agreement, the linking of Germany into the Western alliance, and the creation of further multinational units ensure that a German army that continues to be strong does not present any threat.

Whether the identity of security policy in the united Germany of the late 1990s will tend more to one position than to the other is an open question. The answer to it does not depend solely on the internal political debates in Germany. In the obvious interests both of the Germans and of their European neighbours it is to be hoped that that identity has as great a civilian content as possible.

NOTES

1 In total, 213 Federal Army garrisons are to be closed by 1994. The total number of garrisons then left in Germany as a whole will be 617 (*Frankfurter Allgemeine Zeitung*, 1991c).
2 In September 1990, 51 per cent of GDR citizens were in favour of a 'neutral Europe' as a safeguard for peace, and only 31 per cent in favour of NATO (Veen, 1991: 40)
3 See the historical retrospective, with contributions ranging from 1963–90 in Bahr, 1991b.

4 See the systematic catalogue of justifications given in the collection edited by the General Inspector of the Bundeswehr, Admiral Wellershof (Wellershof, 1991).

REFERENCES

Bahr, E. (1991a) Press conference, reported in *Frankfurter Allgemeine Zeitung*, 18 May 1991.

Bahr, E. (1991b) *Sicherheit fur Deutschland: Vom Wandel durch Annaherung zur Europaischen Sicherheitsgemeinschaft*, Munich and Vienna: Hanser.

Bahr, H.-E. (ed.) (1990) *Von der Armee zur Europaischen Friedenstruppe*, Munich: Knaur.

Brandt, W. (1991) interview in *Der Spiegel*, 11 February 1991.

Bredow, W. von and Jager, T. (1991) 'Die Aussenpolitik Deutschlands: Alte Herausforderungun und neue Probleme', *Aus Politik und Zeitgeschichte* 1991, 1–2: 27–38.

Bulletin des Presse (1990) 'Vertrag uber die abschliessende regelung in bezug auf Deutschland vom 12 September 1990', *Bulletin des Presse und Informationsamtes der Bundesregierung*, **109**, 14 September 1990.

CDU-Bundestageschaftsstelle (ed.) (1991) *Deutschlands Verantwortung in der Welt*, Bonn: CDU.

CSU (1990) *Heimat Bayern: Zukunft Deutschland: Mit Uns: CSU* Programme der Christlich-Sozialen Union zur Bundestagswahl, 2 December 1990, Munich: CSU.

Czempiel, E-O. (1990) 'Die Modernisierung der Atlantischen Gemeinschaft', *Europa Archiv*, 1990, 8: 275–86.

de Maiziere, U. (1991) 'Pladoyer fur die Wehrpflicht', in D. Wellershoff (ed.) *Frieden ohne Macht? Sicherheitspolitik und Streitrafte in Wandel*, Bonn: Bouvier.

Deiseroth, D. (1991) 'Die Bundeswehr und militarische Einsatze im Rahmen der Vereinten Nationen', *Frankfurter Rundschau*, 24 June 1991.

Der Spiegel (1991) 12 August 1991.

Enders, T. (1990) 'Militarische Herausforderungen Europas in den neunziger Jahren', *Europa Archiv*, 1990, 10: 321–9.

Europa Archiv (1990) 'Das KSZE-Treffen der Staats-und Regierungschefs in Paris im November 1990', *Europa Archiv*, 1990, 24: D607–54.

Europa Archiv (1991a) 'Das deutsch-sovietische Vertragswerk vom Herbst 1990', *Europa Archiv*, 1991, 3: D63–85.

Europa Archiv (1991b) 'Vertrag zwischen der Bundesrepublik Deutschland und der Republik Polen uber die Bestatigung der zwischen ihnen bestehenden Grenze, unterzeichnet in Warschau am 14. 11. 1990', *Europa Archiv*, 1991, 13: D310–33.

FDP (Federal Committee) (1991) 'Liberale Aussenpolitik fur das Vereinte Deutschland', *Freie Demokratische Korrespondenz*, 26 May 1991.

Frankfurter Allgemeine Zeitung (1991a) 5 March 1991.

Frankfurter Allgemeine Zeitung (1991b) 18 May 1991.

Frankfurter Allgemeine Zeitung (1991c) 25 May 1991.

Frankfurter Allgemeine Zeitung (1991d) 3 June 1991.

Frankfurter Allgemeine Zeitung (1991e) 7 August 1991.

Genscher, H.-D. (1990) 'Die neue europaische Friedensordnung', *Europa-Archiv*, 1990, 15: 473–8

Giessman, H.-J. (1991) 'Der Umbruch in Mittel- und Osteuropa', *Sicherheit und Frieden*, 1991, 2: 94–7.

Gillesen, G. (1991) 'Deutschland Hauptbasis fur den Truppenaufmarsch am Golf', *Frankfurter Allgemeine Zeitung*, 5 June 1991.

Hofmann, G. (1991) 'Wieder einmal ein neuer anfang: Deutschland soll sich nicht als Reservat betrachten – ein Gesprach mit Willy Brandt' *Die Zeit*, 24 May 1991.

Horn, E. (1990) 'Positinspapier der Arbeitsgruppe Sicherheitsfragen der SPD-Bundestagsfraktion und des Arbeitskreises I des SPD-Volkskammerfraktion', unpublished paper, 6 September 1990.

IAP-Dienst Sicherheitspolitik (1990) '"Ein Staat – ein Armee". Streitkrafte im vereinten Deutschland', 1 August 1990.

IFSH (1990) 'Ein geeintes Deutschland in einem neuen Europa: vom Blocksystem zur Sicherheitsgemeinschaft', *Sicherheit und Frieden*, **8**, 2: 74–85.

Isensee, J. (1991) '"Recht und Freiheit des deutschen Volkes" – Legitimation und Schutgut der Bundeswehr', in D. Wellershof (ed.) *Frieden ohne Macht? Sicherheitspolitik und Streitrafte im Wandel*, Bonn: Bouvier.

Jopp, M. (1981) 'Politische Interessen und militarische Planung bei der Integration der Bundeswehr in das NATO-Bundis', in R. Steinwag (ed.) *Unsere Bundeswehr? Zum 25-jahrigen Bestehen einer Umstrittenen Institution*, Frankfurt, Suhrkamp: 15–51.

Kamp, K.-H. (1990) 'Die westliche Allianz: Rahmenbedingungen ihrer kunftigen Entwicklung', Sankt Augustin, Forschungsinstitut der Konrad-Adenauer Stiftung, Internal Report no.19.

Kiy, M. and Lobbe, K. (1990) 'Verteidigungsausgaben der Bundesrepublik und volkswirtschaftliche Auswirkungen verminderter Rustungsausgaben', *RWI-Mitteilung*, **41**, 4: 331–61.

Krell, G. (ed.) (1991) *Searching for Peace after the Cold War: Conceptual and Practical Problems of a New World Order*, Peace Research Report 19, Frankfurt: PRIF.

Kuhlmann, J. and Lippert E. (1991) *Wehrpflicht Ade? Argumente wider und fur die Wehrpflicht in Friedenzeiten*, Working Paper 48, Munich: SOWI.

Meyer, B. and Zadra, R. (1991) *Friedens-und Sicherheitpolitische Positionen der Grunen und der Liste Vendi*, Bonn: PRIF.

Muller, A. (1991) 'Fremdbestimmt, ohne Debatte und im Kern ohne Not: zur Diskussion in der SPD uber die Beteiligung der Bundeswehr an Blauhelm-aktion' *Frankfurter Rundschau*, 29 May 1991.

PDS (1991) *Deutsche Sodaten in Alle Welt? Nein*, Arbeitskreis Frieden und Antimilitarismus der PDS/Linke Liste, Landesverband Hamburg: PDS.

Portugalov, N. (1990) essay in *Der Spiegel*, 8 October 1990.

Ruhe, V. (1991) interview in *Frankfurter Rundschau*, 11 February 1991.

Schlotter, P. (1991) 'Die 2 + 4 – Verhandlungen und der KSZE-prozess', in B. Kohler-Koch (ed.) *Die Politischen Konturen eines neuen Europas*, Baden-Baden: Nomos.

Senghaas, D. (1990) *Europa 2000: Ein Friedensplan*, Frankfurt: Suhrkamp.

Senghaas, D. (1991) 'Die Neugestaltung Europas: Perspektiven und Handlungangebote', *Aus Politik und Zeitgeschehen*, 1991, 18: 11–20.

Siegler, H. von (ed.) (1979) *Dokumenttation zur Deutschlandfrage*, Main Volume I, St Augustin: Siegler.

SPD (1990) *Bundeswehr im Ubergang: Positionpaper der Arbeitsgruppe Bundeswehrstruktur*, Bonn: SPD.

SEF, in cooperation with Institut fur Entwicklung und Frieden (1991) *Globale Trends*

1991: Daten und Dokumente zur Weltentwicklung, Bonn: Stiftung Entwicklung und Frieden.
Stoltenberg, G. (1990) 'Kunftige perspektiven deutscher Sicherheitspolitik', in Der Bundesminister der Verteidigung (ed.) *Informationen zur Sicherheitspolitik*, Bonn: Bundeministerium der Verteidigung.
Stolting E. (1991) '"Wer will weg aus Osteuropa?" and "Ist Nagorny-Karabach bald uberall?"', in Die Tageszeitung/World Media (eds) *Die neue Volkerwanderung. Die Migrationen der 90er Jahre*, 8 June 1991: 22–7.
Suddeutsche Zeitung (1991) 1/2 June 1991.
Tandler, G. (1990) unpublished speech to the CSU congress on military policy, Munich, 27 October 1990.
Tuckfeld, M. and Muller J. (1991) *Welt-Kriegs-Ordnung*, Bonn: Die Grunen-Bundesvorstand.
Veen, H.-J. (1991) 'Die Westbindungen der Deutschen in einer phase der neuorientierung', *Europa Archiv*, 1991, 2: 31–40.
Vogt, W. (1990) 'Positiven Frieden wagen: zur Transformation militarisierter Friedenssicherung in zivilisierter Friedensgestaltung' in W. Vogt (ed.) *Mut zum Frieden Uber Moglichkeiten einer friedensentwicklung fur das Jahr 2000*, Darmstadt: Wissenschaftliche Buchgesellschaft.
Weidenfeld, W. (ed.) (1990) *Die Deutschen und die Architektur des Europaischen Hauses*, Cologne: Wissenschaft und Politik.
Weizsacker, R. von (1991) interview in *Die Zeit*, 8 February 1991.
Wellershof, D. (ed.) (1991) *Frieden ohne Macht? Sicherheitspolitik und Streitrafte im Wandel*, Bonn: Bouvier.
Wellman, C. (1989) *Abrustrung und Beschafttigung – ein Zielkonflikt,?* Frankfurt/New York: Campus.
Woyke, W. (1991) 'Zur internationalen rolle des vereinigten Deutschlands: die wirtschaftliche weltmacht muss politisch reifen', *Das Parlament*, 28 June 1991.

Index